THE BIG BUCKS

THE BIG BUCKS

ALBERT CORY

Edited by SAMANTHA MASON

Illustrated by JONATHAN SAINSBURY

Foreword by DAN GILLMOR

CUBBYBEAR PRESS

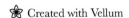

CONTENTS

FOREWORD

Dan Gillmor

The Big Bucks is a time capsule. It's fiction, but it captures a time in the history of a place, and an era, that helped create the digital world in which we live today.

I arrived in Silicon Valley a decade after the events in Albert Cory's novel take place. Based on my conversations over the years with people who were there, and from my reading of the valley's epic history, it feels like what it is, an historical novel in which great care has been taken to get the details right.

They should be, because Cory (a pen name chosen by the author) did live and work in the belly of the technology beast that was then in one of its major expansionary phases. Silicon Valley as a concept dated from the 1950s, though the nickname didn't arrive until the early 1970s, and the advent of microprocessors — now part of so much of what we touch, and how we communicate every day -—became the foundation of massive hardware and software industries that have become the world's most powerful enterprises.

For people like me, the 1980s were the decade of personal

computers. I bought my first computer in the 1970s, but in the '80s I let my full geek emerge with machines only old-timers will remember, with names like TRS and Osborne, and then the ones that became the foundation of the personal-computing era, the Apple II, IBM PC, and Macintosh. I was online, but to services (also only remembered by older folks) like the Source and CompuServe. America Online, much less the commercial Internet, was years away.

But while people like me reveled in our personal computers, software that was clumsy yet enormously powerful, and online conversations that hinted at the free-for-all to come, people like the characters in this book were assembling some of the key pieces of what was to become the network of networks we all use today.

Those pieces included, above all, something that wasn't a technology or tech-based service, per se, at least not in the sense of processors, memory, disk drives, software (operating systems and applications), and the companies that made them. The key pieces of what became the Internet was, from my perspective, *ideas and rules* that spawned hardware and software and the vast connections that followed.

Networking did exist back then, and had been around for some time. But apart from some government installations and labs in a few universities, networking was governed by the rules of giants like AT&T and IBM and a few select companies. They believed in "local networks" and, for longer distances, "dedicated" circuits from one entity to another and, in effect, appointments for one person (or machine) to talk to another.

The breakthrough was embedded in the notion, which had emerged in the 1950s and 1960s, that it would be interesting to break up messages into lots of small packages, called packets. Each packet would contain information, apart from its piece of the message, saying where it was coming from, where it was going, and what its location had been in the overall message. Routing devices would send the packets via the best-available route, and when all the packages got to the destination — some wouldn't get there on the first try and would have to be sent again — the message would be reassembled. If networks were fast enough — and they were becoming faster and faster — this might turn out to work just as well, or better, than the "authorized by the Big Guys" technology, and it would be far, far cheaper. Packet-switching, as this was known, was the basis of rules that engineers agreed on informally, and which became standards.

This novel is, in part, about the early days of how that breakthrough made its way from brilliant ideas to a set of rules and then into hardware and software that could be deployed far beyond governments, big companies, and major universities (though it would work brilliantly for them, too). A key invention in the hardware category, Ethernet networking (from 3Com's founder, Bob Metcalfe), turned out to be ideal for packet-switching. The teams that put all of the ideas and rules into the marketplace, and helped connect entities like universities and government installations to the emerging Internet, were people like the ones who populate this novel.

They worked hard, but they were people, with emotions and ambitions and passions. Much of the novel is about the outside-of-work parts of their lives, taking place across — at first — a wide geography but then, as the major characters find their way to California, in Silicon Valley as it existed back then: places like Cupertino and Santa Clara in the South Bay, which was a hike from San Francisco even before nightmare traffic arrived in the 1990s.

I got my initial direct Internet access in 1991, a dial-up account from the first commercial ISP in Michigan, where I was working at the time. My arrival in Silicon Valley, to work at the San Jose Mercury News, came in 1994. By then, the ideas and rules that animated the characters in this book were fully embedded in the technology scene. AOL thought it might capture the commercial online user base, and Microsoft, the dominant tech company of that era, disdained the Internet — in both cases largely because they couldn't see a way to control it themselves — and lost to the freedom to communicate and innovate that the Internet offered.

The radical decentralization that the 1980s and 1990s technologists created has been a wondrous thing. We may lose it to authoritarian governments, corporate monopolists, and our human preference for convenience. But I'll put my hopes on people like the ones in this book who see the possibilities for the future, and do their part to bring it about — and are human beings, with all their foibles and richness, in the process.

May, 2022

PREFACE

The Big Bucks is Book II of my series on building our modern computer society, the first of which was *Inventing the Future*. That book covered the building of the Xerox Star, which, as we all know, preceded the Apple Macintosh. You don't have to have read that book to appreciate this one, although some of our characters, especially Janet and Dan, are introduced there.

When we built the Star, none of us expected to get rich from it. Suddenly Apple went public, IBM introduced the PC, the world changed, and the 80s happened.

It's hard to imagine a world without the Internet nowadays. It's even harder to imagine a world where almost no one owns a computer. But that's the world *The Big Bucks* starts with. Imperceptibly, our modern world was getting built. The Internet *was* getting built in the Eighties, but most people didn't notice. Even if you did notice it, like I did, you never imagined it as it is today. Most people dismissed it as "just something those academics do."

This is a novel like the first book, not a history. It features characters who are not famous and who have lives outside of work. "What was it like to live then?" is a question that a factual history usually won't answer. It's a subjective question, and I hope I've put you into the 80s so you can see for yourself.

The Big Bucks is more heavily fictional than *Inventing the Future:* the computer events are (mostly) all true except as noted, but some major plot events never happened. I think of it as the characters getting up off the page and having a life of their own. I hope you enjoy it.

If you haven't read *Inventing the Future*: as I said, it's not necessary, but if you want to read the backstories of Janet and Dan (and Grant, although he only appears in one chapter here), you can read a plot synopsis in the Afterword.

1

THE AFTERMATH

Dan Markunas had just called the famous headhunter Kim Burdette. He wondered, *"Do I need to introduce myself?"* He was only a first-line manager on Xerox Star in El Segundo, not a big name, but Kim seemed to know all about him. *"She must have her own org chart. No wonder all the startups use her!"* It was June 5, 1981, a month after the National Computer Conference demo of the Xerox Star, and all the gossip seemed to center on who was quitting and what Xerox technology various startups were trying to exploit to get rich.

Dan had never talked to a headhunter before. He pictured a gruff person who didn't give a damn about you, rattling off some languages and operating systems to find out how to pigeonhole you, and ending by demanding a resume. But Kim wasn't like that at all. She seemed to have all the time in the world for him. Occasionally, she'd mention a startup she was working with but would then say, "I don't think that's the right one for you."

Eventually, he worked the conversation to the next time he was going to the Bay Area and whether she could set something up for him. *That* would require a resume, for sure. If she were going to pitch him to some VP of Engineering, they would definitely ask for one. He would send her a resume, but he *had* to write it on a Star, or else what's the point? He would go back into the office one night to print it out so that no one would see it on the printer.

Now that the phone call was over, he opened his office door, and Peter Eisen walked in. Dan felt guilty that he'd turned over the Records Processing group to Ron Powers, an XDS old-timer who had no particular affinity for the project or the people, but he had grudgingly agreed to take over.

"So, how's it going with Ron?" he asked.

Peter looked resigned, "Okay, I guess. I wanted to ask you about the paper, though."

Dan was the lead author on a paper about Star Records Processing, and Peter was a co-author. There was a third guy, Joel Byrne, working with them in Palo Alto. They spent some time talking about who was doing what and agreed to have a phone conference with Joel later that day.

2

MOVING UP

Janet Saunders left Xerox on Friday, June 5, 1981. She'd loved working on the Star, but she'd realized, sadly, that Xerox had no clue that they could now take over the entire computer industry. Apple, on the other hand, was the aggressive startup that appeared to understand that. She was starting there on Monday the 15th.

Janet had been married to an engineer she'd met in college when she started at Xerox, but she was divorced now. She and her cat, Rocky, were living in an apartment in Manhattan Beach. The movers were coming on Monday, so she spent Saturday and Sunday tossing stuff. She was warned that they would pack *everything*, even the contents of the trash cans, so this was her opportunity to slim down. Out went all the clothes she didn't wear and all the books she would never reread or lend—good riddance to the crappy furniture she'd bought when she divorced.

On Monday the 8th, the movers packed up her stuff. She spent the rest of the day cleaning up the apartment so that she could get her security deposit back. After finishing, she called her dad, Len. He first told her about the Apple II being used in the Finance Department at Chrysler, where he worked, so she knew he was especially interested in her adventures at Apple.

"Hi, Dad! I'm all done cleaning the apartment, so I thought I'd give you a call."

"Hi, sweetie! When do you leave for Cupertino?"

"Driving up tomorrow, and then looking for an apartment."

"I'm looking at the map. It looks like I-5 is the quickest road."

She made a face, "Yeah, but it's *so* boring! I was going to go up 101."

"Well… I guess there's no hurry, right?"

"Yeah. I don't start work until next Monday."

Len thought for a second, "So that gives you, what? Five days to find a place? Is that enough time?"

"Well, I hope so. I'll keep you posted."

"Good luck, sweetie. Let me know when you get to your hotel tomorrow."

She knew he'd be worrying about her all day, so she said she would.

She was about to hang up, but Len had one more thing. "Hey, your apartment is completely empty now, right?"

"I know what you're going to ask. My bed's gone, but I kept my sleeping bag for tonight!"

"That's my girl. You think of everything! Talk to you tomorrow."

On Tuesday, she drove up to the Bay Area and checked into the Best Western on Stevens Creek in Santa Clara and called her dad. On Wednesday, she bought a copy of the *Mercury News* and set out to look for an apartment somewhere close to Apple. She spent a couple of days driving around, and on Friday, she finally found a place on Rainbow Drive, just off of De Anza Boulevard, in a two-story block of condominiums. It was maybe a mile and a half south of Apple, so it was *possible* to walk, but she was realistic enough to know she never would. She was thankful that the condo owner had moved out, so she could move in the next day.

Monday the 15th was the big day. After working at two giant companies, Apple was a shock! There was no giant HR department, just a couple of people who handled pay and benefits. She reported to a two-story building at the corner of De Anza and Lazaneo in Cupertino, nicknamed Taco Towers. The towers came from the fact that it was two stories, and Apple had always been in single-story buildings before that. Taco, she later found out, was because the roof tiles resembled those of a Taco Bell.

She was going to work on the new computer called the Lisa, which either stood for Local Integrated Software Architecture or the name of Steve Jobs' daughter, depending on whom you talked to. The Lisa would have a graphical user interface and use a mouse, technologies Xerox had pioneered. Apple engineers, along with Steve Jobs, made two visits to Xerox Palo Alto Research Center in December 1979, which many of Janet's Xerox friends were bitter about. Apple people were quick to tell her that the Lisa project was already underway when the visits happened, and in any case, Xerox had no realistic plan for capitalizing on the inventions. She had concluded that they were right about the second part.

The Lisa team moved here from its original home behind the Good Earth restaurant on Stevens Creek when it became too large to fit there. She found it a much different environment than she'd joined at Xerox so long ago. On this project, they already had their hardware chosen! The software environment was settled, too—no leisurely ruminating on how to do things, like Xerox had been doing when she joined.

Traditionally with a new computer, the engineers had to develop for it using some other machine first, and it was a big milestone when they could develop for the machine *on* the machine. Although some engineers were developing on the Lisa, there were still many working on an Apple II. She couldn't wait to tell her dad about this! He'd been the one to tell her about the Apple II last December, and he'd ended up buying one so that he could run financial analyses on VisiCalc for his work. But now, she had her very own Lisa, which had wooden feet because the case wasn't finished yet. It had a fitted canvas cover that she was told to put over it when she left for the night because they didn't want people taking photos through the windows.

That night, she took her Pascal manual, went home, and called Len again. "Hi, Dad! Well, I'm an Apple-ite now!"

"I'm dying to hear all about it! How is it?"

"Well… it's *way* different from TRW and Xerox!"

"Oh, yeah? How so?"

"Well, it's smaller. Just a few thousand employees. Still scattered among different buildings, though."

"How close is it to your apartment?"

"Just a couple miles. I want to start riding my bike."

Len had never imagined riding a bicycle to work. That was just not something you did in the Detroit area. "I guess you don't get snow and ice there, huh?" he laughed.

She changed the subject, "There *is* something I didn't realize when I interviewed there. You know the computer I'm going to work on is called the Lisa?"

"I'd forgotten, but yeah. What, did they cancel it already?" he chuckled.

"Not yet, but there's another computer project competing with it!"

Len was amazed, "What? In a company that small they have competing projects? Chrysler had that once, but the management put a stop to it pretty quick."

"Well, I don't know what's going to happen with this. This other thing is called the Macintosh."

"Like the apple, huh? Are they going to cancel your project and go with that?"

She didn't like to think about that. "It doesn't seem like it.

The Lisa's been going for a couple of years now, and we have our own building."

"And when's it supposed to come out?"

"1983, but don't tell anyone I told you."

"My lips are sealed. All I can say is, if this Macintosh is the coming thing, maybe you should transfer to it as soon as you can."

"We'll see. Thanks, Dad!"

Len still wanted to hear about her office, what hours she was expected to work, whether she had coffee breaks, and all those other things that existed in his world back in Detroit but not in hers. They also talked about what was new in his life, and then, she went back to her Pascal manual.

3

NOTHING'S AT STAKE

I t was fall of 1981, and Matt Finegold scurried up the stairs to the apartment at his usual time, 6:30 pm. He wore his normal street-wary look that growing up in Queens had given him, even after years away.

He and his wife, Miriam, lived in a grubby building in the complex for married grad students near the University of Minnesota in Minneapolis. Miriam was cooking dinner, and she didn't seem to be especially cheerful, but then, she hadn't been lately. She also had that look of vague irritation customary for New Yorkers.

He put his keys down on the counter and said, "Hey."

She answered, "How's it going?"

"Oh, about the same. How about you?"

She was silent for a few seconds, "Today, all my clients at the clinic canceled. I don't know how I'm going to get my hours in this way."

"Fuckin' losers. How many more hours do you need?"

"Oh, shit... I'm not sure anymore. It depends on which states I want to be licensed in. I'm so fucking sick of this."

"Really?" He thought, "*You did sign up for this, though.*"

"Licensing! It's a good thing programmers don't have to

get a license." Changing the subject, "So, how's your research coming?"

Matt had a pretty good day, actually, but he didn't want to seem too cheerful since that would annoy her. "Poking along. Today, I discovered some papers by a Minnesota Professor, W.R. Franta, about networking. Seems like interesting stuff."

"Networking? That's not what your research is about, is it?"

He knew she'd say that. Anything that didn't lead to earning their degrees and getting the hell out of Minnesota with its brutal winters was a waste of time for her. Miriam had also grown up in Queens in a family considerably wealthier than Matt's. Although their families only lived a few miles apart, they didn't know each other until they met at The State University of New York (SUNY) in Binghamton. And for some reason, which they couldn't remember anymore and sometimes argued about, they had decided to go to grad school here in the frozen tundra. They both thought they knew what winters were like, but they'd never lived in a place where your key wouldn't open the car door in the morning because the lock froze overnight.

Matt was in the doctoral program in Computer Science, and Miriam was in Clinical Psychology. In her program, she not only had to do a dissertation, which she'd procrastinated about since they arrived a couple of years ago, but she also had to get her supervised hours in. These, of course, were completely unpaid. She was at a clinic where unwed mothers, drug users, people diverted from the criminal justice system, and other troubled people went. When someone with less severe problems came in, one of the more senior psychologists took them.

They'd both become disillusioned with the academic world and had long since stopped laughing at the joke among grad students:

Q: Why are academic politics so vicious?

A: Because there's nothing at stake.

He considered her question about whether he was shifting focus. "No, not really. Networking seems like a hot area, though."

"Does this thing, whatever it is, have a name?"

"It's called Hyperchannel. Dr. Franta wrote a paper about connecting dissimilar CDC machines. You know CDC, right? Control Data Corporation. They're right here in Minneapolis."

Miriam looked slightly more interested, but not much. "Vaguely. Would this help you get a job with them when you finish school? I don't *want* to stay in this godforsaken place! Just thinking about the coming winter depresses me."

Matt laughed, "You and me both! No, I don't want to work for CDC. Or Cray Research."

She patted him on the arm and went back to the stove. "There are lots of hot areas. When you earn your degree, you'll have plenty of time to explore. Someplace with a decent climate."

Over dinner, they talked about things to do outside of school. This was always a fraught topic since Miriam was sure to say it was better in New York, no matter what *it* was. Nonetheless, Matt ventured, "I read Patti LuPone is starring in *As You Like It* at the Guthrie in February!"

"She's slumming it here in Minneapolis, huh?"

"We saw her in *Evita*, remember?"

Miriam was briefly lifted out of her funk. Patti LuPone was at least a legitimate Broadway star.

"Should we buy season tickets to the Guthrie this year?" he asked.

"Sure, why not?"

"I'll order them. Also, do you want to see *A Prairie Home Companion* this week?"

Miriam made a face, "You got me in a good mood, but did you think I was going to go for that one?"

"Just thought I'd try," Matt snickered. He was always more willing to try out this Midwestern stuff than she was. Last year, he'd taken her to a University of Minnesota football game, and she still hadn't let him forget that one.

THE NEXT DAY AT WORK, Matt reread the paper about Hyper-channel and talked to some of his research colleagues about it. He also resolved not to tell Miriam any more about his side interests.

His research supervisor, Logan, apparently had some knowledge of Hyperchannel, so he dropped in on him. All the other grad students were in shared offices, but Logan had his own. He was still officially in the Ph.D. program, but that was more out of inertia than anything else. He'd long since stopped thinking about a dissertation.

Logan had wild, messy hair and dressed in that sloppy way that telegraphed, *"I'm a lifer here, and I don't care anymore."* He didn't have a beard, though, and Matt figured he probably just couldn't grow a decent one or else he would. He'd hung around the Computer Science Department long enough that it was almost easier to give him a job than to kick him out. When Matt joined the project, Logan was not even a little bit helpful to him. When Matt was just starting and asked Logan how to connect their PDP-8 to the CDC machine, Logan had said, "With instructions!"

Now that he was a paid University employee who ran their project, Logan had the fancy graphics Terak terminal, the one that cost almost $9,000. And when some of the faculty saw it, they started lobbying to have their terminals upgraded.

"Hey, tell me about Hyperchannel. I found this paper sort of interesting," he held out the Franta paper.

Logan looked at it, "Yeah. It's a local area network for Big Iron. Super-expensive."

"Oh yeah? How does it work?"

"Well, as I recall, you have these four trunks of coax cable, each carrying 50 megabits. There's an interface board with ECL components, although maybe they've replaced that with microprocessors by now."

Matt raised his eyebrows at ECL. Emitter-coupled logic was something he didn't know much about, except that it was fast, hot, and way more expensive than other circuit types. "How does the computer know when it can send some data? Or if it got there successfully?"

"Good questions. You might want to ask Dr. Franta about that, but I think the board listens on one trunk first, and if it's busy, it tries another one." He gave Matt some names to look up and then turned back to his Terak, which Matt understood as a signal to leave.

He went to the department library and spent the morning reading papers. *"Damn, this is what I should be doing!"* He went to lunch with the other guys in his research group. They were always up for any topic that did *not* involve their actual work, so local area networks held their interest for a while.

One of them, Roderick, had an Apple II that he kept at his desk. He left the cover off it since it was generally believed that they ran cooler that way. Everyone made fun of him for that, pausing whenever they walked past to blow imaginary dust out. He'd found the secret society of Apple II owners at the school, and they were constantly dropping off floppies at his desk. Matt learned that they referred to that as SneakerNet.

Roderick said, "I think one of those Hyperchannel adapters must cost about ten times what my Apple costs."

Matt laughed, "Only ten? Probably more like fifty. Plus, it's no good if there's only one. Everyone has to have one!"

Everyone chuckled. Roderick said, "Someone's going to create a local area network for *cheap* computers. Someday."

Vince remarked, "They're already doing it. Datapoint has

one, and there's this company Nestar in California that's selling one. And 3Com is selling Ethernet cards for the IBM PC." Vince had bought an IBM PC as a reaction to Roderick's Apple. It was a novelty at first for everyone, but now it sat unused most of the time.

Roderick said, "And the Ethernet card is pretty expensive."

Matt took his notebook out of his pocket and wrote down those names. "What's the Datapoint one called?"

"ARCnet, I think."

"And the Nestar one?"

"Cluster/One, I think."

Roderick instantly answered, "Clusterfuck!" They all smiled.

"Ethernet, I know about. Supposedly, DEC and Intel are in on it, too."

That topic being exhausted, they moved on to the *Mommie Dearest* movie, which they all claimed was about *their* mothers.

Back at the office, Matt thought about his dissertation, which was starting to seem more and more pointless. The Cray-1, which had been donated to the University, seemed to be vacuuming up every research dollar in the department. It was generally considered the fastest computer in the world, and Matt used to feel really cool to be working on it. When he talked to his old Computer Science friends at SUNY Binghamton, they were all impressed with how Matt had come up in the world. Business magazines ran fawning profiles of Seymour Cray, the chief architect.

The Cray ran at 160 MFLOPS, or million floating point operations per second. Floating point was the hardware that serious number-crunching required, and it was almost never found on the cheaper personal computers. The Cray specialized in vector operations, where you had an entire row of numbers that all needed the same operation done on them—add, multiply, whatever—and it supposedly did them all at once. Matt had learned that they weren't really done all at once, but still, it was pretty damn fast.

When the Cray was announced, a bidding war broke out between Lawrence Livermore National Laboratory and Los Alamos National Laboratory for the first unit. A few giant labs like those, plus the National Security Administration, were always the first to get the latest and greatest computers. As an expert on the Cray, Matt could look forward to guaranteed employment with one of those behemoths, if he were willing to live in Livermore or Los Alamos or maybe the D.C. area. The NSA was reportedly using theirs for analyzing crypto-graphic algorithms so that they could decrypt the communications of hostile nations, but no one who knew anything about that area would ever talk about it. When he was working toward his bachelor's at SUNY, Matt had interviewed with NSA on campus, and the interviewer told him that part of the process was to go to the campus police station and be finger-printed. He might even have to take a lie detector test. He didn't bother.

Now whenever he saw the NSA in the news, he felt a personal connection. The interviewer was actually pretty nice. He told him the NSA had the largest computer center in the Free World, which Matt guessed was meant to impress him.

Matt's research was on register allocation in high-level languages, which meant using its extremely expensive and scarce special memory efficiently in FORTRAN. He'd spent countless hours at Cray's headquarters in Minneapolis.

Naturally, the University had thrown up a huge bureau-cracy around access to the Cray and kept it in a glass-walled room with a raised floor. Gaining access to it required a process similar to entering the priesthood. As a privileged researcher with full access, Matt had a certain cachet with the undergraduates, which, he had to admit, he'd enjoyed at first. But now, he was completely tired of it. Still, his work was progressing steadily, but it seemed like every other week, some new hotshot came to him with a theory on register allocation in vector operations. Or they took it to his advisor, or worse yet, to some *other* professor in the department who hated his advisor. Matt had become sick of how all the professors seemed to hate each other, and he continually struggled to put together a team of dissertation advisors who wouldn't blow up in his face when two of them had a falling-out.

"*Back to the grindstone!*" Matt said to himself as he logged onto the Cray.

4

MARKING TIME IN EL SEGUNDO

D an, Joel, and Peter had finished their paper on Star's Records Processing in late September and submitted it to the conference, where it was promptly accepted. The Xerox Star was hot, hot, hot in the academic world.

Dan was flying up to Palo Alto every week now, and he always took the 8:00 am United flight because that didn't force him to wake up obscenely early. He left the house at 7:15 am, leaving him time to board the plane with a few minutes to spare[1]. His new group, Advanced Development, reporting to Martin Whitby, was made up entirely of Palo Alto people, except for him. After he left work for the day, he'd sometimes interview with some startup, so he had acquired a pretty good picture of the startup scene in Silicon Valley.

It seemed like "Unix on a Motorola 68000, with a graphical user interface!" was everyone's elevator pitch. He wondered how many of those startups the venture capitalists were going to fund. *"Maybe you're not really accepted into the VC club unless you have at least one of those!"* If you were a founder and didn't have "graphical user interface" or "mouse" or "microprocessor" or "Unix" (okay, those last two hadn't come from Xerox) on the first page of your business plan, the venture capitalists wouldn't even speak to you. Or so it seemed.

It was tough to find the right fit, though. Nearly everyone was happy to talk to him since "Xerox Star experience" was *the* golden credential. But often, the startups wanted some specific skill that Dan didn't have. He wasn't a Unix kernel guy—someone who knew how to get Unix working on a particular microprocessor, the kernel being the inner heart of the operating system. Every startup seemed to want those guys.

He wasn't a specialist in user interfaces, either, although he came to realize that in their minds, he was! *"In the kingdom of the blind, the one-eyed man is king,"* he used to say. But he didn't feel like selling himself as the expert on that stuff. Databases were the obvious career direction, but after all, the Star database was a single flat file. It was not a relational database where different data types could be combined in arbitrary ways. Oracle was doing that. Dan didn't want to work on databases anymore, anyway. He had joined the Advanced Development group at Xerox partly to gain more exposure to other technologies.

There were some weird startups, and he enjoyed those. Grid Computing in Campbell was trying to build a laptop-sized computer, but the problem was the weight. Compaq had a portable PC that was referred to as luggable because it weighed twenty-eight pounds. You didn't really want to put that on your lap. Grid was trying to make one you *could* keep on your lap.

To reduce the weight, they had to limit the amount of memory, and to do that, they used a language called Forth, which was highly compact in its binary code, but weird in its syntax. There was a license plate frame you could buy, a takeoff on "Honk if you love Jesus," which read "Forth love If honk then." Dan had no desire to program in Forth.

Another fun one was Rational Machines, whose employees he thought could best be described as a cult. They were developing entirely in Ada, supposedly the new standard language for defense-related software. At the end of his interview, he asked the usual questions for a startup about their stock, total capitalization, who the investors were, how many shares were outstanding, how many rounds of capital-raising they'd had, and so on. Dan had found that every employee at most startups knew all those numbers by heart. The interviewer at Rational answered wearily and condescendingly, "Well, I *guess* we *could* have someone explain all that to you, if you were really interested." Apparently, a true believer wouldn't ask such things, he gathered.

Later, one of Dan's friends interviewed at Rational Machines as well and told him that he'd been interviewed by every single one of the twenty-eight employees. They told him there was a basketball game every afternoon, and participation was mandatory. This friend didn't go to work there either, but Dan figured he must have feigned devotion better than Dan did—at least well enough to make it that far.

At Xerox, he was working on adding voice annotation to documents. The Advanced Development group had many lengthy and inconclusive meetings on the topic, where the number one problem was that voice files were large. While there was research on compression, the technology hadn't reached the point of being standardized. And if you did nothing clever, you sampled the audio forty-four thousand times a second—twice the highest frequency the human ear can hear—and you encoded each sample with 64 bits.

That was almost 22 megabytes per minute! This was way, way too much for documents to hold. And suppose a Star user added a minute of voice comments to a document and mailed it to twenty members of their staff? Would that be twenty copies of that voice annotation? Think of all the Ethernet traffic! It would never fly.

So now, they considered putting the actual data on a file server, where there was, in theory, plenty of disk space. The voice icon, whatever it was, would be a reference to the file on the file server. Problem solved! But wait... then if you mail the document to twenty people as before, now you have twenty pointers to it? If one recipient deletes it, you still can't delete it off the file server because there are still nineteen people holding the pointer. Maybe if all twenty delete it, you can, but what if you miscount, or someone squirrels a copy away on a removable disk, or they mail it to some people on a different file server so that they get their own copy?

It was ugly. Dan's instinct was just to pick some reasonable choices and go for it. This was only a prototype, after all. But he discovered that the sort of people who work in an Advanced Development group are not necessarily used to making quick back-of-the-envelope calculations and running with them. They want to think about everything and discuss it. Forever. Nonetheless, hacking the Star document code to get something working was what they hired him for, so he set about doing it.

Out in the startup world, every available niche in the ecosystem was filling up. Graphical user interfaces with icons and mice were hot, and the IBM PC was, too, so naturally several startups were trying to marry the two. It was very difficult, and most programmers thought the Intel 8086 processor at the heart of the PC just didn't have the power to handle it. Also, it would have to be intimate with the MS-DOS operating system, and Microsoft's Bill Gates would never stand for that. If it did catch on, Microsoft would announce their own version or maybe make the company a lowball acquisition offer with the implicit threat that they *would* do their own. Rumor had it that Microsoft was trying to create a window-based interface, too. In fact, a PARC guy had supposedly taken on this fool's errand.

One of Dan's Xerox friends had gone to Sun Microsystems, which had a reputation for being a sweatshop. They were trying to do Unix with windows—a system where each Unix process ran in its own window. The graphical user interface revolution hadn't made much of an impression on some of the Unix old-timers. They referred to the mouse as a rodentiary device intended to replace typing, an idea they took grave offense at. Some of them said ironically, "The mouse is what I use to indicate the window I want to type in." He visited there one Friday night, and since it wasn't a full-fledged job interview, nothing more was expected unless he initiated it. He didn't

5

JUST BEFORE THE DAWN

Matt left his regular meeting with Professor Herriman, his advisor, more discouraged than ever. His dissertation proposal had been sitting on Herriman's desk for a couple of weeks, and these meetings usually made him catch up, at least. He hadn't realized when he started here how many different things Herriman was involved with and how little time he would have for Matt. When Matt thought back on his time at Minnesota, he realized it was his second semester before Herriman even knew his name. That was why he'd hired Logan to manage their software effort—he couldn't possibly manage everything himself anymore.

At any rate, Dr. Herriman pronounced Matt's proposal excellent, but he had just a few comments. *"Just a few!"* Matt muttered to himself as he contemplated redoing most of his last month's work. It seemed like he always had some niggling complaint about the illustrations, which today included the shade of blue he used. Each of these *teensy* complaints took him most of an afternoon on the computer, although it would be ten seconds with paper and pen.

On the way back to his office, he stopped in the department library. He'd been spending a lot of time there lately, looking through the computer magazines and reading networking papers. He read the Metcalfe paper about Ether-net, and he was entranced. *"Plus, it's a joint standard with Xerox, DEC, and Intel!"* There were many citations of it, and he read those, too. People were claiming it would never work because the time to send something was non-deterministic, meaning you didn't know for certain how long it would take. Matt was a practical-minded guy from Queens, and the people trashing it reminded him of hoity-toity rich kids who grew up in suburban Connecticut and went to Ivy League colleges. He hated them already.

The personal computer revolution was taking off, but Matt always thought that one big problem with a bunch of cheap computers was that most of them needed something occasion-ally—a printer, or more hard disk space than their machine had, or *something*. When you had a terminal to a big machine, like the Cray, you had access to all the resources it had, but with just a little Apple II or IBM PC, you had nothing. With a network, you and all your coworkers could share a central file server or a printer. This made so much sense. It had to be the future.

He needed to get into that stuff! This grad school life sucked. Somehow or other, he had to sell himself to one of these startups out in Silicon Valley. How was he going to do that? And even if he did, what would Miriam say? Their plan had always been to earn their doctorates and then move to some town where they could both work, him in industry or academia and her as a clinical psychologist. They'd have nice comfortable lives. He had to bring her around. But how?

That night after dinner, she brought up her clinical work, which was frustrating as usual. Her clients were not motivated, and they resisted everything she tried to do for them, if they even showed up for appointments. The management was completely incompetent, except at writing grant proposals. It seemed to her sometimes that grant writing was all they actually cared about. But she had to get in her supervised hours to be licensed as a clinical psychologist, so she stuck it out.

Matt was used to this kvetching, and he had to move beyond it. She hated Minneapolis and the Ph.D. program, but in her profession, unlike in his, a Ph.D. was almost mandatory to do the kind of work she wanted to do. He had to plant the seed and make her think it was her idea, somehow. *"Okay, here goes!"*

"So, how goes the dissertation topic search?"

She made a face, "Yuck. They're pushing me to work on one of two big projects that are already underway, and neither one excites me."

"What are they?"

"One is a gerontology project, where you're working with old people, and the other is for developmentally disabled children."

Matt couldn't resist, "Damn, they're always either too old or too young!"

She chuckled mirthlessly, "Yeah. Why can't I work with regular old neurotic adults?"

"I don't see why not," he observed. "By the way, doesn't MMPI stand for Minnesota Multiphasic Personality Inventory? We took that at SUNY, remember?"

"That thing's a joke. I'm sure I could join the project to revamp it for people other than rural married whites."

Changing the subject, she asked, "So how about your project, whatever the hell it is?"

Now it was Matt's turn to make a face, "Same old shit. Herriman complained about my diagrams some more. That's about all he ever cares about."

She was hardly paying attention now and was ready to explode. "So, Matt. What the *fuck* are we doing here? I hate this fucking place."

"Where would you want to go?"

"I don't know. For starters, someplace with decent weather."

"Like where? California?"

"Where the only cultural advantage is, you can turn right on a red light?" she sneered, quoting *Annie Hall*, although it was more out of a sense of obligation as a New Yorker.

"Woody Allen was talking about Los Angeles, actually."

She smiled briefly, "Okay, LA is out. Can you turn right on red in San Francisco?"

"Pretty sure you can. Plus, it has Stanford and Berkeley. And lots of computer jobs."

She looked wistful, "Stanford had the famous Prison Experiment. Do you remember that?"

"Oh, was that the one where they turn ordinary people into sadistic torturers?"

"The very one. I want to manipulate adults, too!"

"That's the girl I married," he said. "And *I* want to jump on the future of computing, which is not Big Iron."

"Big Iron? Is that what you call your computer? I thought it was a song by Marty Robbins."

He sang a line from that song,

"... with a *big iron* on his hip."

"So, what's *not* Big Iron? Those little personal computers? Do they call them Little Iron?"

Matt became righteous, "Little Plastic, I think. They might be toys now, but in five years, everyone's going to have one."

"Even me? Never!"

He laughed, "Okay, maybe not you. But everyone else. They're already using them in big companies."

"So, how come your computer department isn't all over that?"

"Probably because Control Data and Cray Research are in Minneapolis," he said, rubbing his thumb against his fingers in the money gesture. Matt was happy to drop the topic. That was enough for one day.

THE NEXT DAY while bicycling to work, he wondered how he could sell himself to one of those Silicon Valley startups. "Hey, I know all about optimizing vector operations on the Cray!" was not going to do it. He needed some experience with local area networks, however lame. It was rare enough in the industry right now that almost any kind of experience sufficed. There was no certificate to obtain.

Then on his morning walk around the department schmoozing with people, Matt realized that *that* was something he was good at, collecting information. Everyone liked to talk to him.

It seemed like every third person he talked to had a personal computer, was about to buy one, or knew someone who had. A few days later, he dropped in on Logan, his supervisor. "Hey. What's up?"

"Not much. You?"

Logan had an idea. "Hey, you were interested in networking, right?" Matt agreed that he was. "You ever heard of CSNET?"

"Some kind of network for Computer Science?"

"Very good. How about ARPANET?"

Matt brightened, "Now *that*, I've heard of. How come we're not on it?"

"We're in good company. Most CS departments aren't. CSNET is a proposal by DARPA to connect ARPANET to the CS departments of the world. Like us."

"Sounds good. So, when do we get it?"

"Well, the University was on the initial committee to get it started, but now, the project is proceeding without us. Which is where you come in.[1]"

Matt looked skeptical. This wasn't what he was hoping for. He wanted to install a departmental LAN and be hired by some startup in California, not take on bureaucratic drudge work.

"Me? What would you want me to do?"

"Take it off my hands, mainly. I seem to be tagged with it."

"Oh, boy. You make it so appealing."

"That's the spirit! I'll send you some articles, and you can get started." He did some quick typing and hit Return with a flourish. Logan stood up, "Okay, I've gotta run to a class now."

Matt returned to his terminal, opened the documents Logan had sent him, and found the other documents that those referred to. ARPANET. Packet-switching. He discovered what RFC stood for—Request For Comment. This seemed so unpretentious, compared to the pomposity he was used to from the big computer companies—a bunch of computer researchers meeting in nice cities but at off-season times when the costs were lower and settling disputes by rough consensus, rather than by voting. He loved it.

He spent the rest of the day reading all that instead of doing his dissertation work. If anyone asked, he was working on something for Logan.

6

LIFE IN THE CIRCUS

J anet had settled into her new job on the second floor of Taco Towers. She'd been at Apple for three months. They had no local area network and no email, and that was pure hell after Xerox. When you wanted to tell everyone something at Apple, you printed up a memo and put it in their mailboxes. If it was urgent, you walked around and handed it to them. Or else you waited for the right meeting. In a dire emergency, you just stood up and yelled. At Xerox, she'd had a private office, but she realized now that those were relics of a bygone era, and she would be in cubicles from now on. Not even necessarily single-person cubes! Yuck.

But no email? *"My God, how do people live?"* At Xerox, if she needed to tell someone something, she just did it. Or if she wanted to ask a question to an entire group of people, she'd receive an answer from one of them ten minutes later. She learned pretty quickly that lamenting this too often would make you one of Those Xerox Snobs, so she restrained herself.

But what was even worse were the printers. The laser printer revolution was still in its infancy, and most of the world was still stuck with those godawful dot-matrix printers. She felt like she'd jumped back in time ten years.

Mostly though, she felt desperately lonely here. She hadn't made any close friends at Apple. She found herself missing her friends at Xerox so much, and she started hanging out with the other Xerox alumni. But there weren't many of them. Since they'd all lived in the Bay Area for a long time, they had their own social networks, but she managed to insert herself into some of them. They had a wine-tasting club that met every week, and even though she'd never been much of a wine connoisseur, it was a nice diversion. She found out that every Thursday, some Xeroids met at the Dutch Goose after work. So, she decided to drive up to Menlo Park and try it.

When she arrived, the trestle tables were full of the usual assortment of golfers, bicyclists, motorcycle riders, locals, and tech types. Peanut shells littered the floor. On the back patio, Porter Berwick was holding forth about bicycles, one of his favorite topics. Porter had a big bushy beard that immediately reminded her of Jerry Garcia, and he was clearly in his element, smiling and laughing. Four or five other people were all eating peanuts and sharing a pitcher of beer. Fortunately, they recognized her, even though she'd never spent much time with any of them.

"Hi, I'm Janet Saunders! I think I know most of you."

Porter shook her hand, "Welcome! So, where are you now?"

She'd already figured out that "where are you now?" was the standard conversation opener for anyone you hadn't seen lately. You assumed that they must have changed jobs.

"Apple. Along with Tesler, Belleville, and a bunch of others."

They laughed. Ray Holmberg shook her hand and reminded her of his name, which she appreciated since she'd forgotten it. "And more to come, probably!"

She sat down, "I wouldn't know about that!"

Porter asked, "So how is that Lisa project coming along?"

"I guess pretty well. They're on the 68K now. You can build for the Lisa *on* the Lisa… it's moving pretty fast."

Ray said, "If we'd only waited a year or so, we could have been using the 68000, too."

Everyone had an opinion on that, and the debate raged for several minutes. Janet noticed that there was no issue that energized computer guys like what a given chip could or couldn't do. Motorola had their 68000 microprocessor chip, which all the cool kids were using, and Intel was pushing their crappy 8086 family of chips. Unfortunately, the Intel chip was what IBM had chosen for the PC, and therefore, most of the world was stuck with it. The Xerox Star didn't use either of those because it had been designed before microprocessor chips really came of age.

All this was rehashed endlessly while Janet congratulated herself for turning the focus onto something other than her. Eventually, Porter held up his hands in the time-out sign. "Okay, we can spend the rest of the night talking chips." No one felt like talking about Xerox anymore, though. That was yesterday's news. The conversation turned to where everyone was going *after* Xerox. Most of them seemed to wish for a research-oriented place rather than the startup world, and they weren't sure where to go yet.

The one other woman at the table looked vaguely familiar to Janet, but she hadn't ever met her. She introduced herself, "Hi, Janet, I don't think we've ever met. I'm Audrey Renner."

"Ah, yes, I remember the name. Nice to meet you finally."

"So, I wanted to ask you. How do you feel about all the management turmoil at Apple? It must be pretty distracting!"

Janet made a face, "Yeah, I'm still getting used to avoiding riding an elevator with Jobs. You hear stories about him asking someone what they do, not liking the answer, and firing them on the spot." Everyone laughed.

Audrey continued, "And, reading about it all in the *Mercury*

News! Good grief. At least at Xerox, they have the decency to carry on their feuds in private."

The San Jose *Mercury News* regarded Apple as its *enfant terrible*. Everything that happened there was considered newsworthy, regardless of whether any other newspaper in the country was following it. This was also new for Janet, and she didn't particularly like it.

"*What am I supposed to say to that?*" She smiled and said something non-committal.

But now Porter picked it up, "So, we hear Jobs is making a competitor to the Lisa, and he's stolen a lot of the good people! True?"

"Yep. I don't know much about that, though. I think it's called the Macintosh. They're over in a different building."

"Cute!" said Porter. "Apple, Macintosh, get it?" They smiled, but no one laughed.

Audrey said, "I remember hearing your name as the Buildmaster on Star. Is that what you're doing at Apple, too?"

"Yeah, among other things. They hand me their floppies, and…" She was interrupted by laughter.

Porter said, "A floppy! I think I saw one of those once." He put his hands out and said, "They're smaller than ours, right?"

Janet answered, "Those are the eight-inch ones. You guys should get with the times." She had them there. Eight-inch floppies were a relic.

Ray said, "So, there's no local area network, I guess. That's going to make it tough to sell to businesses."

She was about to say, "Especially now that Xerox has that market all sewn up."

But Audrey interrupted, "I hear they use Hungarian notation in their code, too![1]" Everyone laughed.

"Hungarian" was the nickname for the almost-unreadable coding conventions that Carroll Molnàr, who was from Hungary, had introduced at Xerox. It had caught on in the

Star project. It was called that because he eliminated all the vowels in variable names to save on memory, and people imagined that was what code in Hungarian must look like.

Porter held up his hands. "I kinda like some of those names, like ctArray," spelling out the word. "At least the name itself tells me it's the count of items in the array. Anyhow, time out. I think we've now completed the hazing ritual for new members! Welcome, Janet." Everyone raised a glass and echoed Porter.

Janet was relieved. She asked, "So, what's happening at ex-Rocks these days? Anyone still there?"

Ray spoke up, "Same old shit. They're in denial about what's happening. A bunch of new people were hired to replace the ones who left."

"Depressing," said Janet. "People all over the Valley are starting up companies to steal their stuff."

Porter said, "Speaking of which, has anyone heard from Metcalfe since he started his company?"

Ray replied, "3Com? No. Building Ethernet cards for the PC is a business that at least makes some sense."

Janet made a mental note of 3Com for later. There was silence for a while.

Norm, another guy Janet knew vaguely, changed the subject. "We're thinking of buying a house. Does anyone know an agent they like?"

Porter laughed, "There are two questions there!"

Norm agreed, "Mainly the *like* part."

Porter said, "I don't know about these guys, but I got my place in Palo Alto a long time ago, and I don't even know if my agent is still in business."

Janet hadn't thought about buying a house until this minute but jumped in, "I kinda resisted it down in LA. Where should I look, if I were looking?"

Norm chimed in again, "It depends. We have kids. Do you?" She shook her head.

"Palo Alto has the best school district. But damn, you *really* pay for it!"

Everyone nodded in agreement. He asked her, "Where are you living now?"

"I'm renting a condo in West San Jose, almost in Cupertino. It's pretty close to Apple, but I don't know how long I'll be working there."

"Yeah, that's tough. About all you can do is be centrally located."

Porter said, "I don't have kids, but the people who might buy my house probably will, so it still makes sense to look at the schools."

She asked, "Is Palo Alto the only good school district? What's in second place or third?"

Ray answered, "Cupertino. Maybe Mountain View. Los Altos."

They discussed the various high schools in the area. They told her that the farther east you went, the less desirable the neighborhood was, but all the jobs were out near 101. If you were really rich, you lived in the hills to the west, like Portola Valley or Los Altos Hills, but then you had a hellish commute. But presumably, then you didn't care because you were so rich.

"I would suggest spending some Sundays driving around going to open houses. It's free… you find out what things cost, and you don't even have to give your name if you don't want to."

Everyone agreed with that. Ray added, "If you meet a real estate agent you like at one of those, then you've got it! That's what I did."

They returned to the topic of bicycling. She remembered Grant Avery, who used to live in Palo Alto, talking about the Western Wheelers, so she asked about that. A bunch of them had gone on rides with them. They had rides for all different skill levels, so she was encouraged to get their newsletter and go riding some weekend. She said she would.

The food at the Goose was famously mediocre, but since they were already there, several of them went to the front and ordered. Janet begged off. She said it was nice meeting them and left. On the way home, she thought about a house some more. Her dad would be opposed, but that was because he'd be thinking of shoveling snow in the winter. Plus, in his day, single women didn't buy houses.

On Sunday, she bought the *Mercury News* and found some open houses in Cupertino and Los Altos to visit. Several were within walking distance of her condo. Maybe she'd buy here, she thought. At least there'd be no surprises since she already knew what the neighborhood was like—solidly middle class and neither rich nor poor.

7

DON'T HEAD FOR THE HILLS

The novelty of working for a team in Palo Alto had worn off, and Dan was bored. He'd already interviewed with a bunch of startups in Silicon Valley, but either they weren't the right fit, or they needed someone who could start immediately, which he couldn't because he owned a house in LA.

Dan had a trip planned to Palo Alto for Monday, January 4, 1982, but he received a surprise phone call on Sunday from one of the admins up there, "Don't come!" It was raining cats and dogs. Being from the Midwest, Dan was never particularly impressed by the big storms in California, which might drop (horrors!) two to four inches of rain. He thought it was a bigger Bay Area story that the 49ers beat the Giants and were going to the NFC Championship Game next Sunday. Maybe they'd make it to the Super Bowl for the first time.

Back in Chicago, it could rain that much in an hour. No one ever canceled an indoor event because of rain. You might cancel for a tornado warning. Those were issued all the time, although there never seemed to be an actual tornado. Maybe for a giant snowstorm, such as the one in 1967. But for a regular old rainstorm? Grab an umbrella and carry on.

Anyhow, they were having rain up there, and in fact, there was a chance of rain in LA, too. On Monday, the *Times* said that the storms that drenched northern California would visit LA all this week. Dan went to work as usual. The email from Palo Alto was much different than usual— people arriving late or not coming in at all and exchanging stories about the roads that were flooded in their neighborhoods.

In San Jose near Cupertino, Janet's condo complex backed up onto Calabazas Creek. In the morning, the residents were standing around watching the waters rush by. In the summer when she'd moved in, the creek was completely dry. Everyone was amazed to see it full of brown water now. Some people worried about how much higher it was going to go.

She tuned into the news station on the car radio. The San Lorenzo River in Santa Cruz had overflowed its banks, and there was flooding all over the area. People up in the hills had to evacuate their homes. Nineteen inches of rain fell in twenty-four hours.

It rained all day. When she returned home, she turned on the local news on TV, which was non-stop storm coverage. Up in the mountains, people had actually been killed by debris flows and landslides. All reporters were photographed in heavy rain gear at some disaster site, usually in front of a house that had been swept away or a road completely covered in rocks and mud. She left the TV on until it became repetitive and then turned it off.

Shortly after that, the lights went out. She walked down to the stairway landing where residents had gathered. A few were holding flashlights. At least she knew it wasn't just her unit that was out. These were her neighbors, but she'd never met most of them. She introduced herself.

One of them, Max, was an old-timer, "Is this your first disaster?"

"Yeah. Is this a common thing here?"

"Oh yeah, every time there's a big storm a limb falls on a power line somewhere."

She laughed, "Wow, you'd think they'd bury them eventually!"

"You would think. But that would require too much intelligence." Outside, they could see the PG&E truck parked with its lights flashing and several workers in yellow rain suits moving around.

Another neighbor, Joan, asked her, "Sweetie, do you have any emergency supplies? Water, flashlights, candles…?"

Janet admitted that she didn't. Joan said, "Come on up to my unit, and I'll give you some candles."

Janet said, "Nice meeting you all!" and followed Joan back up the stairs, where she gave Janet three candles. Janet went back to her condo.

She thought she *might* have a flashlight somewhere, but she wasn't sure. She set one candle on a plate on the kitchen counter and took another to the closet to look for a flashlight. Success! Now at least, she could read a book while waiting for the power to return.

The next day, the storm was the entire front page in the *Mercury News*. People were killed when trees fell on their houses or cars, they were hit by cars or trucks that lost control, power lines fell on them, and most spectacularly, fast-moving debris flow came right through their house and buried them.

Back in LA, Dan had been watching the news on TV. The Bay Area seemed to have worse rainstorms, while LA always had forest fires, and they both had earthquakes. As Roseanne Roseannadanna said on Saturday Night Live, "*Well, Jane, it just goes to show you, it's always something—if it ain't one thing, it's another.*"

8

THE REVOLUTION WILL BE TELEVISED

M att had two networking tasks, up from zero at the start of the school year. He had the official one and the unofficial one, plus he still had his regular dissertation work, which he was actively looking to get out of. He was officially working on register optimization for vector operations on the Cray, and he found that he loathed that subject more and more daily. But that was what paid his salary, so he needed to at least give the illusion of progress.

The official networking task was to get the University onto the nascent CSNET so that users could do email, file transfer, and remote login, even though they weren't on the full ARPANET. CSNET was a proposal to give Computer Science Departments who couldn't join the regular ARPANET a sort of second-class status. At least, they could exchange email and files and log onto the main computers. ARPANET only had about twelve hosts and was not even contemplating adding everyone who wanted in.

The plans for CSNET were now on their third iteration. Minnesota had been one of the universities interested in the first go-round, but that plan had failed when many of the prospective customers balked at the cost. Nonetheless, the

National Science Foundation had been patiently encouraging, and the third time seemed to be the charm. Now, the University of Wisconsin at Madison, Purdue, RAND Corporation, and the University of Delaware were up and running, and more schools were joining. It galled Matt that Wisconsin, just the next state over, was in, and Minnesota was not.

Matt's unofficial task, which had no backing at all from the CS Department, was to create a network for the Apple IIs and IBM PCs that were springing up like weeds. His network, whatever it turned out to be, was going to replace SneakerNet, the informal name for the network of people walking around (in their sneakers!) with floppies. How many obstacles stood in his way? First, it required laying cable. The University had contracts with the electricians' unions specifying who could do that. It would cost money, too, and a lot of it.

There was more. The Department was heavily into Big Iron, i.e., the massive supercomputers from the vendors headquartered in Minneapolis—Control Data and Cray Research. Those companies were not exactly jumping on the personal computer bandwagon. They considered personal computers toys. What do you get if you connect a bunch of toys together? A toy network. They were not the least bit amused at the thought of a toy network connected to their machines, like tying tin cans to the back of their Porsche.

Above all that, he'd have to convince a bunch of faculty members to agree on which network to install. *"Good luck with that! These are people who can't agree if water is wet."*

Even assuming he managed to slip sideways into networking and get out of the Ph.D. program altogether and into Silicon Valley, he still had to convince Miriam that this was a good idea. She was making imperceptible progress towards her Ph.D., but since she hated Minnesota, he had at least some chance of prying her out of that. Maybe she could switch to a doctoral program somewhere else, and she wouldn't have to listen to Matt complaining anymore. But for now, she was dubious.

Matt's father had served in World War II in the Seabees, the construction unit of the Navy that built bases all over the South Pacific in insanely short periods. His father always said, "The difficult, we do immediately. The impossible takes a little longer." Matt tried to emulate his dad. If he pulled this off, he'd have no trouble landing a job in this industry.

How would those tasks relate to each other? Matt almost laughed out loud when he pictured himself sitting at an IBM PC and sending an email through the ARPANET! *"Everyone says you can't do that! Oh yeah? Watch me."*

His first task had been to ask around and find out who the local experts were and make them his allies. He'd learned already that people who possessed arcane knowledge were often very lonely and desperate for attention. Universities, especially, tended to collect these people. His boss, Logan, was definitely not one of those people. Logan knew everything but only told you what he knew on some topic when you'd said the wrong thing about it.

Instead, Matt's colleague Roderick had been very helpful. Roderick was a clean-shaven, good-looking guy, reasonably well-dressed for a grad student, with a quick wit. He had won Matt's undying admiration the time Logan commented, after a party, that Roderick's house seemed to have a three-hole punch that belonged to the CS Department. Roderick said in a flash, "Those pricks! They must have snuck into our house and stuck the Department's three-hole punch in our living room!"

"Hey, Roderick! What do you know about X.25?"

"X.25. Some kind of public packet-switching, I think. Why?"

"Oh, Logan asked me to look into getting us on CSNET. X.25 is one way you can do it."

"CSNET... wasn't that going to be a way for unimportant places like this to get on the ARPANET?"

"*So, people have heard of this!*" Matt replied, "Right. But now, it's really happening, and we're not."

"Figures. How come? Money?"

"I'm not sure. That's what I have to find out. Who would know?"

"About X.25, you mean, or why we aren't on CSNET?"

"Well, either one. Both, actually."

Roderick said, "For X.25, you might try Dr. Caron. She's into all that international shit."

"Figures. French stuff. How about CSNET?"

"That one... I have no idea. I suppose you tried Logan already?"

Matt made a face, "Well, he gave me this to get it off his plate, so I'd rather not bother him right away. Thanks, Roderick!"

When he wandered up to Associate Professor Françoise Caron's office, she was there, intently studying her screen. She was neatly and conservatively dressed, with that elegant look French women seemed to have without even trying. She turned around, stood up, and extended her hand as he introduced himself.

"Dr. Caron, I've heard that you're the expert here on X.25. Is that true?"

She smiled, "I would not say I am an expert, Matt. There are so many things I don't know. What is your interest in it?"

"Well, Logan Arnold asked me to look into CSNET..."

Françoise's face was impassive. Was she hiding something? He wondered if she knew something and wasn't saying.

"... and from what I can tell, X.25 is one low-cost way we could connect to it."

"Okay, okay. So, there's a service somewhere you want to connect to, and you want to use X.25 to talk to it?" Matt nodded. "Do you know how X.25 works?"

He said, *"Un peu,"* but that was about all he could remember from his high school French.

She smiled thinly and proceeded to show him some introductory texts on the subject. "I'm afraid I can't lend these to you since I'm referring to them all the time, but I think the library has copies. You might want to write down the titles."

He copied down the titles, and he thought maybe she wanted him to leave, but her eyes brightened and said, "Do you know about Minitel?" He shook his head. "How about videotex?" Again, no.

"Well, we French are leading the world in that. In some French cities already, you can rent a terminal from the telephone company and look up people and businesses yourself, without calling Information. Soon, it will be throughout France, and there will be all sorts of services you can use besides number lookup.[1]"

Matt had never heard any of this. He didn't know what to say at first. He asked her how a customer would pay for these wonderful services and found that they would appear on your telephone bill. He was dumbfounded. All these problems of getting online that people here didn't even know were problems—the French had solved them already.

Without being asked, Françoise told him all about the CCITT, the Consultative Committee for International Telephony and Telegraphy, which was an association of the world's telephone companies, ultimately under the United Nations. CCITT was the reason you could pick up the phone and dial France or anyplace else. The CCITT was responsible for X.25, the public packet-switching network that Matt had originally asked about, and it was busy standardizing electronic mail, too. She had attended some of their meetings and spoke rapturously about the organized, stately way it was proceeding.

When the CCITT finished its work, you would be able to access your email through the phone, just the way you made phone calls now, and all of it would just be part of your communications bill every month.

"*Why haven't we heard about all this?*" Was it because the telephone company was a government monopoly in most of the world, and in the U.S., it was a private company? In fact, the government had been suing AT&T to make it even smaller, and AT&T had recently agreed to break itself up. Françoise did not try to hide her feeling that the Americans were shooting themselves in the foot over this, and pretty soon, they would regret that the rest of the world was steadily advancing without them. Very soon, the French would own the tech world!

An hour later, Matt remembered a class he had and left, failing to get the practical information on X.25 he originally came in for. His head was spinning with all the jargon she'd thrown out. "*Telephone companies are going to own the online world. How depressing.*"

He was still no closer to figuring out why Minnesota wasn't on CSNET or how to get it there. He suspected Dr. Caron must know something but wasn't saying. Logan surely knew. Was there some alternative to asking him? He decided that an email was the easiest way. Logan would probably give a one-word answer, but that would be enough. A half-hour later, he had his answer—Dr. Bruce Chapman, a fairly new Assistant Professor. When he finally managed to meet with Dr. Chapman, all he received was some eye-rolling and a vague reference to department politics. He began studying up in his spare time, or rather, the time he stole from what he was supposed to be doing.

～

IT WAS the start of the spring semester, and he'd been seeing references to The OSI Model, as though it was the Holy Writ that explained everything. He ran up to the library and found a journal that described it and set about reading. *"My God, this is thick stuff!"* It became clear to Matt that it was a conceptual model and not a description of anything that actually existed. Presumably, there would be detailed specifications developed and software written to conform to the model. Still, it was impressive as a description of a lot of things he'd wondered about.

When Matt knocked on Dr. Chapman's office door, he was admitted. "Hi, Dr. Chapman, I've been asked to look into CSNET... " Chapman nodded warily. "... and I've been doing a little reading in my spare time. I came across something called the OSI Model."

Dr. Chapman had certainly heard of that. He said sardonically, "Right, the answer to all the world's problems!"

"So, I take it you're not a big fan of that, huh?"

Chapman snorted and turned his terminal screen around so that Matt could see it. It had some email exchanges about protocols, but Matt didn't know what any of it meant.

"What's that? It looks like people discussing networking, I guess?"

Chapman snorted again and turned the terminal back around. "It's called rough consensus and running code. That's what the IETF values, not abstract design."

"What's IETF stand for?"

"Internet Engineering Task Force, and it's what's behind TCP/IP."

Matt was onto something! *"Keep this guy talking."*

"Is the University a member? Or are you a member? How does it work?"

"Anyone can be a member if they contribute. There are people with no degrees at all, and there are full professors. I would say so far, it's mostly grad students and other research people, but there are some people from the industry, too."

"And how does something get adopted? Do they take a vote or what?"

Bruce became more animated, "There is *never* a vote in the IETF! As I said before, rough consensus. It's a technical group, not a bullshit political group like the CCITT, pardon my French." Matt smiled at the word French, thinking of Dr. Caron. Bruce continued, "... and your code has to work, and it has to interoperate with other people's code. That's how we know if you're full of it or not."

This was strong language from a faculty member. Matt figured it had to do with his not having tenure yet.

"Sounds pretty good to me. So, the CCITT doesn't do that?"

"They think actual coding is a task they can delegate later to their lackeys."

Matt was silent for a while. He was beginning to get an idea of what happened to CSNET at Minnesota. He tried, "So, on CSNET... you said it was department politics when I asked you before. I don't want to push you into incriminating yourself, but does it have to do with this conflict between CCITT and IETF?"

Bruce leaned forward and dropped his voice an octave, "Look, Matt, I don't have tenure here. I have to be careful what I say."

Matt nodded, "Sure."

"But I *will* say this... backing Big Telecom is always going to be the safe choice. Like buying IBM for an MIS director."

"Yeah. Yeah. So, they're not involved in IETF at all? I would think they'd be able to steer it their way."

"They send people to the meetings, and they're on the mailing lists. But basically, no, they're not in control."

Matt was amazed. There really *was* a revolution underway. He wanted to be a part of it.

9

FATHERLY ADVICE

I t was the end of May 1982, and Janet was stubbornly trying to make Lisa a business computer, part of the original concept. Whenever people argued about that, as they often did, she pushed for it, but she was losing those arguments.

She'd worked on the Star, which was way too expensive for home hobbyists, and Xerox had never even considered them a market anyway. Businesses obviously bought computers, and they weren't as frugal as individuals. If numerous people in a company had computers, then they needed a network because they needed to exchange files, share a printer, and send email. This seemed pretty clear to Janet, but it was not going her way.

The Apple engineers and marketers didn't want to use a network unless it was Apple's own, and they weren't ready for that yet. There was talk of AppleNet, which was their own, but AppleNet's existence ruled out Ethernet and all the other popular ones like ARCnet. She really tried to push ARCnet because it was very well engineered and cheaper than Ethernet. But to her dismay, both Ethernet and ARCnet were damned as NIH—Not Invented Here.

She thought of her dad, Len, who'd first turned her onto Apple back in 1980 and raised it with him one Saturday during their regular phone call. "Hi, Dad!"

"Hi, sweetie. How's the big fancy job treating you?"

"Well… I wanted your advice as my PC-in-the-office expert!"

"I'm honored! Shoot."

"So, you guys started bringing in your own computers to the office because Chrysler wouldn't buy them for you, right?"

Her dad worked in Finance for Chrysler in Detroit. His people had started bringing in their personal Apple II computers to use VisiCalc in their financial analyses. This had opened Janet's eyes to the fact that the world was not standing still while Xerox, in its slow bureaucratic manner, made the Star.

Len laughed, "It was worse than that! They actually threatened to cut off our support if we tried to connect the Apples to *their* computer."

"And how are things now?"

"Well, now that IBM's blessed them, it's like night and day. You can put in a purchase request for an IBM PC, and maybe, maybe Chrysler will buy you one. I'm trying that myself."

"But not an Apple, huh?" she chuckled.

"I'm hoping. Are you guys making one that Chrysler will buy? I promise I'll make them get me one!"

"That's what I wanted your advice on. Apple doesn't seem serious about the business market. It's all individuals and hobbyists to them."

Len was silent for a second, "Really? How much are they going to sell those things for?"

Apple employees were lectured on confidentiality almost daily, so this was an easy answer. "I can't tell you, Dad, sorry. I could be fired for that."

"Okay, sweetie, I don't want to get you in trouble!"

"Anyhow, if an IBM PC costs $6,000 instead of $2,000, would Chrysler still buy it for you?"

"Well, that's a tough one. In finance, we have to look at the return on investment of capital equipment. So, it depends... maybe."

"It would be a yellow light and not a red light? Is that what you're saying?"

"Yeah, that's about it. But there's no way in hell, pardon my French, I'm paying $6,000 for a toy for home!"

"That's about what I thought. I keep telling them that, but they won't listen."

"Really? I thought Apple was the up-and-coming genius company. This seems pretty obvious to me."

Janet sighed, "Well... yeah. Anyhow, I have some other news. I'm looking at houses!"

"Houses? You mean, like, to buy?"

"That's the idea, Dad. Me, a homeowner! Did you ever imagine?"

Len put his hand to his forehead, "I have to admit, no, unless you marry again."

Janet would have been offended if anyone else had assumed that single women couldn't buy houses, but this was Dad. He gets a pass.

He asked, "But what are you going to do when it... oh wait. I guess it doesn't snow out there."

"No snow. And the houses don't have basements."

Janet had spent many a rainy day down in the basement as a kid, playing ping pong, reading, or watching TV. It seemed like almost every house in their neighborhood had a finished basement. It was hard to imagine living in a house without one, but after eight years in California, she'd become used to the idea.

Len still didn't feel comfortable. He didn't see what a single woman needed a house for. Families needed houses, but people living alone didn't.

"Why don't you just buy a condo? You still have the bene-fits of ownership, but you don't have all the chores and hassles."

"I don't want a condo, Dad. I'm tired of living in apart-ments, and that's all a condo is. Plus, you have homeowner boards to deal with. And if the price goes up, they can just build more."

He knew he wasn't going to win this one, and she did know how to press his economics button—supply and demand. The supply of condos is too elastic. She was right on that one.

"Well, if you're sure that's what you want. I hesitate to even ask, but how much are houses selling for out there?"

She knew what he'd say next. But he'd probably get over it. He worked in finance, so it was all just numbers, after all.

"The ones I'm looking at are around $130,000."

He gasped, "A hundred thirty thousand! How can anyone possibly afford that? Do you know what our house cost?"

"I think you told me once, but I forget. How much?"

"In 1952, we paid $20,000 for it, and we thought *that* was expensive."

"Well, times change, Dad. And California's always been more expensive."

"I guess." He tried to imagine the mortgage payments.

"And you're sure you can afford that on your salary? Do you need any help with the down payment?"

"Well, thanks, I might take you up on that. I cashed out my Xerox pension, so that should take care of most of it."

Len cringed at those words. It was unthinkable to cash out his pension. That was what he'd been working toward all these years! But Janet would do what she wanted to do, so there was no point in arguing.

They talked for a long time about mortgage rates, prop-erty taxes, commute times, schools, and all the usual home-owner things. She mentioned how property values seemed to only ever go up in California. He was unimpressed but didn't say it. In the Midwest, you could own a house for twenty years and make less money on it than you would have gotten from a savings account.

When they hung up, Janet thought he wouldn't be as completely positive about it as her friends out here, but at least he was in her corner.

THE NEXT DAY, she checked the newspaper for the open houses. There were quite a few right in her neighborhood and some in Los Altos and Mountain View.

In Los Altos, the houses were all too expensive, but that sure was a nice neighborhood. The closer you were to the hills on the west, the more astronomical the prices became. Sigh. Very close to Los Altos on the east was the Cuesta Park section of Mountain View. It was sort of a poor man's Los Altos—still west of El Camino, a very short drive to Apple and anywhere else she'd be likely to work after that. In every house she went into, she made a point of talking to the real estate person staffing the place, like the guys at the Dutch Goose had told her. At one of the Mountain View houses, she hit gold.

Bob, the fifty-ish agent, was affable, down to earth, and not at all pushy. He wore a sport coat with no tie, large metal-frame glasses, and was very slightly overweight. He had a British accent that had almost faded away after years in the States, but it was still audible. She liked him immediately. He'd been in the real estate business forever, had seen it all, and was friendly without being obsequious. He wanted to know what she was looking for and her budget, like any agent, but once she said she worked for Apple, he seemed to relax about money. He had a way of letting her tell her story without seeming to drag it out of her. She took his card and promised to call him in the coming week. After that house, she'd had more than enough real estate for one weekend and went home.

Bob's office was in Los Altos, and she met him there the next Saturday morning. They hopped into his car, and he said, "Well, shall we go terrorize Cuesta Park first?" They went to four or five houses in Mountain View, and Janet was not overly impressed. They were okay, but nothing special, and the asking prices were considerably more than she felt like paying. At each one, she would go out in the backyard and look over the fences into the neighbors' yards, something her father had taught her. You never knew when someone might have a car up on blocks, or chickens, or a swimming pool, or something else you'd rather not live next to.

She didn't see any houses she was really interested in. Bob just said, "Well, what did you think of that one?" after they left each house, but he didn't seem too concerned about selling her a house. When they parted, he said, "Shall we hit Cupertino next week?" She agreed and thanked him.

Thinking it over, Janet felt encouraged even though there was nothing she wanted to buy yet. Bob wasn't showing her the crappy houses first so that she'd jump at the first decent house, the way people had told her the slimy realtors did. Instead, she was getting a realistic idea of what $130,000 would buy. So many renters had an image of a gorgeous house in Palo Alto and just refused to accept living in South San Jose or Santa Clara with all those yucky working-class people. She didn't think even that would be such a total come-down, but she was more optimistic that at least she could live in a middle-middle class area. Hell, even the neighborhood she was renting in wasn't that bad... if it came to that.

It hadn't come to that yet. The next weekend, Bob thought they should go check out Cupertino. Even though Apple was in Cupertino and she lived just across De Anza Boulevard from it, she didn't have much of a sense of what it was like.

They exited 280 at De Anza and headed south. Janet felt like she was seeing it all with fresh eyes. At the corner of Stevens Creek on the left, she noticed the Cali Mill, a very old-looking building that she'd never really looked at even though she'd driven by a million times. "Have you ever been inside that?"

"What, the Cali Mill? No, I don't own a horse! Or poultry," he laughed.

"Is that what they sell there, horse chow?" she giggled.

"That, young lady, is a relic of our agricultural past. Take a good look at it because I'm sure they're going to tear it down soon."

"Wow. Maybe I should go in there sometime."

"You should. I don't know what you'd find to buy, though, unless you acquire a pet rabbit or want to grind some grain."

They drove down De Anza in silence, and Bob turned right at the first light. "Valley history aside, this first house is a three-and-two, built about 1955. I haven't had a chance to go inside it, so I can't tell you too much about it."

Janet walked through it. It hadn't changed much since it was built in the 50s. The windows all looked like the cheap single-pane jobs she was used to in apartments, and the kitchen wasn't too inspiring, either. Although a little less than the Mountain View houses, the price was higher than she wanted to pay.

Bob didn't say much about that one. The rest of the Cupertino houses were a variation on the same theme—so-so quality, nothing exciting, prices still too high. Janet's reactions told Bob all he needed to know, so he didn't quiz her too closely about what she thought about them.

On the way back to his office, she was curious about his background. "So, Bob, I have the feeling you weren't born here."

He laughed and put on a posh BBC accent, "Why, deah, what on uth gave you that idea?"

"Oh, I don't know."

"Yes, I came here from London in the early 50s with my wife. Been here ever since."

This left so many questions in her mind, but maybe he wasn't going to tell her much. "So, when did you get into real estate?"

"When did I get into real estate? I think it was in the mid-50s if I can think back that far. It's been so long!"

"So, you probably remember when this area was all fruit orchards."

He laughed, "Not quite all of it. The part we're looking at next time was, definitely."

"Where's that?"

"Well, it's exactly where you're living. West San Jose, which just happens to be in the Cupertino School District. Cupertino, you probably didn't know, has the second-best school system in the Valley, after Palo Alto."

"Really? I guess I wasn't paying much attention to that."

"I'm not surprised. Most people don't unless they have kids."

Janet got the point immediately, "But that has to be a big part of the real estate value, right?"

Bob smiled, "You're learning well! Let me know when you're ready to go out again. Next week, I have some other clients, but after that, I'm free."

Janet congratulated herself for picking Bob. He'd find her the right house.

10

MATT AND MIRIAM GO FOR A DRIVE

I t was a few weeks into that heavenly time on campus when there were no classes. Matt had a summer internship with Datapoint down in Texas starting next Tuesday. Miriam wasn't terribly pleased about Texas, but he'd appeased her with the promise that San Antonio would be just for the summer.

He landed the internship by installing ARCnet, Datapoint's local area network, in the CS Department at Minnesota and letting Datapoint know about it[1]. Matt was particularly proud of how he'd done that because it took a lot of chutzpah. Everyone said you couldn't possibly do it, given the contracts with the electricians' union and the opposition from some of the faculty, especially Françoise Caron, the champion of international standards. ARCnet was emphatically not one of those standards. It was also not what his graduate fellowship said he was supposed to be doing. But somehow, he'd pulled it off. His research group colleagues and Assistant Professor Chapman looked at him with a new sense of respect. Associate Professor Caron bided her time until she could derail the entire thing, but Matt figured by the time that happened, he'd be long gone.

He'd started by finding three people, not in the CS Department, who all had Apple IIs or IBM PCs in their offices and wanted to share a printer. Even more crucial, they all had adjacent offices. The fact that they were in Electrical Engineering, a different building from the CS Department, meant that Dr. Caron and her allies didn't know what he was up to until it was too late.

The four of them had come in on the weekend and pulled cable through the ceiling over their offices. They carefully taped the ARCnet cable to other wires with electrical tape to make it look official. A couple of weekends later, they had it all running. Word spread among the EE faculty, who all wanted in, and then inevitably to Computer Science. The EE faculty just *loved* taunting their CS friends that they had a 2.5 megabits per second local network, and the hotshots, supposedly on the cutting edge, did not.

This could not stand. CS had to keep up. The faculty pressured their Chairman, who pressured the Dean, and one thing led to another. Pretty soon, the CS Department had a special experimental agreement with the union and the Computing Services Department. Cable was pulled throughout the building, and ARCnet became a semi-official network. You didn't have to be on it, but everyone wanted to be. Matt was going to work for the Department as a full-time employee in the fall and finally move on from this stupid Big Iron dissertation he was so sick of. Freedom!

The CS faculty made sure to point out whenever the network was discussed that this was not the real network, and real soon now, they'd have Ethernet everywhere, or IBM's Token Ring, or Sytek, or WangNet, or... the list went on and on. Each standard had its own local champion.

How would they ever agree? Matt didn't care. It would be some kind of bureaucratic dogfight. He had a start on what he wanted, joining a networking startup and leaving the University. This summer job was the beginning.

He went to say goodbye to Roderick and Vince for the summer, his two favorite guys in the research group. They were in shorts and flip-flops, going all out for this summer thing. "Hey, see you guys in September!"

Roderick put out his hand, "Yeah, have fun in San Antone. Remember the Alamo!"

Matt laughed, "I don't think you're allowed to forget it down there."

Vince asked, "So, this ARCnet thing... it was just a gigantic scam to find a summer job?"

Matt stood up straight and feigned seriousness, "Why Vince, how can you say that? I only have the good of the CS community at heart. You know that!"

They all laughed. Vince asked, "So, how hot is it there in the summer?"

Roderick said, "I hear it's a dry heat, though!"

Matt answered, "Yeah, that's what I tell Miriam."

Roderick asked, "Do you know what you're going to be doing there?"

"Something to do with ARCnet, I guess. I'll find out on Tuesday."

They talked more about their summer plans. Roderick and Vince were staying around for the summer, which was actually the most pleasant time of the year at school. Most of the students were gone, everyone was more relaxed, and the women made up for their heavy coats all winter by wearing as little as possible. Matt would miss it.

When he arrived home, Miriam was in the bedroom packing for their drive down to San Antonio over the weekend. She had adjusted surprisingly well to the Texas thing since it was a vacation from the Psych Department and the free clinic where she logged hours for her therapist's license.

She had six boxes full already. He said, "Whoa! This all has to fit in our little car, remember!"

She looked annoyed, "What, were you planning to bring some friends, too? It'll fit!"

He sat on the bed, "I thought I'd just bring a few T-shirts, a pair of shorts, and some flip-flops."

Miriam replied, "Good because that's all you'll have room for!" He laughed and showed her the TripTik he'd picked up from AAA, with road maps all the way down to Texas. Going to the AAA office was his assignment today. He opened the maps for Minnesota, Iowa, and Missouri and showed her the routes AAA recommended. She didn't pay much attention at first since he usually did most of the driving. But man, oh man, this was going to be two *long* days of driving. Miriam was going to have to take the wheel some of the time.

ON SATURDAY, they finished loading the car and headed south on I-35 with Matt driving. The FM stations faded out pretty quickly, and they were stuck with AM radio and their tape collection. They figured they'd listen to AM until that became intolerable and then switch to the tapes.

The AM radio was barely tolerable if you kept switching the station, which was Miriam's job. "Ebony and Ivory" by Paul McCartney and Stevie Wonder was playing everywhere —insipid garbage, they agreed. "Rosanna" by Toto, same thing. "Break It Up" by Foreigner—wasn't it bad enough that this stupid band dominated the 70s? Do we *still* have to listen to them? What's next, Kansas with "Dust Up His Nose," as he referred to that godawful "Dust in the Wind"?

Out in the wilds of southern Minnesota and northern Iowa, there might be one rock station, and all the rest were country, religious, or farm news. If the one rock station was playing one of those hit songs, they were screwed. But "867-5309 (Jenny)" and "Hurts So Good" by John Cougar would come on now and then and keep them motivated.

They talked about how far they'd make it today, where they'd stay in San Antonio and whether Datapoint was going to pay for it, the leads Matt had on an apartment for the summer, and what Miriam was going to do with herself while Matt was at work.

Miriam was curious, "So, Matt, do you *want* to go back in the fall and work for the University?"

"Well, if all else fails, it's a pretty good gig."

"All else being what?"

She had him there. He decided to come clean. "I think I'd like to move into the industry. Do you feel like getting rich? It ain't going to happen at the University."

"That's for sure. But how are we going to get rich? Are you buying lottery tickets and not telling me?"

Matt laughed, "Lottery tickets are a tax on stupid people. No, I was thinking of joining some startup and receiving a whole bunch of stock. Then when they go public... boom!"

"Just like that, huh? Boom. Like getting free money?"

Matt had been researching startup companies. Datapoint had been around too long to be a startup, and anyway, they weren't going to give a summer employee any stock. But he told Miriam how many Apple employees became instant millionaires when Apple had its initial public offering.

She was only a little impressed. "Okay, that's one company. How many other ones go out of business, and you never hear of them?"

"Probably a lot."

She felt smug and pressed her advantage, "Who are the really big companies in this networking business? That's who you should join."

He played along, "Well, Datapoint is doing pretty well now, but it probably won't last."

"Why not?"

"Well, it's a closed system. They don't have any allies."

"Allies? Why do you need those? Does IBM have allies?"

Matt felt like he was in control, but she didn't know it yet. "IBM is in a different business where they control everything. You can't do that in networking."

"If you own all the computers, then isn't that everything?"

"Okay, we have an answering machine, right?" She nodded. "You know that at one time, those were illegal?"

"I guess. Were they?"

Matt had been doing his reading. "Ma Bell used to insist that connecting anything at all to their telephone system would endanger it. The Supreme Court put the kibosh on that in 1968."

"Okay, so?"

"So, nobody can own *all* the communications anymore."

She was silent for a while and then observed, "Not even Ma Bell. Now we have, what is it? U.S. West."

"Meet the new boss. Same as the old boss," Matt sang.

"Anyhow, how far are we going today?"

"I was hoping for Wichita," he said, glancing at his watch.

"Will we see the lineman?" she asked, and they both sang the opening line of "Wichita Lineman." Those were all the words they could remember, so the song petered out. They stopped for lunch in Des Moines, and Miriam took over the driving afterward.

There were a lot of FM stations for most of the way to Kansas City, so the music was a little more tolerable, and they didn't have to dip into the shoebox with the tapes. After Kansas City, it was godawful flat and boring, with endless wheat fields and cornfields.

Matt rummaged through the tapes. Miriam cried, "Driver controls the music!"

"Okay, fine. What's it going to be?"

"Pink Floyd, *The Wall.*"

Matt groaned but inserted the tape and looked out his window. After that, she called for *Slowhand* by Clapton. Matt said, "If I never have to hear 'Lay Down, Sally' again for the rest of my life, it'll be too soon." Listening to guitar god Eric Clapton debase himself with pop garbage like that was pure torture for him.

After that was over, he said, "Okay, I think I remember an addendum to that driver rule... it only extends to two tapes."

Miriam considered challenging that non-existent rule but thought better of it. They drove on. Kansas City. Topeka. Matt said, "How are you feeling? Wichita tonight?" She nodded.

As they approached Wichita, they couldn't believe their luck. They saw a worker climbing up a telephone pole and said "The Wichita Lineman!" together. She honked the horn, and they both waved, and he waved back. Matt said, "He's probably used to that since the song came out."

After an unmemorable motel room, dinner, and breakfast, they hopped back into the car with Matt driving. This time, Matt exercised his driver's prerogative and chose *Moving Pictures* by Rush, with Miriam's least favorite lead singer, Geddy Lee. She knew she'd earned this with the Clapton album yesterday, so she didn't grumble. Matt felt like he needed something high-energy to get him going in the morning.

After the tape finished, she popped it out, "Thank God that's over."

Matt just smirked and said, "I hear they have a new album coming out next month, too!"

She asked how he could sleep nights knowing that and then said, "So, you really want to work at one of these little networking companies?"

"It's worth a shot, right? If you never play the game, you can't ever win."

He thought she was going to throw cold water over it again, but she surprised him, "So, we'd have to move to Silicon Valley, is that what they call it?"

"Well, that's where most of them are. And if one fails, you just move on to the next."

She was silent for a while, "And, what would I do while you're getting rich? Or not."

He corrected her, "While *we're* getting rich."

In any case, he was ready for this. He'd visited the school library and looked into Ph.D. programs in Psychology in the Bay Area and also the licensing requirements for therapists. They talked about all that, while Matt was careful to let her do most of the talking and not make it seem like he had it all planned out. She ranted about how fucked up the clinic she volunteered at was. He knew he didn't have to convince her that she wanted to be out of Minneapolis.

When they hit a lull in that conversation, Matt picked a tape that he knew Miriam liked, *For Your Pleasure* by Roxy Music. They grooved along to that in silence.

They arrived in San Antonio late Sunday night and moved into the apartment Datapoint had reserved for them. Tomorrow was going to be sightseeing and settling in, and Tuesday, he'd start work. Neither of them had ever been to Texas.

On Monday, they went to the Alamo and then walked the Riverwalk. There weren't too many tourist attractions in San Antonio, so they agreed, "Of course, we have to do that! Everyone's going to ask us if we went to the Alamo." It was charming. Even Miriam liked it.

On Tuesday, Matt went to work at 8550 Datapoint Drive in northwest San Antonio. He knew Datapoint must have been there a while if they had a street named after them. There seemed to be Datapoint buildings all along the street, but this was the Software Development and Testing building.

His task this summer was writing test programs for ARC,

the Attached Resource Computer, which was what they actually called it, not ARCnet. His primary supervisor was a guy named Marty, who looked like he'd come straight from Brooklyn—he had a straw-colored fedora with a wide striped band around it, dark hair with a goatee and mustache, and spoke with a wide Noo Yawk accent. Matt wondered if they chose a New York guy to manage him so that he'd be comfortable, or maybe Marty had chosen him for that reason. Anyway, the two of them hit it off immediately. Marty led him to a conference room and started drawing boxes and lines on the whiteboard.

ARC programs were already being written and run by a lot of Datapoint customers, and Matt found out that they went well beyond what the Minnesota faculty was doing. Marty said the engineers were continually surprised by what users came up with out there, and usually, they'd only learn about it when a salesman called in and said his customer was having a problem. Normally, Marty said, they'd ask each other if what the customer was doing should work since none of them had ever tried it. It was a point of pride for Marty and the other engineers that it almost always did work! Datapoint sales were booming, and they all expected to be living very comfortably from their stock, if they weren't already. Matt noticed a very positive vibe in the building, and people seemed proud of what they were doing. He was looking forward to this summer.

Matt's job was going to be to set up some really ambitious network configurations, so whenever they had a new release of the Resource Management System, the software that ran on the computers, they could test it on Matt's giant test networks. They had a big room set up for him as a lab, with what seemed like a couple of dozen computers, a bunch of telephones and hardware that he guessed was their new **PBX** product, spools of cable, and all sorts of odds and ends. He spent the rest of the day looking it all over, reading the manuals, and making a preliminary sketch of his design for the lab.

On Wednesday, Marty dropped in to see how Matt was doing. Matt had a million questions about the ARC features he'd never used and the PBX system, and Marty was patient in answering them. When they were taking a break, Matt asked him some things he'd been wondering about. "So, ARC is basically the leading local area network right now, right?"

"Yep! If you go by installed base, we're way ahead. We came out with it before the world even knew what a LAN was."

"That's so cool. How come I never see ads for it in the magazines?"

Marty looked annoyed, "Yeah, we're always asking the Marketing guys about that."

"And… what do they say?"

"Oh, they say the product sells itself. We actually have customers reading the hype about Ethernet and asking us if they can get a LAN, and we tell them they already have one if they have ARCnet. They're amazed."

Matt laughed, "So if you advertise, you're just helping the competition. Is that it?"

"More or less," agreed Marty.

"So, what do you think about Ethernet? Xerox makes a big deal about it."

Marty looked like he was used to this question, and his answer sounded rehearsed, "We read the papers about it and discussed all the options when we designed ARC. We even talked to Bob Metcalfe about his early Ethernet designs."

"And?"

"We thought it was a joke. You can't even determine how long it's going to take to send something. You might be retrying all afternoon."

"Why's that? Because of the contention-detection?"

Marty was rolling now, "You go to send, and if someone

else is also trying to send, you both have to back off and try again. And again. You can't put any bound on it."

"And ARCnet doesn't do that, right?" Marty shook his head. "You have to wait for your turn to send, and then it's yours, I guess?"

"Right. You wait for the token to come around, and then you're good. Furthermore, your Send doesn't return until the receiver has it, and everything is correct. With Ethernet, you don't even know if they received it."

"So, you always know the maximum time you'll have to wait?" Matt could tell Marty enjoyed this little colloquy, so he encouraged him.

"Right. If the network is saturated, Ethernet completely falls apart. ARC just approaches maximum throughput smoothly."

Matt wasn't done yet. "How about the cabling? Is that different? I know I pulled the cable for ARCnet in the EE Department at school."

"That's another thing. We use the exact same cable as an IBM 3270 terminal, which many companies already have installed. Ethernet has a special coax cable, and then you have these vampire taps you have to punch in it."

"What's a vampire tap?"

Marty explained how with Ethernet, you had to punch a hole in the coax to penetrate to the center connector, and the Datapoint engineers had scornfully rejected that early on. They just put plugs on the ends of the coax, the way God intended.

Now, Matt was wondering something, "We keep hearing the word standard about Ethernet. They make a really big deal about how DEC and Intel are onboard with it, the IEEE is formalizing it, and so on. But ARCnet is not doing that?"

This was another hot button for Marty, "No, we need to control how the thing evolves. Once you give that up, then the competitors can dick you around in committees for years, and you're helpless."

Matt agreed again, "IBM just releases a product, and *that's* the standard, right?"

"Now you've got it. You must have that account control, where the customer just does what you say. DEC is trying to do the same thing."

Marty looked at his watch and stood up, "Well, anyway… you're doing great here. Let me know when you have a layout for your test system, and we'll go over it."

"Okay, thanks, Marty!"

11

THE GARAGE INDUSTRY

I t was mid-June when Janet went out looking at houses again. The politics at Apple had her depressed enough to want to qualify for the mortgage while she was still there and before she quit. Steve Jobs had been kicked out of the Lisa project, and he was not happy about it. The Lisa team was of two minds about that—first, glad he was gone, but second, unhappy that he was now throwing his energy into the competing Macintosh project. They were being a bunch of little assholes with their pirate flag, as Janet saw it. Most of the Lisa team didn't see it that way. They figured they'd be absorbed into the Mac team eventually if it succeeded, so who cares? They were still the glamor company of the Valley.

She envisioned someday being at some little startup that might go under at any second and figured that would not look good to a loan officer. Better to buy the house now. Having been out looking at houses with her realtor Bob twice already, she had a more practiced method of doing it—ignore the things you can easily change like paint and carpets. Especially, ignore the furniture since real estate agents stage the house with rented stuff to impress unwary buyers. She was hip to all that now.

Bob had taught her to look at the things you cannot change, especially the location, and the things that are very difficult to change, such as the floor plan. So when he took her to West San Jose, she knew already that it was a decent neighborhood with good schools, and the people who'd buy her house from her years from now would pay for that.

They drove down De Anza Boulevard again, past her office, and this time, they kept going and turned left, not right. The right side of De Anza was Cupertino, and the left was San Jose. It was a different zip code, and the houses seemed noticeably cheaper, but not dramatically so.

"This area here was all fruit orchards when we first moved here in the early 50s," he noted as he parked on a street near Bollinger. Janet thought it looked not new but not old, and the street was not narrow but not wide either, and it had sidewalks. The houses all looked like they were built at about the same time. It was middle class in every way. Bob read off his clipboard, "Okay. This little beauty is offered at $129,999. Three bedrooms, two baths—one with a tub and one in the master bedroom with a shower stall—built in 1958."

Janet thought it was clean, well-maintained, and had a nice yard. She came out smiling. Bob asked, "So, what did you think?"

"I liked it. What's next?"

He looked at his clipboard, "Our next one is right around the corner, very similar to this."

Bob was right, the next house had the identical floor plan, and the asking price was only $5,000 more. They had upgraded the original kitchen, and the bathroom didn't have that nauseating Pepto-Bismol Pink tile that the older bathrooms used to feature.

He knew this was her house, but he wanted her to say it.

She'd seen maybe twenty houses by now. This was it. They went back to his office and discussed money, and he suggested she could offer $130,000 for it, and probably the seller would counter-offer, and then, we'd be off to the races, as he put it. He called the seller's agent and made the offer, and the agent said she'd take it to the seller. Janet's heart was racing. She thought of calling her dad, but she decided to wait until the deal was final. That night, she walked over to the house to get a better sense of the neighborhood she'd been living in.

It was on a street that didn't connect to any major street, so she wouldn't have a lot of car traffic. Check. The neighborhood seemed to have a lot of kids, but not a lot of teenagers hanging around. Check. The street was not jammed with parked cars, which happened with a lot of renters. Check. She was happy.

Sunday, Bob called back with a counter-counter-offer from the seller. She made a counter to that, it was accepted, and the deal was done. On Monday, she had to drive up to Bob's office in Los Altos to sign her name again and again. Bob helped her with the mortgage application and told her that escrows usually took about sixty days. She called the Xerox pensions office to start withdrawing her pension in cash to meet the down payment, which was over $26,000, more money than she'd ever seen in her life.

She arrived home tingling. It was time to call her dad, Len. "Dad, I found a house!"

"Oh, that's wonderful, sweetie! When do you move in?"

"They say the escrow usually takes about sixty days, so sometime in August, I guess."

"Wow, are you excited?"

"Scared. I haven't lived in a house since... since I lived with you."

Len remembered those days wistfully, "Well, I can't wait to see it!"

They talked about the mortgage payment, the down payment and how she was going to come up with it, how big the house and lot were, the property taxes, and all the usual house things. Len thought, but didn't say, that for $130,000, you'd get a palace on a quarter acre of land in suburban Detroit.

"Can you come out and help me move in and settle in, Dad?"

Len thought about that, "I have to put in for vacation way in advance, sweetie. I'll see what I can do, but I'm not promising anything."

"Okay, thanks. Should I start buying stuff... hammers, saws, drills?"

He laughed out loud, "Whoa there! You'll have plenty of time for that after you move in."

She giggled, "I can't help it! I want to start now, but I have to wait."

"Yeah, it's tough. Why does it take so long to close on the house?"

"Good question. Everything is on paper. It's like they've never heard of computers."

"Most of the world hasn't. You people out there in Silicon Valley, or whatever you call it, are in a special world."

"I guess," she said resignedly. They talked about the kitchen and bathrooms and the landscaping. She didn't know anything about trees, and he didn't know anything about California trees, so they didn't make much headway on her ideas of growing fruit. It had a lawn, and she'd never thought much about watering lawns, except that for their house in Michigan they just put out a sprinkler now and then. It rained a lot more than in California.

She mentioned that Xerox PARC had a rule for naming their software, which was that the name had to appear in the *Sunset Western Garden Book*. He laughed at that, and she made a note to go out and buy that book. It was a long conversation with not very much decided since Len's experiences with houses didn't apply much to California.

On Monday, she went around telling everyone about her house, and they congratulated her. It seemed like a fair number of the senior engineers already had houses in much wealthier areas than hers, like Saratoga and Los Altos. Furthermore, since Proposition 13 had been in effect since 1978, their property taxes were capped at one percent of the price they paid, plus a small annual adjustment—no matter how much prices went up. They consoled her by saying that the same thing would apply to her in a few years.

She checked the Apple stock price. It had been climbing lately, after falling for the first half of 1982, but her four-year vesting period meant that it would be mid-1985 before she really owned all her hire-on stock. Still, they also had an Employee Stock Purchase Plan, where you could contribute part of your salary, and you bought the stock at a discount at the end of each six-month period, so that could potentially be a nice bonus. At Xerox, the stock never did anything dramatic, so she'd never paid much attention to it.

She waited out the days for escrow to close, gave her notice on the condo she was renting, and tried to ignore the turmoil at Apple. Finally, the big Saturday came in mid-August. Her Dad had failed to get vacation time off, so he sent his regrets. Down in LA, her friends had a tradition of moving parties, where all your friends show up to help you move, and then you buy pizza for them afterward. She'd carried boxes for more people than she could count. Up here, she just didn't know enough people to have a proper moving party, so she hired movers, feeling vaguely ashamed because in your twenties, that meant you didn't have any friends.

She stuffed her cat Rocky in his cat carrier, which he absolutely hated. She apologized to him, but there was nothing for it. They were moving. When they arrived at the new house and she let him out, he ran away looking for a place to hide.

The neighbors were attracted by the moving truck and came over to welcome her to the neighborhood. None of them worked in high tech, and they all seemed bemused by the novelty of an Apple employee moving in. Larry, her next-door neighbor, a tall middle-aged man with a graying mustache, worked at Lockheed.

One fifty-ish lady, Kay, lived across the street. She wore white shorts and a floral top, had her hair pinned up, and was more than a little overweight. She said they'd never had a single lady owning a house on the block before, but things were changing, and it was fine with her. Kay and her family had been there since 1958 when the neighborhood went in. Even after only twenty-four years, there weren't too many original owners left.

After asking Janet whether she had any children, Kay asked what she did for a living.

"Oh, I'm a programmer at Apple," she answered.

"Apple! We're all so proud of these electronics companies around here. What's it like to work there?"

Janet wasn't sure what kind of information Kay wanted. Probably not the same thing her friends at Xerox would want. "Oh, it's pretty good. Good pay, good benefits, and they treat you pretty well."

"Do you ever see that Steve Jobs guy? We see his partner Wozniak at Cicero's Pizza all the time. He seems like a very nice man."

"I've seen Jobs once or twice. We try to avoid talking to him if we can."

"Really! Why is that?"

Janet wasn't sure how much inside dirt she could share because this was Apple's original neighborhood after all. The company was featured in the *Mercury News* almost every day. "Well, there are these stories of Jobs asking what you do at Apple, and if he doesn't like the way you answer, you're fired!"

Kay was shocked, but not very. It was a different world with these electronics companies, she said. She changed the subject, "You know... we used to do work in our garage for National Semi."

This was genuine news for Janet. "For National Semiconductor? What kind of work?"

"Oh, we used to stuff circuit boards for them, on a piecework basis. Sometime in the 70s, we worked for Fairchild and Commodore, like Scotty down the street, but mostly we stuck with National. They paid on time, at least."

"Stuff circuit boards? Don't you need a lot of skill for that?" she said but hoped she hadn't offended. Maybe Kay did have a lot of skill, but she didn't seem offended.

"Yeah, they'd deliver the parts and come pick them up when we were done. You'd just stuff the little integrated circuits, or ICs they were called, into their carriers, and that was it. If you were very good, they might ask you to solder, but I never soldered."

"Wow! I've never heard of this. Did Apple hire people to do that, too?"

"I think Harry over on the next block did some assembly for Apple on the first little computers they sold. We never did."

Janet absorbed all this. Electronics really *was* a garage industry around here.[1]

Kay became philosophical, "Nowadays, there isn't much of that anymore. The parts have just become too tiny. You can't even see them without a microscope. Anyway, if you need anything, just come over, and ring the bell!"

"Okay, thanks. Nice meeting you, Kay!"

Since she didn't have any food in the house, she decided to go to Cicero's Pizza for dinner and see if the Woz was there. He was. She didn't go over and introduce herself. She was pretty sure he wasn't into the celebrity thing.

On Monday, she asked people at work if they'd ever heard of this garage piecework business. No one had, and some of them looked like they doubted that it was even true.

12

BACK TO THE FROZEN TUNDRA

Summer was over, and it was time for Matt and Miriam to return to Minneapolis. They were depressed because San Antonio had been so fun, even though it was stinking hot most of the time.

Miriam had spent a good part of the summer at the adult pool in the apartment complex. She had a nice tan now, something she'd never managed to acquire up North, and her backstroke had become quite good. On rainy days, she'd gone to the library to look up doctoral programs in the Bay Area and the licensing requirements. She had her heart set on studying at Stanford, and she resolved to lobby her professors at Minnesota to have them make phone calls on her behalf.

Matt had been happier at work than she'd ever seen him. Quite often, he'd go back to the lab after dinner "just to finish up some stuff." She could have been annoyed with that, but it was so nice to see him enthusiastic about what he was doing that she didn't have the heart.

His summer task was to build a test suite to do proper regression testing on new software releases. Regression testing was meant to solve the software problem where things broke when you hadn't even touched them, as far as you knew. In reality, you *had* touched them by changing some other thing that they depended on, and you didn't realize it. It was pretty tedious to test every single feature of a system you'd tried a thousand times before, over and over again, and it was human nature to just assume that it should still work.

So, a regression test would mechanically test everything. The computer never gets bored.

Datapoint had a guy, Ted Nelson[1], who was sort of a celebrity as a futurist and thinker. Matt had even heard of him before arriving. His life's work was a project he called Xanadu, a global system of hypertext or linked documents. Nelson had been dubious about Texas as a place to live, like most people who weren't from there, but upon arriving, he found it very mellow. Matt had really enjoyed lengthy conversations with Ted, which rarely had anything to do with his actual work but were fascinating all the same. Nelson was not popular among the executive class, which meant that his days were numbered. He believed in the mouse and worked on a design for a new word processor, which utilized his theory that software was a presentation art, like cinema, and the computer was basically putting on a show for the operator. Instead of having the text display line by line as it came in, the way word processors had always worked, it showed up all at once—bang! There were other special effects that most of the executives hated.

Near the end of the summer, one conversation with Marty stuck in Matt's mind. He and Marty had been talking about Datapoint's future, and Matt brought up, very gingerly, the Groundhog Day event in February of that year that shaved almost a third of the stock's value in less than a week. They'd offered him the summer job long after this happened, so he figured it couldn't be that important, and indeed, Marty didn't think it was.

Matt asked, "So, that big stock market thing back in February... haven't heard anyone talk about that all summer. Was that not a big deal?"

Marty expelled some air forcefully, "Nah! A buncha executive shenanigans. It's all been cleaned up by now."

"So what happened, again?"

Marty answered, "After thirty-nine straight quarters of increasing earnings, we missed a target. By a dime."

"That's all it was?"

Marty nodded. He knew there was more to the story, but there was no need to rehash it all now.

Matt continued, "Weren't there some fake sales numbers or something? I forget what I read."

Marty had been hoping not to talk about this anymore, but he liked Matt and was very happy with his work, so he went along with it. "Yeah, some of the salesmen were booking sales at the end of the quarter that weren't real, just to make their quotas. Then, they'd let the customers return the items at the start of the next quarter. Stuff like that."

Matt remembered reading some other nasty things, such as non-existent customers whom they'd shipped to and early shipments when the customer hadn't agreed to an early shipment, but he just shook his head. "Salesmen. They're all the same, aren't they?"

"You got that right. Unfortunately, Wall Street doesn't trust us anymore."

"Is that bad?"

"Well, it is, and it isn't. It doesn't affect the customers, obviously. They're still buying our stuff like crazy. But raising more money becomes harder."

This seemed to be leading into esoteric areas of corporate finance, which Matt knew almost nothing about, so he changed the topic. "What about IBM PCs? Aren't they going to cut into our market?"

"Well, we got there first. The suite of software that they'll have to develop over time, we already have. We don't view IBM as a threat... more of a validation of what we've been doing for twelve years."

"So, it shows that there's a market there, and Datapoint already dominates that market."

"Yep," said Marty. "Also, we have what they call account control. Once the customer is committed to us, it's pretty hard for them to switch. IBM's been doing this forever."

"Account control... that seems kinda sinister."

Marty was not sheepish, "That's what business is all about. The customer keeps on buying from you. We just have to encourage them." He smirked.

Matt went back to work. But his suspicions grew that the Datapoint guys weren't totally in touch with reality. Maybe they'd been too successful in the 70s, and now, they couldn't adapt to the 80s or didn't want to. And this sales scandal really worried him. "There's never just one cockroach," as everyone in New York always said about apartments.

Marty had said several times that they'd like to offer him a full-time job, but since the stock market debacle, there was a hiring freeze. In fact, bringing someone on for the summer was a way of getting more work done without violating the freeze. At least this spared him having to decide whether to accept an offer.

13

CONTACT

I n late September 1982, Dan was still at Xerox. He'd
gone on a three-week trip to Europe in the spring, his
first time there, but the glow from that had faded. And
his job search among the startups was becoming monotonous.
He'd go there late in the afternoon for an informal interview
and learn what they were doing and walk away thinking,
"Nope, that's not it." Either they just had a dumb idea or a
good idea but ten other startups were doing it, or it just didn't
appeal to him, or he didn't appeal to *them*. Often, they wanted
someone local who could start in two weeks.

The El Segundo office had moved west on Rosecrans to a
brand-new office building, and now at last, you could walk to
actual restaurants. No more going across the street to the
crappy old cafeteria. The corner of Pacific Coast Highway
and Rosecrans was a mini-shopping center with several
reasonable places to eat. An entire crew of new people had
been hired to work on Star, and they seemed to have swallowed the company line completely and believed that there
was no problem with Star that another release or two wouldn't
fix. Dan found it utterly depressing.

And then, two events in rapid succession made things

dramatically worse. The first was Michael Adams, the head of Star since the beginning, and Harold Esposito, his boss in Dallas, left Xerox to start their own company, along with Martin Whitby and Brooks Landon, two of the main architects of the Star user interface. Their company, Metaphor Computer Systems, was supposedly not competing with Star, and they were careful to say that they were not giving up on Star after all these years. Metaphor was going to attack a different problem than Star, namely the need for office professionals to access big databases on IBM mainframes. For example, marketing and salespeople needed up-to-the-minute data on orders, which you could only retrieve from the mainframe.

This was a related market that Xerox wouldn't be able to focus on for years and years, and they were going to use a Star-like workstation to do it. So, it was *validation* of what everyone was doing, not *abandonment*. At least that was the official story.

"Nothing to see here! Move along," was how Dan interpreted all this marketing-speak.

"Yeah, sure, they're not bailing out! Not at all. Xerox is still one hundred percent committed to Star," he said, unable to hold his tongue. Now that he wasn't officially in Star development anymore, he was freer to be sarcastic, which he knew was not a career-enhancing behavior.

Even worse, Xerox made a corporate acquisition that had nothing whatsoever to do with copiers or computers or anything else they'd ever done. They bought an insurance company, Crum and Forster, for about $1.6 billion in cash and stock. Xerox's stock went down on the news, while Crum and Forster's went up. The stories in the business press emphasized that Xerox was expanding into financial services, and that must mean they'd given up on their core business, copiers. It was not considered good news for Xerox.

The internal corporate line on this move was similar to the Metaphor deal, "We're still one hundred percent committed to Star." Supposedly, the financial stability of an insurance company would be counter-cyclical to Xerox's regular business, going up when the regular business was going down and vice versa. And it was not at all a signal that the company was giving up on office automation. Or copiers. No, not at all.

To Dan, it was another "Nothing to see here. Move along!" message. *"How can people fall for this?"* he wondered. Crum and Forster's management said in an interview that they did not talk to any other potential acquirers before making the deal. Dan thought that when they saw Xerox coming, they must have said, "Hello, sailor!"

In January 1983, his paper on Records Processing was published in the first issue of *Transactions on Office Information Systems*, a journal from the Association for Computing Machinery (ACM). Publishing the paper didn't make much of a difference in his life except that he started receiving letters from people in other countries asking for a copy. Since he had plenty of reprints, he was usually happy to send them one.

IN MARCH, he received a phone call. A female voice asked, "Hello, is this Daniel Markunas?"

"This is he."

"Mr. Markunas, I'm a recruiter for an exciting new startup in the Bay Area. They're particularly interested in you. Would you be interested in talking with them?"

"Maybe. Can you tell me a little more about them?"

She wouldn't but arranged for the founders to call him at home that night. He was slightly optimistic, but this kind of thing had happened too many times for him to take it very seriously.

That night, a guy named Clay Nelson called him. They had seen Dan's paper and engaged the recruiter to call him. Dan thought, *"Jeez, I'm already looking for a startup. You don't need a recruiter! You could have just picked up the phone.*" But he was too polite.

Clay said he and two other founders were developing a graphical database for the IBM PC, which did not mean a database of graphs—it meant a database with a graphical interface, which just happened to be exactly what Dan's paper described. They were so excited to see that Xerox had developed one and were not at all worried that Xerox would steal the market. Two of the founders were from Apple, and they were also not concerned because Apple was too tied up with the Lisa and the Macintosh. The database would run on the IBM PC, like Lotus 1-2-3, which had taken over the spreadsheet category from VisiCalc.

It would also be an analytical database, which meant that it would be tailored to analysis, like VisiCalc and Lotus 1-2-3, but look like a database and not like a spreadsheet.

Would Dan like to meet with them on a Saturday sometime up in the Bay Area, when they'd have enough time to really talk? Dan was interested. He figured he'd travel there on a Friday for work and then spend the night with Henry Davis, his friend from Xerox. Clay gave him directions to a house in Saratoga.

Henry lived in Los Trancos Woods in the hills near The Alpine Inn, a favorite Xerox gathering place and biker bar where Dan had been once or twice. His wife Sally taught piano, and they had three children, one of whom was a toddler who sat in a seat attached to the beamed ceiling with a spring so that he could jump around in safety. It was cute.

Henry was the person who had invented icons, a fact that he often noted had not made him rich. The other two guys in Palo Alto who had designed the Star user interface had left to join Metaphor, but for whatever reason, Henry hadn't gone with them. He and Dan had a frank talk about startups and how they were both looking for one. Henry asked Dan what he thought about a new company that was trying to develop a

Star-like windows-and-icons interface for the IBM PC. Dan was dubious that anyone could do this successfully since the PC was pretty underpowered. Henry seemed inclined to join them anyway.

On Saturday morning, Dan drove down to Saratoga. It seemed like a fairly wealthy area. When Dan arrived, he met Miles Watson and Jacob Brucker, the other two founders. Clay had gone to Harvard, Miles to MIT, and Jacob to Brown. These were some high-class guys. And here they were pitching to poor old Dan from the University of Illinois! He realized that being from Xerox had vaulted him up several rungs on the status ladder.

Clay had come out of the banking industry in New York, which was not a badge of honor since banks generally attracted the stupidest people around. Clay was conscious of this prejudice and took pains to assure Dan that that wasn't the case in New York City, where there weren't any high-tech jobs except in finance. He had a goatee and dressed as though he didn't care how he dressed, with khakis and an unpressed and probably unwashed Oxford shirt that was half untucked. At times, he could make everyone, even Miles and Jacob, laugh out loud. He was a little manic, and Dan wondered if he ever swung to the other extreme of anger and depression. Not today, anyway.

Miles and Jacob had both come from Apple. Miles had curly hair and a sort of smirky expression. He was nice to you only if he wanted something. He seemed vaguely reptilian, but that was par for the course for marketing people. "*It might even be a job requirement,*" Dan thought.

Jacob had curly black hair and a neatly trimmed beard and had come from the Apple Lisa project. He asked Dan if he knew Janet Saunders, which of course he did, and he spoke very highly of her. He seemed to know every engineering detail about everything, including the Motorola 68000 processor ("the 68K" in engineer-speak); the Intel 8088, processor for the IBM PC and why the startup trying to build a Star-like interface for it was doomed; the Apple II; the Star; and everything else. He knew every startup Dan had talked to. Jacob was into engineering in a way that awed Dan. He told Dan that when you arrived at many Silicon Valley parties, someone asked you at the door, "Hardware or software?" You were then directed to the appropriate group of people. They just assumed you mainly wanted to talk about work.

They spent an hour or so talking about the software market—how Lotus 1-2-3 made everyone realize that IBM PC software would not be advertised in the back pages of *Byte* magazine. Lotus had spent a million dollars on their launch, a record, and almost immediately, it had pushed VisiCalc, the product that had owned the term spreadsheet, into oblivion. Miles explained how Lotus had invested heavily in training salespeople at computer stores to sell the software intelligently, and their new company was planning to do the same. You had to sell to the resellers.

In Miles' and Clay's minds, their product would be as basic as Lotus or dBase—the leading database product. It would be one of the standard things every business user bought.

Venture capitalists, who had concentrated on hardware up to now, were scrambling to find a software play, and this company had attracted some top-drawer investors. When Dan left to go to the bathroom, they exchanged glances with each other, and apparently, they agreed to show him their demos. Before that, they just weren't sure about him, he guessed.

The demos were impressive. Clay had coded them and used them to sell Jacob and Miles and the venture capitalists. They showed an interface where you could ask questions about your data and test them, similar to a spreadsheet. They used a mouse, something a user had to buy separately since PCs didn't come with one. Dan wondered how you could get away with requiring users to buy special hardware just to use their software. Miles, the marketing guy, handled this one, and he claimed to have research suggesting that mice would soon be standard since lots of other new software applications also used them.

From his extensive experience with databases, Dan's first question was, "How can this possibly be fast enough?" Disk access was slow. A huge part of what he had spent the last ten years doing was designing software to avoid the disk. The data on hard disks was carefully organized to make absolutely sure you didn't do too many accesses. These analytical functions obviously required reading all the records, not just one or two. They said the database would all be in memory!

Dan was flabbergasted. PCs could only have 640K of memory. How could any meaningful database fit in so little memory? Miles had researched that, too. He calculated that a personal database, as opposed to a big mainframe database, could be as small as two thousand records, and personal databases were a market that the big players had completely ignored. A marketing person, even if he were accessing a mainframe of millions of records, could do very meaningful analysis on a small aggregate or subset of them. Maybe the mainframe database guys would create those summary data sets every day—who knew?

Of course, a user could also have additional memory on their PC, but none of the popular software could take advantage of it. This product would use it but wouldn't require it.

Personal databases. A graphical user interface. Analytical functions. Dan loved it. It appealed to the same taste for unconventionality that had led him to Xerox so long ago. And maybe, just maybe, he could get rich from it, which he certainly had not from Xerox.

Then, he asked who the President of this new company was. It turned out that the company already existed, and it had a President and was called Taurus Software. Taurus had a completely different product for CP/M, the operating system popular on PCs before the IBM PC came out, but this new product had no relation to that one. The old product would be retired.

This seemed strange. Why graft a totally new idea onto a presumably failed startup? It turned out that this venture capitalist desire to have a software play had previously created Taurus, and the VCs were salvaging it. Taurus was headquartered in Lafayette, a city far out in the East Bay, but the new company would not be there. Needless to say, the current President was not here interviewing him, and Miles hinted that they would probably replace him with a real CEO with the help of the VCs.

What about the engineers at Taurus? Would they be part of the new team, too? They said that a couple of them would, while others would probably be allowed to leave on their own.

What about other new engineers, for the new product, if there were any? Shouldn't he meet them, too? Apparently, this wasn't necessary.

Dan left with a positive attitude, despite that large helping of weirdness. The product seemed awesome. He'd been looking for a very long time, and this job was a perfect match for his current qualifications at least. He'd done a system at Xerox that was "data processing for the noncomputer professional," as his paper's title put it, and that's what this product was.

IN A FEW WEEKS, he received an offer. They matched his salary at Xerox, which was nice—frequently startups made you take a cut in salary, he'd heard. They added in a hundred thousand shares of stock, which was currently valued at $0.25 a share. Dan did the math over and over in his head. If it went public at $15, that would be $1.5 million. Of course, there would be stock splits and lots of other financial business before that

Initial Public Offering, so there was no telling how much he'd really make. But it would be a lot. He could retire from computers and buy a radio station or something.

He solved the problem of selling his house by just putting it up for sale and leaving it vacant, moving up to the Bay Area. He hoped it would sell quickly, but right then, the housing market was terrible. Mortgage rates were around thirteen percent, and often, the seller had to cushion the blow by giving the buyer a second mortgage at a lower rate. He lived in a rental house until his house sold.

He started work in their office in Fremont, where there was virtually no high-tech at all and no good restaurants. The office building was one story looking out at Paseo Padre Parkway, and Taurus shared it with the phone company. Dan had never realized how many people paid their phone bills in cash until he saw the steady lines of people.

There were four other engineers to meet, two of whom had worked at the original Taurus and one who was a prestige hire because he'd worked on Lotus 1-2-3. The Lotus guy was a fairly intellectual and high-strung person named David Cohen, who'd grown up in New York, attended Harvard, and then worked on the Lotus launch, also headquartered in Boston. Dan wondered if he would be like the Boston office-mate he had back in the early days of Xerox, another East Coast snob. That guy was continually bemoaning the lack of mass transit in LA to the point where you were careful to avoid that topic with him.

The Bay Area had a mass transit system, the BART, and David lived in Berkeley, so theoretically, he could commute on BART. The Fremont BART station was walkable from the office, if a long walk. Maybe, just maybe, he'd be happy here, but more likely, he was just here to make some money and then move back. Certain people just made you wonder, "Why did you *ever* leave the East Coast?" and David was one of them. Dan felt that he and David were destined to become competitors. They'd both come from highly influential companies, but David's at least had been a financial success, unlike Xerox.

Ed Huber was a longtime PC engineer who'd worked on CP/M with Digital Research, the early leader in PC operating systems that had become a famous "opportunity lost" legend in Silicon Valley. Supposedly, Gary Kildall, the owner of Digital Research, was out flying his private plane when IBM came looking for an operating system for its new PC. Accounts differ on what exactly happened, whose fault it was, and who stole from whom, but the upshot was that Bill Gates snagged the deal for Microsoft, and the rest is history.

Ed was tired of talking about this since everyone asked him about Gary Kildall. He was a pleasant guy who laughed a lot but was pretty reserved and seemed to have a very deep reservoir of knowledge about PC hardware and software. He seemed to know all about the C compilers available for the PC, which was especially important since the product was going to be written in C. Dan remembered the joke about C posted on someone's door at Xerox PARC:

C: *All the control and flexibility of machine code*
plus all the type safety and abstraction of machine code

He thought this would not be a wise thing to say now. C was what everyone used in the industry, and he just had to get used to it. He bought the Kernighan & Ritchie book ("K&R" for short) on C at Stacey's Bookstore in Palo Alto and carried it with him everywhere. It was a thin book, so it wasn't hard to read it cover to cover.

And then, there was Tuan, a Vietnamese-American guy who'd worked with Clay before. He seemed a little more outgoing and opinionated than most Vietnamese Dan had met.

The last new guy was Gershon Janko, who had joined Taurus in Lafayette, and was probably the youngest person there. He was short and intense, and his father had been in the Israeli Army. Gershon, like Ed, was a hardcore personal computer guy without any deep thoughts on human interface. Ed and Gershon both thought of the user interface as just one of those froufrou things real men didn't touch.

Dan didn't have much rapport with Ed, David, Tuan, or Gershon, nor did they have one with each other. They didn't seem terribly impressed with Dan's Xerox experience. To them, Xerox maybe had some interesting ideas, but they'd completely failed to commercialize them, and the Star was a joke. Xerox was history. The future belonged to Apple or maybe Microsoft.

Everyone there had been attracted by the product and the prospect of making a lot of money, not because they liked the team. The trade press was full of stories of instant millionaires being minted when their startups went public. It seemed that all an entrepreneur had to do was put "personal computer" in the prospectus, and Wall Street would throw money. The personal computer makers rushed to go public before the spigot turned off. If they hadn't gone public already, it was in the works—Kaypro, a name that sounded like a cosmetics company; Osborne Computers; and now Eagle made history.

ONE DAY IN JUNE, shortly after Dan joined Taurus, a company named Eagle Computer had its IPO, and its founder Dennis Barnhart celebrated his sudden riches. He was driving his new red Ferrari in the mountains near Los Gatos, and the car spun out of control, crashed through a guard rail, and came to rest in a ravine, killing him and making him an instant Silicon Valley legend.

Clay was nominally the VP of Engineering since the product had been largely his idea, but his experience on personal computers was pretty thin. Jacob was the aggressive technical guy whom all the engineers looked up to.

Ed and Jacob jointly decided to use Lattice C. Lattice was an independent company based in Chicago, and Microsoft did not have a decent C compiler. Ed worked out a way that the code could use the PC's "expanded" memory if it were present, without using full 32-bit pointers everywhere in the code. Clay approved of all this, officially, but then, he wasn't given a choice.

Dan set to work on the database for the product. He'd only ever designed data structures for traditional hard-disk-based systems, so this was a new experience. It was also strange since there was no specification for how it was supposed to work or what the product would do. Also, he'd never worked on an IBM PC or written anything in C. The engineers were unanimously unhappy with what he came up with, and Gershon was handed the database task.

Despite his official role, Clay wasn't much involved in this decision. Dan had done lots of functional spec work at Xerox, participating in the design of graphical user interfaces for Star, but he was unable to claim any ascendancy over the titanic egos of Clay, Miles, and Jacob. The company only had one product, and no one was willing to give up influence over it, and why would they, after all? You only had one shot to get it right.

Design meetings took place daily with Clay, Miles, Jacob, and most of the engineering staff. The meetings were contentious and often featured Clay losing his temper and inducing David to lose his. Miles tried to play peacemaker without much success. Jacob listened to him but was unwilling to defer to him. The two of them could be allies on important issues, but on everything else, they argued.

The company President had no influence whatsoever and wasn't even there for most of these meetings since he had no connection to the product they were designing. To make up for his absence, the venture capitalists were onsite a lot. But they were no help in resolving design issues, either. They were corporate guys, not product guys.

Clay threw enough tantrums that he soon had no credibility left, and no one looked to him for decisions. One weekend, things came to a head, and it seemed that almost everyone was calling the lead investor, Bill Walker, about Clay. If you didn't call him, eventually he'd call you, and everyone else did, too.

Dan spent a large part of the weekend on the phone with Bill, Jacob, Miles, Clay, and several of the engineers, and it was clear that they had all been calling each other. There were no in-person meetings, but on Monday morning, it was announced that Jacob would be the new VP of Engineering. Clay was outwardly supportive of Jacob and had accepted some vague title that made it clear that he was still an active participant in product strategy.

It seemed pretty weird. Dan would have thought that if you're deposed by your own people, with the connivance of the lead investor, that had to be the end. You'd quit, take whatever loyal troops you had—Clay only had one, Tuan—and start another company. But no, Clay was staying. Everyone felt Jacob should have been the VP all along.

An executive search firm was engaged to hire a permanent CEO. Dan and the other engineers saw a parade of middle-aged guys in suits who all looked like they'd been President of their fraternity. Sometimes, Dan would talk to them while they waited, and since they had no idea who might have influence, they were on their best behavior with him. It was somewhat fun in a sadistic way.

Miles hired experienced people at a blistering pace, and money was no object. If they were making a huge salary at some top firm, he would match it. He brought in a top advertising guy with ten years experience at McCann-Erickson, several experienced salespeople, a MarCom (Marketing Communications) manager, a finance manager, and a training manager for setting up the classes for computer store salespeople. Of course, all those high-powered people needed support staff, and many very young women were hired to work for them. Dan found all these people much more interesting than the engineers, and he spent a good deal of time hanging out with them. One of them got married, and Dan went to the wedding.

A Quality Manager was hired for testing the software and a Technical Writer for the user manual. Dan wondered how they had the money for all this. He'd always had the impression that startups ran on a shoestring budget until they hit success, and everyone did a little bit of everything. That was the romance of a startup, and he'd been looking forward to it, but it wasn't that way at all. He was an engineer, and he just did engineering. The marketing and sales work was done by people who were trained for that. In that respect, it wasn't much different from a large corporation except that the non-engineers were in the next room instead of in a different building. He found out that he was mistaken about startups, and they all ran like that. Live and learn.

Apparently, the venture capitalists also idolized Lotus and were determined to build a first-class software startup—costs be damned. The software would sell for $495, the exact price of Lotus 1-2-3. Bill Walker gave a barbecue party for the entire company at his Los Altos Hills house. It was catered by MacArthur Park, a well-known restaurant in Palo Alto. Taurus had free memberships at a health club near the office, and Dan started playing racquetball again, one of the few sports he was any good at. They also had free snacks for a while, but eventually, the costs got out of hand, and those went away.

Dan's job now was to develop on top of the basic graphics library that Jacob had written so that he could draw things on the screen. He created the List View, which was a tabular representation of the data, and he had quite a bit of *déjà vu* for that since it was something he'd worked on at Xerox. He added the feature where you could adjust the width of a column by clicking on the vertical column divider and dragging it, and he was constantly amused that that was the first thing everyone tried. It was such a simple thing, but people just love direct manipulation.

14

CORPORATE LIFE, HOME LIFE

At Apple, Janet's businesslike attitude had been a big positive. They had so many ideological fanatics around that a mature adult was a pleasant contrast. People knew she'd be fair to everyone and just get the job done, whatever she thought about it privately.

The Lisa computer was not slated to be an open system like the Apple II had been, where outside developers were allowed or encouraged to create their own products around it. The Xerox Star wasn't open, either. What that meant, though, is that Apple had to create the main applications itself. She'd just finished updating the LisaWrite program, and they were creating other applications as well, such as LisaCalc and Lisa-Draw. Now, she'd been given the job of managing all those. It was a major promotion for her, and she had people under her who, in turn, had people under them.

For all of her career, she'd thought of managers at the second level and above as mucky-mucks. And now, she was a mucky-muck herself, and she never had time to look at code anymore. Although Apple wasn't nearly as organized at training managers as Xerox, you did receive some corporate indoctrination in the form of off-site training classes when you reached her level. She seemed to spend most of her time in meetings and, often, had to bite her tongue when the other managers dismissed the business market as a target. "Look, you might hit ten thousand businesses if you're successful. We can hit a hundred million consumers." "*Yeah, but each business is worth…*" she wanted to say.

Apple seemed to be a company that just wanted to make computers for individuals, not for corporate purchasing managers, and there wasn't much she could do about it. Besides that, the Macintosh team had Steve Jobs behind it, and his charisma and massive ego were pretty tough competitors.

Still, she had to admit the extra money was nice. If she went to interview for a managerial job at another company, there wouldn't be any question that she was qualified.

She noticed that everyone seemed to assume that her next step was VP of Engineering at a startup. That was your ticket to Silicon Valley royalty. If you were in the original management team at a startup that went public, you'd be living in Portola Valley or Los Altos Hills and starting your own charitable foundation. She wasn't exactly sure what she'd start a company *about*, though. Usually in startups, the VP of Engineering was the technical driving force behind the company, who has the vision to sell it to the venture capitalists and helps recruit the rest of the executive team. She couldn't see herself as that person.

In her daily life at work now, after a long day of meetings, she conducted performance reviews. She also instructed her people on how they should do performance reviews, read schedules, and mollified the egos of other mucky-mucks. She ended her day feeling as though she hadn't done anything. Yet, she was exhausted. Making any progress at work seemed impossible.

Janet had seen many executives in that situation search outside work for achievement. Raising children could definitely eat up all your time and then some, and that was something almost all of them did. Sometimes, they drank, and others participated in demanding sports, such as marathon running or mountain climbing. None of those pursuits really appealed to her, and she didn't have kids.

Yet, here was a house she now owned, and it was in desperate need of improvement. The main bathroom in the hallway didn't even have a shower—just a bathtub. If she had a guest, such as her dad, she didn't want to make him take baths. If she did put in a shower, the water would destroy the drywall around the window. The walls had this awful red patterned wallpaper. The ancient vanity looked like it was cheap even when it was new twenty-four years ago. There was a built-in diaper-changing table in one corner and linoleum on the floor.

She wasn't ready to sell the house and move up yet, although some people advised her to do exactly that. Her real estate agent, Bob, had told her about this event called the show house, where the owner of a house moves out and turns it over to a group of designers, and each one does their best work on a single room. They compete to show off their skills, and the public pays $10 or $15 to tour it, with the proceeds going to charity.

One Sunday, she went to a show house in Menlo Park near 280. It was inspiring! They had a lot more space to work with than she did, and some of the furnishings looked like the kind of thing you bought when you did become Silicon Valley royalty. She walked from room to room with a sense of bemusement.

One of the bathrooms had been done up in a way that screamed money! The two designers were standing there, greeting people, and Janet told them how much she loved their work, but her house was just a typical tract house that didn't justify all this expense. She meant extravagance, but she avoided that word.

The main designer, Ida, was friendly and not at all snob-bish. She said, "That's okay! I like working on a limited budget." Janet felt comfortable with her, and they talked at length about her house and what the bathroom was like. Janet took her business card and called her the next day.

Ida was enthusiastic and practical-minded about the job. She told Janet that she knew a great contractor, Walt, with whom she'd done a lot of work. Her mode of operation on this would be to find the toilet, sink, and everything else and tell Janet to buy them herself. This way, Ida's time would be minimized. Janet would pay Walt herself, and Ida would not be supervising. The entire cost would be under $5,000. Janet was thrilled. She was going to have a nice bathroom without a gigantic bill!

Walt came over a few days later, and Ida talked over the job with him. The two of them spoke with absolutely no formality. Ida thought they'd put in a pedestal sink in place of the vanity, and Janet was a little worried because then you wouldn't have any place to put your stuff. She'd always had one of those cheap vanities in the bathroom. You just threw all your junk in the cabinet under the sink. But Ida explained that she was going to rip out the diaper-changing table behind it and put in a floor-to-ceiling cabinet so that Janet would end up with even more storage space.

Walt asked if the cabinet would just be paint-grade wood, and he was relieved to hear that it would since that's a lot cheaper than finish-grade wood. Ida asked how Janet felt about painting the cabinet herself, and she gulped and said, "Sure!" Walt said that he could do it, of course, but he'd have to charge.

He pointed out that the tub was original construction, just

cheap enameled steel. He asked Janet if she wanted to go all the way to a cast iron tub. She had no idea. Walt explained that cast iron is a lot better, and in his house, he had an extra-long cast iron tub. He'd sit in there in the morning with a cigarette, relaxing, and it was just so sweet. She didn't have that much room, though, so she'd have to settle for a standard tub.

Walt explained that he could prepare a complete estimate if Janet wanted, but he preferred to work based on trust. He'd give her periodic bills after doing some work, and he was pretty sure that the total would come in below Ida's $5,000 figure. This wasn't what she was expecting from a contractor! She thought it would be some big formal contract with lots of arguing, inevitably ending in lawsuits. From what she'd heard, the contractor arrives, rips out a wall, takes your check, and then disappears for a few months while he works on someone else's job. This wasn't going to be like that.

Ida said the tile around the tub could be mostly field tile. Janet had no idea what that meant, but Walt seemed to know it was just standard white tile. She was going to put in a single row of green marble tiles laid on the diagonal, with gold ribbon tiles around the row—just a little bit of jewelry, as she put it, that wasn't very expensive, compared to all marble. Still, it would give the room a special look. The floor would be black and white vinyl tiles, so between that and the pedestal sink, it would be Art Deco, more or less.

That almost covered it, except for doing something about the walls. Ida asked if Janet knew what a *faux* finish was. Janet had a vague idea since some of the rooms in the show house had a paint finish that looked like marble. She had no idea how that was done but was sure it must be expensive. Ida explained the various ways of doing *faux*, like ragging on and ragging off and sponging on. She said she and Janet could do it together. It sounded like fun.

All done planning! Walt would probably start the job next week.

~

THE NEXT MONDAY, Walt came over, she gave him a key, and they talked about the job some more. He was smoking a cigarette when he arrived, but he put it out before coming inside. He'd been thinking about the job, and he measured everything again just to be sure. Janet felt like dealing with him was like dealing with any engineer at work. It felt comfortable. He had a practical way of just asking what the task was, telling you what your choices were, and explaining what he would do if it were him. Often, he seemed to be obsessing over a quarter-inch of space and giving you way too much information, but that was kind of endearingly engineer-like, too. Usually, his choices were reasonable and made perfect sense if you thought about it.

Around 10:30, he called her at work in a panic. He thought her cat Rocky had escaped when he left the door open carrying in his tools. He felt terrible. She drove home, and Walt greeted her anxiously, and Rocky strolled out of his hiding place, where he'd been all along.

Now, Walt felt even worse. He'd made her drive all the way home for nothing on the very first day of the job. This was not the way a good relationship with your customer was supposed to start. He apologized profusely.

Janet felt nothing but sympathy for him. These things happen, she told him. And, his reaction seemed human, not something some corporate handbook prescribed for dealing with customer issues.

At the end of the week, he left a bill for the week's work on her kitchen table. He called that evening and asked if she'd seen it. Janet knew that being paid on time was the bane of every contractor's existence. Some customers, especially the corporate ones, question every item and delay and delay, and the contractor has to keep calling and calling. It was the rich exploiting the poor, if you really thought about it.

She had a revelation about working with contractors, "*Don't be that way, pay him right away.*" She offered to write him a check then and there, and he said he'd come over and pick it up. When he did, he went over all the things he'd done in the bathroom and what he was going to do next. She listened attentively, although she didn't understand most of what he said.

The next week, Ida gave her the part numbers at Home Depot for her sink, faucets, drain, and other bathroom hardware. She went and bought them. Walt arrived most days, except that when he used a subcontractor, he often had to wait for them, which held up the plumbing, floor, and tiling. Still, the job went reasonably quickly. The subcontractors were all people Walt had worked with before, and she liked almost all of them and paid them directly, too. Since she had a separate bath in the master bedroom, it wasn't a great inconvenience to have a bathroom out of commission for a few weeks.

The cabinet did indeed need painting. Janet decided to go all-out—to hell with cost and inconvenience. She chose an expensive oil-based paint. Oil stinks up the house, and you need paint thinner to get the paint off your hands, but what the hell, she thought, this is forever. She bought an expensive brush and worked obsessively to feather over every brush mark and get it *perfect*. It took a *long* time, but it was satisfying to know she could look at this cabinet every single day and say, "Oh, yeah, I did that!" She went back again and again to admire her work.

Ida came over, and they put a *faux* finish on the walls together. Janet applied the yellow base, and Ida did the ragging off, where she used a rag to remove glaze from the walls, to create the textured finish.

When it was all done, Ida asked if they could do a story in

the *Mercury News* about the bathroom remodel and its budget cost. Janet said that was fine as long as it didn't use her name or address. The house was one of the three remodel jobs featured in the Sunday magazine section of the *Merc*, described as "a house on a quiet street in West San Jose." Ida told her later that she landed eleven new clients from that story. Janet didn't begrudge her at all.

15

A NAME AND A CEO, FINALLY

The Super Bowl in January 1984 had one of the most famous, and to Dan, pretentious TV commercials ever shown—the Apple "1984" commercial. By this time, Dan's former boss on the Xerox Star, Mark Banks, had left Xerox and joined Apple, and he invited the old gang up to his house in Los Altos Hills to watch the game. Many of Dan's other friends had also moved to the Bay Area, including Brian Lerner and Howard Fisher, and they regularly gathered at Mark's house, just like in the old days.

Mark was unapologetic about joining the company some Xeroids viewed as the enemy. When one of them asked him why he was working for Apple in an accusing tone, he said, "For fun." Mark was a survivor.

The Mac was Apple's second try at a Xerox-style graphical interface, Lisa being the first, and this one was a serious Steve Jobs production. The commercial was directed by Ridley Scott, the famous Hollywood director. It featured a crowd of acolytes staring slack-jawed at a political speaker on the screen, just like in the movie *1984*, when a female athlete runs into the room and hurls a sledgehammer at the screen. This, the voiceover intoned, demonstrated that "1984 won't be like *1984*." Dan wanted to vomit. The dominant computer was the IBM PC, and supposedly, the Mac was going to strike a blow for freedom. Right.

Jacob and the other engineers at Taurus admired the Mac. Jacob had known some of the engineers who worked on it and considered them awesome. There was no possibility that Taurus would change its plans and develop for the Mac, though. It was still the IBM PC all the way. Business is business.

Dan's house in Hawthorne finally sold after almost four months on the market to an Ecuadorian family with four names on the deed. He bought a house in West San Jose near Cupertino, figuring that while it wasn't close to Fremont, it probably would be close to his next job. It was a step up in neighborhoods from the Hawthorne location—more middle-middle class than working class. He announced a moving party at work, but no one showed up, except for Miles, who came two hours late.

In March 1984, after what seemed like an endless stream of CEO candidates, Jacob, Miles, Clay, and the VCs settled on one. He looked indistinguishable from all the other middle-aged executive guys, except he was barely six feet tall. His name was Henry Franklin, and he'd been CEO of a small electronics company. The VCs always tried to find someone who'd done it before, but hardly anyone had run a software company.

There was even more great news! Paul, the senior marketing guy who'd worked in advertising, had been busy coming up with names for both the company and the product. He'd even brought in expensive consultants who specialized in naming things. This was not a topic to take lightly! The entire future of the company might be riding on it, and everyone had an opinion. And it was a familiar pattern at Taurus —*everything* was a matter of life and death, and everyone had a strong opinion about it. The pattern stayed true in that Jacob, Clay, and Miles made a show of consulting everyone and then decided on their own, first running it by the VCs.

One of Paul's suggestions that was seriously considered was Extèn—Dan couldn't remember what kind of accent mark the 'e' had. It had a nice moving forward ring to it, kind of like extend. Extèn, however you spelled it, was not chosen for reasons no one could remember.

The final name was chosen because it suggested what the product was for—analysis. The company would be called Analytica.

One down, one to go. They still had to name the product. Should it be a database-ish name, a spreadsheet-ish name, or something generic but friendly and happy? Numerous names were tried out, and for each, the naming consultants provided feedback on whether someone was already using that name, and if so, whether it was a problem. It couldn't sound too similar to things like Lotus 1-2-3, but the name needed to suggest what the product did.

After many long, agonizing discussions, the name Reflex was settled on because the user interface would be so easy that the user's natural reflexes would just be correct. Or something like that.

Dan thought to himself, *"Okay, we have a CEO, we have a company name and a product name, and I have a house! We're rolling now."* But somehow, nothing much changed at Analytica. Henry did not make any major alterations to the product or the company, which was probably the reason he was hired in the first place. His main job seemed to be meeting with the press, other executives, and investors with the credibility that the CEO title gave him. This was after he put out the fire that threatened to consume the company.

Jacob had been consistently telling the Board that the

product would be shipping in ninety days, and revenue would start rolling in. Dan and the other engineers never believed this but thought, "*Well, we're glad you're talking to those people and not us!*" Ninety days later, he'd tell them again that the product would be ready in ninety days. Henry, Jacob, and the other top managers didn't share many details with the engineers, but eventually, word trickled out that the newer investors had put in money on the promise of revenue in ninety days and were not especially happy now.

Henry had a series of meetings with all the engineers, Clay, and Miles in his backyard in Los Altos. He leveled with them—you must give me a schedule I can believe in and take to the Board. It was a long and painful process, but the outcome was that Reflex would be ready in about a year. The company would not be shut down, and the new investors were surprisingly supportive. This is why you hired a CEO.

Henry came at things with a fresh eye. He wasn't burdened by Reflex's history, which had started in 1982. To him, there were core products that every business PC user bought, like Lotus, dBase, and Word. Those products cost about $500 or so. Then there were add-on products they bought afterward, and those cost much less. Which category was Reflex in? At his house one Saturday with everyone there, he brought this up.

"I've been talking to the investors and to the press, and I can tell you, everyone is just blown away by what you guys are building! You can all be *very* proud of yourselves."

Clay and Miles beamed, as did everyone else, but they wondered if there was a "but…" to that.

"I think we need to work on the positioning now, though."

Positioning was a word Dan had come to dread, although he knew that was why you hired marketing people. If you had only five seconds to tell a reporter what your product did, what would you say? How did it relate to everything else in the market? Millions or even billions of dollars depended on the answers, and a serious marketing VP would hire some very high-priced talent to help craft them.

Miles expounded on the positioning for Reflex that they'd worked out over months and months and made sure to name-drop all the consultants who'd helped with it. Dan thought, *"For a five-second summary, it sure takes a long time to talk about."*

A long discussion followed. This was a topic everyone had been arguing about since the company started. Henry listened respectfully and then said, "I'm wondering if maybe Reflex is an add-on that goes on top of dBase or whatever database you're using. You use the database to hold your data, and then you buy Reflex to help you analyze it. What do you all think of that idea?"

These were fighting words to Clay and Miles. Their entire plan for the company was to produce a foundational piece of software at a premium price. If they'd wanted to make some nice-to-have accessory, they wouldn't have needed seven million dollars in venture funds. They wanted to build the next Lotus 1-2-3.

Another discussion ensued, this one even longer than the first. In the end, Henry backed down. Reflex would be positioned as a core product.

In Dan's world, all the engineers had Compaq computers with two floppy drives so that they could carry them home. They also had Tallgrass external disks, which were about the size of a shoebox and had 10 MB of space. Working from home was now possible, although you had to put all the software you needed on your hard disk before you went home. There was no remote access except by driving to or from the office. Once, Dan had turned in some new software and then worked from home. When he received a call that it didn't compile properly, he had to drive half an hour to Fremont to fix it.

Several of Dan's friends from Xerox had gone to work for a new company in San Mateo, Electronic Arts (EA), which was focused on a new way of building games and other home software. Dan's friend Todd had even contributed its name since the artists were the outside game creators, not the EA employees. EA had a radically different way of creating software from the standard corporate model. Its founder, Trip Hawkins, thought games should be produced the way movies were done in Hollywood.

A Hollywood movie was often done by a production company, which invested its own money in making the movie, and the big studios were often just distribution arms. In other words, Paramount or United Artists did not conceive of and cast every single movie it put out with its own employees and its own money. Maybe in the golden age of the Studio System in the 30s and 40s, it had worked that way but not anymore. Now, it was decentralized.

In Trip's vision, an independent person or group—the artists—would come up with the design of a game or other piece of home software and then take it to EA. If EA liked the game, it would assign a producer to the team and give them what they needed, put its name on it, and handle the marketing and distribution. The game creators would receive royalties but would not become employees.

This created tension with the employees, who were often game enthusiasts themselves. "Why can't *we* create games, too?"

Trip would say, "Okay, if you want to give up your salary and stock options and become an independent contractor, then you can try your hand at it!" Generally, they saw the light, preferred the job security, and stayed with EA.

Dan had never much liked playing games and had no desire to work at EA. He had a very brief flirtation with the first networked games at Xerox, but it wore off quickly. When he was visiting Todd in the Bay Area, he showed him the Pinball Construction Kit, one of EA's first products. It ran on the Apple II and had a Lisa-like interface. The user didn't play pinball—they created their own pinball game, and then they could play it! If they didn't like the way the game played, they could then redesign it. It was a hugely influential game and won all sorts of awards in the gaming world.

Dan thought it was a very nice bit of assembly language programming, but definitely a toy, albeit a great toy. He'd had courses using IBM 360 assembly language in college, which meant you wrote the plain machine instructions instead of some higher-level language like Mesa at Xerox or C like he did now, making it easier for you.

Assembler was a gigantic pain to write, but in theory, it gave you much more control and smaller, faster code. It had almost completely died out in the business world except in some very specialized areas. You'd have to work very hard to convince your manager to let you write in assembler. Games ran on such dinky, underpowered machines, however, that you almost had to write in assembler. Dan had enjoyed it as a student but didn't feel like turning back the clock and doing it again.

DAN HAD the idea of a startup softball league, a league of soft-ball teams from the various startups in Silicon Valley, and began setting up the first game with EA. His efforts finally bore fruit. The two teams met at a diamond in Fremont. Both were led by their company presidents, Trip Hawkins for EA and Henry Franklin for Analytica. EA routed them. Hawkins hit a mighty blast over the left-field fence.

Later in the game, something unusual for amateur softball happened, although it was common with professionals. When there's a runner on first and the batter hits a grounder, the infielders hope for a double play. Although the pros make it look easy, they're using a smaller, harder ball that travels a lot faster than a softball hit by an amateur. And, of course, they're professional ballplayers who've been doing it their entire lives.

It's pretty difficult for a shortstop or second baseman to step on second base and throw to first accurately and quickly enough to beat the hitter coming down the line. If an amateur tries it, he's in such a hurry that he's lucky to throw it anywhere near the first baseman, and if he manages that, the hitter is usually safe. It's a high-skill play, in other words.

Nonetheless, Henry hit into a double play. One of the women players for Analytica said cuttingly, "*Their* president hit a home run!"

Everyone had a good time, though. Analytica didn't play any more softball games, and Dan never heard whether EA played again. They did produce some very successful games, though.[1]

16

WHO CARES ABOUT 'INTERNET'?

Matt and Miriam soldiered on at the University of Minnesota. Matt had settled into his job running the Computer Science Department's local area network, now that he was officially an expert—he had worked at Datapoint after all!

Miriam had gritted her teeth and settled on a dissertation topic, so she was actually going to earn her doctorate there. She'd looked into transferring to a doctoral program in the Bay Area, but it looked too difficult to be admitted into Stanford, much less do it without starting all over again in a new program. She also managed to switch to a different clinic in Minneapolis, which didn't serve only people who skipped their appointments, so she was a little happier.

ARCnet worked pretty well, so Matt's job was not very technical. But it was not taking the computer world by storm, despite having a huge early lead. Datapoint didn't seem willing to do what they had to do to take advantage of it. They were a prisoner of their own early success. The tech world was not very sentimental about those.

It seemed like every week, or even every day, someone

would ask Matt, "Why don't we use Ethernet?" or "Why don't we install Token Ring?" Or some other new local area network fad. There were innumerable committees at the University to decide these things, and Matt spent an ungodly number of hours sitting in their meetings, wondering why *he* wasn't running the committees. At least, he knew something about the topic. He figured two or three half-hour meetings ought to be enough to settle this shit and move on.

Matt liked to repeat what someone had said at a networking conference, "Local area networks are like trolleys. If you miss one, there'll be another one along in five minutes."

One of his more persistent antagonists was Charles Oliver, who was Assistant to a Dean of something or other. Matt had given up keeping track of all the Deans, let alone their assistants. Oliver was never seen without a suit and tie. He was six feet tall, in his mid-forties, with neatly cut short hair, horn-rimmed glasses, and a square jaw. He had impeccable academic credentials, having graduated from Yale and Wharton School of Business and his summer internships with McKinsey. Charles had been chosen to head up the main committee choosing a LAN.

Matt had come to dread the phone calls from Charles inviting him to lunch. It was always in a plush conference room with sandwiches brought in and at least two of Charles' staff joining them to take notes. Charles always had transparencies ready to show on the overhead projector.

It was a Wednesday in early October 1984, and Charles' call came like clockwork at 10:00 precisely, inviting Matt to lunch on Friday. Matt tried to sound enthusiastic. When he arrived at Charles' office, where he had photos of his wife and children at each corner of his desk, he noticed a hardcover copy of *In Search of Excellence* on his bookshelf. On his desk was a copy of the *IBM Systems Journal* opened to an article, "A token-ring network for local data communications." Uh-oh, he thought.

After pleasantries, Charles invited Matt to join him in the conference room. "Well, shall we start? We have a lot to discuss today. I'd like to settle all this before the meeting on Tuesday."

"Great!" said Matt.

Charles' two assistants, Janeen and Nancy, were already in the room. A round of introductions, and Charles said, "Well, dig in," pointing to the box with sandwiches, chips, soda, and cookies. He turned on the projector and put on his first slide. "I'll just go through these while you eat."

Matt's heart sank when the first slide was displayed. As he remembered later, it went:

Why Have a LAN?
• Large databases
• Access by several users
• Frequent updates
• Expensive I/O devices

There were some other bullet points, but those were the ones Matt remembered.

"I thought we should just set the level before continuing so that we know why we're doing this at all." Matt wondered if McKinsey had new hire orientation talks where they taught you phrases like "set the level."

Janeen raised her hand with questions about what large meant in this context. Was it 1 gigabyte, 10 gigabytes, or something larger? Charles said that was a good question, and they would take that up offline—offline meant later or maybe never, Matt had learned. Nancy asked what frequent meant, which received the same answer from Charles.

As the presentation went on, Charles considered the various local area network technologies being offered in the market up to now. ARCnet, the one that was actually relied on by Matt's users, was barely mentioned. Many others were clearly not destined to take over the market, such as Corvus, Sytek, and WangNet. The last of those merited a little more consideration since Wang was, in fact, a leading word-processor company, but their death was just a matter of time.

Matt groaned inwardly as Charles recapped all these. *"Why in God's name do we have to go through all this stuff again?"* he wanted to scream. Janeen and Nancy looked on raptly, asking occasional questions, which were all to be taken up offline.

Then, he had some slides on the strategic considerations for the committee. After all, the University was making a multi-year multi-million-dollar commitment! There were so many considerations—how will it affect the facilities' budgets, the maintenance budgets, compatibility with future software architectures? For the last one, Janeen suggested taking it to the IT Department's Architecture chiefs, which Charles thought was an excellent suggestion.

He focused on what he thought were the two main competitors—Ethernet and Token Ring. Ethernet had an early lead and was standardized by the IEEE, but IBM was mounting an all-out effort to stop them with its token ring architecture.

The arguments about Token Ring made Matt fondly remember the time someone explained Ethernet's contention detection algorithm by comparing it to speakers at a cocktail party. They notice that they both spoke at once and back off. In Token Ring, a "permission to speak" card is handed around from person to person, and you can't speak until you have the card. If you don't need it, you just pass it to the next person. So, one can figure out the longest possible wait for the card.

There had been endless discussions about this, usually involving the word deterministic when techies were talking. Since Charles was not aiming for techies, he didn't use that word. Instead, he seemed to use several hundred words that added up to the same thing.

Ethernet also had technical limitations, among them the

wiring. You had a thick coaxial cable, usually running through the ceiling, with vampire taps coming off it to take the connections down to the floor. Vampire tap means that a metal pin had to puncture the coax all the way to the central wire and was meant to suggest a real vampire sinking its fangs into your throat. Token Ring would use normal telephone wiring—supposedly—although there was much debate about that. Would it be special shielded wire or the normal wire? Would it use the same wires as the telephones or new ones?

Matt knew there were endless debates about that, too. Charles artfully avoided all the technical details and just left it as a choice between special new cable in the ceiling versus wires we already have. He also mentioned that debugging Ethernet usually meant crawling through the ceiling plenum to find the problem.

Now, Matt just couldn't hold himself anymore. "Charles, at this point, shouldn't we mention that there are lots of other cabling alternatives being tested and even being used?"

"Thanks, Matt. I'll add a slide about that at the end."

"By then, no one will be paying attention," he thought.

Charles was almost done. Janeen and Nancy applauded. Matt raised his hand. Charles looked expectantly at him.

"Charles, when will IBM's Token Ring products actually be available? And do we have prices?"

He thought he detected a stony look on Charles' face, but it seemed to vanish quickly. "Our contacts tell us it'll be sometime next year."

"And if you believe that…"

Charles clasped his hands, "Thank you, everyone. And thank *you*, Matt, for taking time out of your schedule to join us!" Matt shook hands with everyone and left.

∿

MATT AND MIRIAM were having dinner that night, and she thought she'd noticed a pattern whenever he talked about work. "So, you don't seem to be having a whole lot of fun at work anymore. Not like at Datapoint."

He looked sheepish, "No, it's a lot of administration nowadays."

"Oh, boy. Don't you hate it?"

"Well, it's important, and it has to be done. If I don't, someone else will do it worse. That's what I tell myself, anyway."

She was honing her interviewing skills as a clinical psychologist at the volunteer site, and she found this intriguing. Was he really telling her what he felt? "And what does your self say when you tell it that?"

He laughed nervously, "He's not totally convinced!"

"No?"

"He tells me, 'I hate this shit!' a lot."

"I bet. I know I would. Or, I should say, my self would!"

"You have to listen to these guys in suits who don't know what the fuck they're talking about, and it never ends."

She decided to be silent. Sometimes, you just had to let the client talk.

"Like today… I had to meet with this guy Charles Oliver and his staff in a pre-meeting for the meeting next Tuesday."

"And, what's he like?"

"He's this typical MBA type in a suit, who somehow or other got himself put in charge of this committee. So, I can't just ignore him."

"But you'd like to?"

Matt snorted, "These management types insist on making everything a question of University strategy, whatever the fuck that is. As if they know anything."

Miriam felt a glimmer of interest, "What do you think they *should* do? I mean, besides putting you in charge!"

Matt smiled thinly at the sarcasm, "Well, there are some

things you just can't prove to them, even though they're true. Ethernet is a standard, and it has the momentum. All the technical people can see it, but the IBM guys in their white shirts and ties walk in and say, 'Oh, Ethernet has all these issues at high traffic volumes, trust us, our Token Ring will be so much better, blah blah blah.'"

"And they buy that?"

Matt snorted again, "Do they ever!"

She thought for a while. Maybe Matt had a people problem more than a technical problem. He had to learn to manipulate these management types, or he'd never make any serious money for them.

She'd been reading up on Silicon Valley and where the desirable neighborhoods were. A few of her friends from college now had rich husbands and lived in the wealthier suburbs of Connecticut. One of them had a child at a top private school, which her parents had never been able to afford for her. Her sister Jeannie, four years older than Miriam, was married to a salesman of industrial equipment and living in a small house in the Long Island suburbs. She pictured lording it over Jeannie.

"So, how do you deal with that?"

"I struggle. Ethernet works just fine, and Xerox's network was *totally* as busy as any other company's. But we call it FUD, for Fear, Uncertainty, and Doubt. IBM is the past master of FUD."

Miriam started to see more and more connections between what she did and what Matt did. But her clients' problems were usually just their own or theirs plus their family's. Matt's were maybe covered more by the Organizational Behavior courses she wished she'd taken.

"How do you deal with FUD?"

"It's tough. FUD really works with these upper management types. That's why IBM uses it so much. I try to talk about the University goals, future compatibility, and all that. But it's tough."

She patted him on the arm. This topic wasn't going to go anywhere further right now. But she resolved to stay on top of it from now on. Unlike when he was just an engineer, she was beginning to think she could be of help to him in his career. It was about managing other people's emotions, not mastering technology. And maybe, it would make him rich, and her too!

MATT MERCIFULLY HAD no committee meetings to go to the next day at work, and the ARCnet was running smoothly, as it usually did. He was going through the set of new connection requests that had come in when Logan, his former boss, dropped by. Logan never tired of reminding Matt that he had succeeded in getting the University onto the Computer Science Network, while Matt had failed. He was about to do it again, but Matt was too quick this time.

Matt looked up warily, "So, how's CSNET going? Are you taking over the universe yet?"

Logan was undeterred, "That's on for next week. I saw an email from you, so I know it's working over here."

"Yeah, it's handy for staying in touch with old colleagues... I'll say that."

"So, when are you going to put TCP on the local network?"

Matt laughed out loud, "TCP? Why in God's name would we do that?"

Logan tried to look serious, but to Matt, he looked wild-eyed. "Transmission Control Protocol, in case you didn't know."

"Yes, I've heard of it. That thing coming out of the ARPANET crowd... the one that's going to solve all our problems."

Logan replied, "The one that'll get us onto the *Internet*," he said, correcting Matt's choice of words.

"Oh, sorry, yes. The *Internet*," emphasizing the word.

"Anyway... we could just have it on a gateway, and the rest of your users could keep using whatever stupid protocol your little network has," Logan said, realizing his first question was kind of an overreach.

"Do you have to write some code for that?"

Logan said triumphantly, "No, dummy! It comes with Unix. We already have it."

Matt expected this kind of thing from Logan. At least now, he didn't have to report to him anymore. "Well, live and learn. Are you going to connect it to the Internet?"

"That's the intent. Can we distribute instructions to your users when we do?"

"*If* you get it working, sure!"

Logan, oblivious to the sarcasm, waved goodbye and left.

Matt thought briefly of the Request for Comment (RFC) docs for the Internet he'd read a long time ago. He hadn't kept up with all the new ones, but Logan apparently had. He remembered enjoying them as a sort of pure, rigorous engineering without the intrusion of business or politics. They were admirable that way.

But what would be the benefit for him in pushing it at the University now? Hardly anyone, except Logan, was bugging him about it. They could have a gateway to the Internet, and anyone who wanted to use it could. In the meantime, most of his users just wanted to share files, use the expensive printers, and send email to each other. Keeping all that up and running and arguing about the next version was more than a full-time job.

He mentioned the Internet to Miriam once, and she just asked if it would make them more money, and he had to admit it wouldn't. "Will it get you a job in California?" was her next question, and he said, "Probably not." End of discussion. But she made a mental note to stay on top of this Internet thing. Matt tended just to be absorbed in whatever he was doing and miss the bigger picture. The bigger picture was figuring out how to siphon off some of the billions to be made in this stuff.

17

LEN COMES TO VISIT

I t was October 1984, and Janet had been in charge of all the Lisa applications for what seemed like forever. But the energy in Apple had clearly shifted to the Macintosh, and even though management officially denied it, the Lisa had been consigned to the "good learning experience" bin. Janet continued to trudge to work and go through the endless management meetings, while smiling at the hints everyone gave her that she really should shift over to the Mac.

She read the news about Bob Metcalfe's 3Com Corporation with envy. They were making good money selling Ethernet adapters for the IBM PC, and her friend, Tim Field, was there. She fondly remembered her big moment in 1978 finding the wrench that caused lightning to blow up the Ethernet, even though Tim figured out how it did that.

3Com had gone public earlier this year in March, and she kicked herself for missing out on that easy Initial Public Offering money. Now, the business magazines were writing fawning articles about them, the way they always do with this month's hot company. 3Com was starting to make software to go with the hardware. Maybe they'd hire her?

She called Tim, who was happy to hear from her. He told

her how he'd singlehandedly held up the production of
3Com's adapter because he'd learned why you had to protect
against lightning! She pictured Tim refusing to let it go into
production until he was satisfied.

He told her 3Com had won an important contest with a
competitor because their adapters had lightning protection,
and the competitors did not, and fortuitously—if that's the
right word—a lightning storm happened during the contest.
Tim promised to bring up the matter of hiring her. She knew
he was a little focused, or perhaps a better term was absent-
minded, so she wasn't surprised when nothing happened.
She'd decided to find another way through the door but
hadn't settled on one yet.

Now that she had a nicely remodeled guest bathroom, she
invited her dad, Len, to visit, and he accepted immediately.
She bought a daybed for the guest room and emptied the
closet. She put in for a week's vacation and felt ecstatic to have
a break from the grind.

SHE PICKED him up at the San Jose airport just before noon on
Saturday, October 13. After retrieving his luggage, they
walked to her car. She still drove a Plymouth out of loyalty,
even though almost no one at Apple had an American car.

"So, what's new back home?"

"Tigers are up, two games to one in the Series! But I guess
you don't follow baseball much, huh?"

"Not too much."

"I want you to know I'm missing today's game to come
visit you!"

"And, don't think I'm not grateful! Is it still on?" She
reached for the radio and searched for it.

"Good thought. It started at…" he glanced at his watch,
"10:30 here."

The Tigers were winning, 4-1, and nothing much was happening in the middle innings. Len had the crossword puzzle started on his newspaper, and he turned back to it. The two of them always liked doing crosswords together, although she never did them any other time.

"Here's a Spanish clue. You guys have a lot of Spanish words around here, don't you? 23 Across is 'something' Gatos, three letters."

"*Los* Gatos!" she said triumphantly. "We can go there for lunch if you decide now." They were on Highway 17, which leads directly to Los Gatos, but they were fast approaching the turnoff to 280.

He laughed, "Maybe some other day. I'm kinda tired now." She turned onto 280.

"10 Across, 4 letters: Merganser."

"Duck!"

"67 Across, 4 letters: Jacob's brother."

That one stumped her.

"I think that's Esau," he said, penciling it in.

"I don't know that one."

"From the Bible, sweetie. Don't they teach you kids *anything* in school?"

She just smiled. They exited 280 at Wolfe Road and drove to her house. She showed him around. He ran to the TV in the family room and turned on the game.

"I hope you don't mind if I watch, sweetie?"

"No, go ahead. I'll just take your luggage to your room." She walked down the hall to the guest room.

Janet had the TV cart facing the kitchen table, but Len turned it toward the couch and leaned forward. It was the top of the ninth inning, Tigers still up 4-1. Jack Morris, the starting pitcher for the Tigers, was still in, going for a complete game, with only eighty-four pitches through eight innings. Tony Gwynn, one of the greatest hitters who ever lived, grounded out to second. In the twilight of his career,

Steve Garvey, the former Dodgers first baseman, came up and hit it off the left-field wall, sliding into second for a double. Now, Len was worried.

Janet heard his "uh-oh" and came and joined him in the living room.

Graig Nettles grounded out to second, with Garvey taking third on the play. Two outs. The crowd rose to their feet, although Len and Janet stayed seated.

A wild pitch to Kennedy, the next batter, and Garvey scored! Len was *very* worried. He gripped Janet's knee. The crowd chanted, "Who cares? Who cares?" Sparky Anderson, the manager, obviously didn't since no one even visited the mound. Kennedy hit a line drive to Kirk Gibson, the right fielder, and the game was over! The Tigers were up, three games to one.

Len wasn't one to watch the endless replays on the post-game show. He walked over and turned off the TV. Janet said, "Yay! One more game now?"

"At least... hopefully, we can finish it tomorrow."

She made lunch for them and told him about how the bathroom remodel had gone. He was very impressed, especially considering that she'd found a good contractor. Len had always had the worst luck with contractors. When she told him how Walt had called her at work when he was afraid Rocky, her cat, had escaped, and she drove home and found Rocky in his usual hiding spot, he imagined himself reading the riot act to anyone who'd waste his time like that. But Janet hadn't. Wow.

After lunch, Len said he was tired from waking up so early and decided to take a nap. Janet went out and mowed the lawn and weeded, and then came in and read the newspaper. Len eventually joined her, and they sat together in companionable silence for a long time. Len put his arm over her shoulders and asked softly, "So, how's my girl?"

She leaned her head against him for a long time and sighed. Finally, "Okay, Dad. How are you doing?"

"Oh, about the same. Nothing changes back there. You know, your mom and I are very, very proud of you!"

"*What can you say to that?*"

"You're a big manager at Apple. *And,* you just bought a house… it's more than I ever dreamed of for you."

"I wish I felt that way more."

"Why? You should!"

"Dad, I'm so *lonely* up here. I can't be friends with anyone at work because it's… well, it's just complicated. Work always gets in the way."

Len thought about that. None of his friends were from work anyway. They were all people he had known from childhood. He decided to let her talk more.

"I never thought I'd miss that group of people Ken and I hung around with in LA. At least they were active!"

At the mention of Ken, he stirred, "He was a loser. You're well rid of him."

She laughed, "Oh, yeah."

"Did he ever remarry... do you know?"

'Yeah, I heard he didn't waste any time. They have a kid on the way."

"So, there's no one up here?"

She looked disgusted, "A few of the guys from Apple asked me out. They're all… I don't know, it was okay, but I just couldn't get too interested."

"Well, sweetie… just when you least expect it, it'll happen. Trust me."

They went back to reading the paper. Finally, Janet and Len went out for a walk in her neighborhood. It was almost dinner time, and children were yelling and riding their bikes. The weather was absolutely perfect as Northern California's so often is, in the low 70s with a light breeze and a few clouds. Movie cinematographers call it the golden hour, when the sunlight goes to the red end of the spectrum, and the shadows lengthen.

The Santa Cruz mountains nearby were bluish with the sunset, while the East Bay hills, farther away, were a little browner. You could see the Lick Observatory at the top of one of them. Detroit didn't have any mountains, Janet reflected.

THE NEXT MORNING, Len offered to take Janet to the hardware store to buy some tools she would need. There was a store, Cupertino Hardware, just across Bollinger. It was a long, narrow store crowded with the useful stuff, and it had obviously been there for a long time, and so had the clerks. A stocky graying man with a red vest and a badge that read Ted greeted them and asked how he could help. Len shook his hand and introduced Janet.

"This is my beautiful daughter, Janet, who lives just across the street there. She's just bought a house!"

Ted shook her hand, "Nice to meet you, Janet. Welcome to the neighborhood!"

"I want to set her up with the basic set of tools she's going to need. Can you help her out? I have some ideas, but you probably know this area better than I do."

"I'd be delighted. What tools do you have now, Janet?"

She was a little embarrassed to admit that she didn't own much. Ted wasn't bothered and invited them to follow him around the store as he pointed out the various tools that he liked, putting them in a little basket on his arm. He added a claw hammer and a screwdriver set and was in the middle of explaining crescent wrenches when she heard a familiar voice. It was Walt, the contractor who'd done her bathroom!

"Hey, Janet, long time no see."

"Hi, Walt. Hey, I want you to meet my dad, Len."

Len and Walt shook hands. Len said, "Hey, you really did

a nice job on that bathroom. I'm going to be using it for the next week."

Walt said, "Oh, no. You're going to see all my mistakes!"

"I haven't spotted any yet."

"So, did she tell you about how on the very first morning... how I called her because I was afraid her cat got out?"

Len laughed, "That has to be the best contractor story I've ever heard."

Walt looked sheepish, "It didn't feel that way at the time. I thought, 'God, what a great way to start a new job!'"

Janet smiled, "Hey, you meant well." Then, she noticed Ted standing there, politely waiting.

"Why don't I go with Ted, and you two can talk?" She and Ted resumed the tool hunt.

Walt asked, "Do you live around here, Len?"

"No, I just flew in from Detroit yesterday, or actually the north suburbs."

"Detroit! So, are you going to watch the game today?"

Len glanced at his watch. Walt said, "You have time. 1:45 today."

"Oh, right. I keep having to remember, three hours *earlier* here."

"Anyhow, the Padres don't have a chance. The Tigers are just too good."

Len smiled appreciatively, "I'm glad *you* think so!"

"Anyhow, it was nice meeting you. You must be very proud of Janet!"

They shook hands, "Nice meeting you, too. You have no idea." Walt resumed looking for whatever he'd come in for.

Ted and Janet walked to the cash register with a basket full of tools, and Janet paid. As they left, Len said, "That Walt's a pretty nice guy." She agreed.

18

WHAT HAPPENS IN VEGAS STAYS IN VEGAS

"Trade shows are the cause of all technological progress" was a favorite saying of Miles, and for once, he was completely correct. Normally when engineers give a date to management, they can say, "Oops, we're going to be late. Sorry." But a trade show has a date that doesn't move. COMDEX—Computer Dealers Exposition— was the trade show in November 1984 in Las Vegas where Reflex would be unveiled. There would be tens of thousands of people attending, and of course all the news media. This was Analytica's one chance to make a good first impression.

The Marketing Department had written a very large check to COMDEX to reserve Analytica's floor space and more checks to the companies who built its lavish two-story booth. Very little of this money would ever return if they canceled. This deadline was real. Every hotel room in Las Vegas was booked, and rooms had to be reserved well in advance.

They needed a product that was demoable, so the engineers' time was rigorously controlled—if a feature wasn't required for COMDEX, it had to wait. As the deadline neared, the controls became even tighter. They only fixed showstopper bugs. Anything an engineer changed *might* break something, so they didn't make a change unless they had to. If they were required to work until midnight and all weekend to finish the work... well, that's the career they signed up for.

COMDEX came, and they all flew to Las Vegas. The town was completely filled with a hundred thousand attendees. The cab drivers, bartenders, dealers, and the rest of Vegas detested the techies. They didn't gamble, they didn't drink, and they didn't go to the shows—all they did was work. At least, that was the stereotype.

Fall 1984 was no longer a boom time for the PC industry. Reflex had missed the moment. The wild euphoria symbolized by the Eagle Computers' founder killing himself in a Ferrari he bought with his IPO cash was over. *The New York Times* story on COMDEX was downbeat:

... the normally boisterous Comdex show has an air of solemnity, the result of the industry shakeout and the relative scarcity of exciting new products.

The new CEO of Apple, John Sculley, gave a similar opening-day speech:

The personal computer industry appears to be, at least momentarily, trapped in a giant rut.

Mr. Sculley said. He asserted that venture capitalists had lost their zeal and that many companies spent too much time worrying about operating system standards, rather than innovation.

Still, there were large crowds. Dan spent the show

explaining the product to hundreds of showgoers, while Henry, Miles, and Clay spent time in the hospitality suite at their hotel, courting the press and other executives.

Dan had been at a trade show before, the 1981 National Computer Conference, where his product, the Xerox Star, really was the hit of the show. Reflex was not the hit of COMDEX, although it was mentioned in stories, albeit well down the page. That same article in *The New York Times* said:

One new category attracting attention is "mindware," the term for programs that promise to help business executives manage their businesses and make decisions. These products are also known as "idea processors" or, more staidly, "decision support systems."

Among the products in this category are Lightyear, from Lightyear Inc. of Santa Clara, Calif.; Reflex, from the Analytica Corporation of Fremont, Calif., and Trigger, from Thoughtware Inc. of Coconut Grove, Calif. These programs, while differing widely, basically advertise themselves as computerized business consultants, helping managers track performance and evaluate alternatives.

This was not the core product positioning that Clay and Miles had been jealously guarding for so long. But at least Reflex made the news, even though computerized business consultant was not the description Miles and Clay would have chosen for it.

Back to work to grind out the final product. Dan hated it, and he was not at all good at hiding his feelings. Work was tedious at best, and downright unpleasant at worst. He resolved to leave Analytica as soon as Reflex shipped. As he saw it, leaving before the product shipped was a serious betrayal of his professional obligations.

He'd written his resume on the Xerox Star, so it had bold and italic text and larger fonts for headings. This was quite unusual for an engineer because their resumes were usually just done on a typewriter. Dan considered it his calling card— Xerox having pioneered all that stuff. He had to go to some trouble to find a Star he could use to update it. He finally found someone at Xerox to let him come in after hours to work on it.

He called Kim Burdette, the headhunter who'd sent him to all those startups when he was leaving Xerox, although not to Analytica. But Kim knew all about Analytica since it was her business to know everything about Silicon Valley. She sent him to a few startups, but now Dan had an Old Boy Network to call on—he'd worked at Xerox.

The months dragged by. Now, he was commuting from west San Jose, not far from Apple, and driving up 17 every day. This wasn't the commute everyone else in Silicon Valley had, which was typically from south San Jose to the Santa Clara area, so there wasn't much traffic.

19

FINALLY, AN ESCAPE

I t was early 1985, and Matt dutifully trudged to his weekly committee meetings on University Network Strategy. His empire as LAN administrator continued to grow in bureaucracy, and now, some of the local area network vendor salesmen had figured out that he was the guy they wanted to talk to, not some Dean of Whatever who'd just waste their time. Of course, he didn't have the authority to say yes, but at least, he asked them a few intelligent questions and regaled them with stories about how the University's LAN was actually working.

Miriam defended her dissertation, a process she absolutely hated, but it was finally over. She was mulling over post-doc opportunities without much enthusiasm and began to pester Matt about finding a way to relocate to Silicon Valley.

Matt had an inspiration! He asked Charles Oliver, the head of the committee, after one of their interminable meetings, "Why don't we invite the various LAN vendors in to give their pitches to the entire committee?"

Charles loved the idea, "That sounds fantastic, Matt! As long as you're their point-of-contact. And they don't bug the rest of the committee or me. You know how salesmen are."

Matt could see it in his eyes—the IBM salesman would blow them away. He assured Charles that he'd get right on it.

"Big mistake!" chortled Matt to himself, as he invited the 3Com representative in first. He glibly explained to Charles that IBM wasn't available right away, so they might as well start.

3Com's salesperson Kate came in the next week, and Matt slipped her his resume and said he wanted to work for them. The next day, he received a call to fly out to California for an interview.

He told Miriam at dinner, and she was ecstatic. Maybe they could finally leave this frigid hellhole. "Finally! Can I go, too?"

Matt didn't want to push it with their goodwill. "Whoa, whoa! Maybe on my second interview or my house-hunting trip if they give me one!"

Miriam's entire outlook suddenly brightened. They spent the rest of the evening talking about what sort of job 3Com was likely to offer him (he had no idea), where they would live, the cost of living in Silicon Valley, and on and on. Time passed slowly until Matt's interview the next week.

MATT FLEW INTO SAN FRANCISCO, which had more flights than San Jose's airport, rented a car, and drove down 101 to Mountain View, where 3Com had its office. 101 was ugly, with billboards everywhere. He watched the signs for Palo Alto since Miriam had figured out from her research that they *had* to live there. At one point, he thought he was there and wondered what she was talking about because East Palo Alto certainly didn't look like any place he'd want to live.

He continued past a Ford Aerospace building and exited at Shoreline Boulevard heading east, turned on Shorebird Way, and parked at one of the identical one-story office buildings that all had very large windows, tile roofs, parking lots in front and all around, and cheap, generic landscaping, heavy on the Agapanthus. The cars were mostly Toyotas, Hondas, and Datsuns—nothing too fancy. If these people had IPO money, they didn't buy expensive cars with it.

The doors opened onto a reception room with a big 3Com logo behind the desk. After signing the guest book, he was offered coffee and invited to sit by the window and wait for Dale.

Dale was a young male engineer who looked straight out of the 50s, with very short hair that appeared to have been greased slightly to keep it in place, horn-rimmed glasses, and a short-sleeved button-down sports shirt. He led Matt through the doors to a conference room where they sat down. He put Matt's resume on the table in front of him and asked him a lot of questions about his current job and what he had done during his summer at Datapoint. Dale didn't know much about ARCnet, so he asked Matt to explain how it worked. Matt thought he'd knocked this interview out of the park.

The next interviewer was a fairly chubby guy, Rich, who had imperfectly tucked his Oxford shirt into his pants. That interview was almost a carbon copy of the first one. Matt asked the guy what he did at 3Com and found out he worked with Dale on their file- and printer-sharing software 3+Share, on the client-side. This meant working on the IBM PC, which Matt hadn't really done, but that didn't seem to bother him. He knew C, so he could pick it up. They talked about the layered protocol architecture 3Com was using, but that wasn't what Matt was being hired for, so they didn't spend much time on it. A competitor in the network software space, Novell, was mentioned, but Rich didn't think very highly of them.

Matt figured those first two probably would have aborted the interview and showed him out if he'd failed, but he was still there! So far, so good. Jim, a tall, rangy guy with a pock-marked face, walked in and introduced himself as their manager. Jim depended on Rich and Dale to rate Matt's technical competence, so he didn't spend much time on that. He seemed to see his job as selling Matt on 3Com.

He talked about 3Com's place in the market, how their name stood for computer communications compatibility, and that openness and standards were their biggest advantage. He mentioned that they were using the Xerox protocol suite, which Matt didn't know a lot about, and Jim walked him through it. He also wanted to know Matt's situation right now, such as did he own a house? What were his commitments to the University? Did he have children? Was his wife willing to move? Matt had a very good feeling about this interview. And then, to cap off the selling job, Bob Metcalfe walked in!

Without any preliminaries, he looked at Matt's resume and said, "So, I see you worked on the Cray!"

"I used to, but it's been a while now." He figured this was just an icebreaker question, which was a good thing since he'd done his best to forget everything he knew about the Cray.

"That *was* the fastest computer in the world at one time. You'll have a little slower machine here at 3Com, I'm afraid."

Matt laughed, "Believe me, I've had more than enough Big Iron for one lifetime!"

Bob smiled indulgently, "So, what can I tell you about 3Com?"

Matt figured he'd better ask something intelligent now. "I'm asked all the time at the University about how the Ethernet stacks up against the Token Ring?"

Bob was ready for this one. "Oh, you mean the Broken Ring?"

Matt laughed, "Is that what you call it?"

Bob's expression became serious as he turned his gaze directly to Matt. "So tell me, where do I buy a Token Ring network this afternoon?" He waited while Matt thought.

"The IBM guys say availability will be soon..." he said hesitantly.

Bob turned to Jim, "And how long have they been saying that?"

Jim answered, "Quite a while now."

"Exactly! But I can name a half dozen places you can pick up Ethernet components on your way back to the airport. I can call up my friend Ralph Ungermann, and he'll be happy to sell you some. Do you have your credit card?"

Matt wasn't quite ready to surrender. Bob wouldn't respect him if he just gave in! But before he could object, Bob had one more comment. "By the way, we made a token ring product ourselves, and it didn't sell very well."

"But isn't Token Ring going to be superior in many ways? More predictable at higher loads, say? That's what they always said at Datapoint, anyway."

"There's that deterministic thing again. Do you know how long I've been hearing that?" Matt shook his head. "At PARC, there was a physicist whose name I can't remember right now. This was about 1973. He claimed that Ethernet would never work because it was not quantum-noise limited, or something like that. Or maybe because it didn't fully utilize all the bandwidth available. I forget."

Jim noticed Bob was looking at him now, "All I know is, we have two hundred people on our Ethernet here, and all these terrible problems we keep hearing about... we never see them."

"Or at PARC," added Bob. "Or SDD."

Matt changed the topic to 3Com's future plans. Bob talked about file servers and their plans to ship their own—a piece of non-public information Matt was requested not to repeat. Then, he glanced at his watch and stood up, explaining that he was late for a meeting, and shook hands with Matt.

Jim and Matt talked more about the company's file- and printer-sharing software and how the LAN worked at the University. Then, Jim gave him a tour of the building, which Matt noticed had no private offices. He'd never worked in a cubicle, but it seemed pretty egalitarian. He was finished before lunch and decided to drive around Palo Alto and see why Miriam was so adamant that they live there.

He drove up 101 to the Page Mill / Embarcadero exit and headed west on Page Mill. Middlefield looked more commercial to the left, and he was hungry, so he went that way and had lunch. Then he headed north again, past Embarcadero.

He thought about the interviews. Dale and Rich, the first two engineers, were obviously there to rate his technical competence, but they didn't blow Matt away. They were good, they didn't flaunt it, and he thought he could work with them just fine if he had to. But he'd had this image of a Silicon Valley engineer as some godlike creature with 800 for an SAT math score and straight As from MIT, so these guys were a bit of a letdown from that. He was pretty sure they'd say he was good enough to work there.

Jim, the manager, was also a no-nonsense guy. He knew a lot of other networking technology beyond what he was actually managing right now, and Matt had the impression that if he did not know something, he'd just tell you without trying to pretend. He seemed like he would be fair and generous, and Matt could definitely see working for him. As a first job in the Real World, this one seemed doable. After he'd been here a few years, maybe he'd leave and start making some real money.

And Metcalfe, the legendary inventor of the Ethernet and founder of 3Com! Even if Matt didn't land the job, he could say he talked to Bob Metcalfe. He certainly knew how to turn on the charm when he felt like it.

He was now across Embarcadero, and the Lucie Stern theater was on the right, all perfectly blended in with the neighborhood. Everything looked either perfectly manicured or carefully allowed to look old. He thought the residents had managed to make it all scream, "We have good taste. And we are smug about it!"

He drove west to see Professorville, a neighborhood Miriam told him to be sure to visit. When Stanford was first built in the nineteenth century, you could only lease the land around it—you couldn't buy it. Professorville was the closest to the University where you could own the land, and several Stanford faculty and administrators had built houses there. Now, the neighborhood had design guidelines, and no one would dream of tearing down a historic house and putting in condominiums. Or, God forbid, a Jack-in-the-Box.

"Miriam would love this place. In the Midwest, every city has suburbs older and prettier than this. But here, they have the 'tasteful and old with big trees' category all to themselves." He drove over to El Camino, which at least looked like a regular commercial street, and then headed back to his hotel near the airport. He decided to check out early and take the red-eye back to Minneapolis

20

TRIVIA QUESTION

I t was a weekend in February 1985, and Janet was making her fourth trip to Cupertino Hardware. One of her neighbors had warned her that no home project ever proceeded without at least three unscheduled trips to the hardware store. Now, she understood.

While she was looking for some English socket wrenches, because she only had metric, she saw someone she knew— Dan Markunas!

"Hey, Dan! What are you doing here?"

Dan looked up, "Janet!" He hugged her. "I was just going to ask you the same question. Do you live around here?"

Dan thought she looked a little harder-edged than she had at Xerox. Maybe it was the effect of the rough-and-tumble of real business, instead of research or whatever it was they did at Xerox. She thought the same about him.

"Yeah… just across the street there," she said, pointing to Bollinger. "How about you?"

"A little farther, but yeah. Over near Rainbow. So, how's Lisa?"

She made a face, "It's work. So when did you move over there?"

"Last March. I'm dying to hear about Apple!"

"*So is everyone*," she thought. "Well, Apple is pretty secretive, so I can't say too much, but let's just say, it's a shitshow."

"So I hear."

"But where are you now?" Everyone from Xerox always asked that question whenever they met another Xeroid. It was important to keep track of each other.

It was Dan's turn to make a face, "I'm at a little startup called Analytica."

Her face was blank, "Haven't heard of that one. What do they do?"

"Oh, we have this database product called Reflex. It was unveiled at COMDEX last November."

She was tempted to ask him what Reflex did, but something in his face made her think he didn't feel like talking about it. Instead, she just made her exit, "Well, it was great to see you! I'll have to walk over and see your house sometime."

Dan had an idea, "Hey, if you're done here, I'll drive you over, and you can walk back! Or you can follow me in your car."

"No, I walked over. Sure, let's go!"

They drove east on Bollinger, turned right on Alderbrook, and pulled in his driveway. Janet saw his house and said, "Oh, my God. This is my house exactly!"

"Great minds think alike," he said, raising the garage door.

They walked in, and Janet knew the floor plan immediately. She walked over to the hall bathroom, saw that it only had a tub, and exclaimed, "I remodeled this room, so it has a shower now."

They talked about contractors, and Dan was full of questions about the bathroom job. He hadn't done much to his house yet, but he had a lot of ideas. They went out in the yard and talked about landscaping and trees for a long time and then sat down on the redwood deck that surrounded the elm tree.

"So, Apple isn't what it's cracked up to be?" he ventured.

She didn't want to just dismiss the question this time. "No, it's *real* different from Xerox, that's for sure. We never even thought about consumers buying the Star, but that's *all* these folks think about. Apple is now all about Macintosh and home users."

Dan didn't know immediately what to say, so she continued.

"But how's this startup you're at? How did you end up there?"

Dan told her the story of how they'd contacted him and all the management turmoil he'd endured.

She was sympathetic. "Yeah, you know, the Xerox people I talk to who've left… well, you hear all sorts of horror stories. You're not alone."

"Yeah. Are you thinking of leaving Apple?"

"For sure. I talked to Tim Field at 3Com, but you know, he's a little… let's say, work-focused!"

Dan laughed, "And you know him from the lightning incident, of course!"

Janet just smiled. Her greatest triumph—saving the Ethernet by finding the wrench.

"Funny, I was thinking about 3Com, too. I know a couple of people there."

They talked about who Dan knew, but Janet didn't know those people. She said, "I don't know… ever since that first trip we made to Palo Alto, I've been fascinated with Ethernet. Even if they're already public, I'd still go."

"Yeah, can't get rich off their stock, probably. But it's still a way to get into networking."

"I guess. Speaking of stock, are you going to receive anything from your Analytica stock?"

Dan laughed, "Wallpaper, probably. But who the hell knows?"

She stood up, "And then, there are people like the Adobe guys, whatever their names are. I bet they're buying houses in Atherton."

"Geschke and Warnock," he said.

"Right. Well, I'd better head back home. It was great seeing you, Dan!"

"Do you need a ride?"

"It's a nice day. I think I'll walk, but thanks."

JANET WALKED BACK to her house, thinking of all the different places the Xeroids had scattered to. Some startups were commercializing Xerox inventions, such as Adobe and 3Com, and of course, Apple was pretty much doing that now, too, although they hadn't started out that way. Sun Microsystems was mostly working the Unix angle, but they had windows and a mouse. Oracle had attracted a couple of Xeroids, although the Xerox connection wasn't very strong with them.

And of course, there were innumerable startups, like Dan's. It seemed like every week, some headhunter called and begged Janet to talk to the latest one. Their pitch was always, "Oh, Ralph Hotshot is the CEO!" or "James Influencer is their PR agent," or the old reliable, "Kleiner Perkins is their lead investor!" The way startups competed for famous names and then used them to attract people was like a politician gathering endorsements.

Dan's not-so-great experiences showed you what was wrong with a raw startup. You just had no idea at all how it was going to turn out, and all the norms of civilized, professional behavior that she took for granted at TRW and Xerox were out the window. People could behave like animals without all those norms, and it sounded like at Dan's company, they had.

She'd heard of Xeroids at startups that had either shut down already or were circling the drain. Sometimes, they'd raised a seed round of financing, and the original investors refused to put any more in, so the execs had to scramble for new backers. Usually if they received new money, the value of the original stock dropped like a stone after the new investors extracted their pound of flesh. She'd been going to the Dutch Goose on Thursdays to keep up with all the gossip, and there was a lot of it.

So, where to go? Since you can't predict which company will make you money, maybe you should just look at whether it's interesting work that you can learn from—and whether it's a nice place to work. As she arrived at her house, she resolved to keep in touch with Dan.

AFTER JANET LEFT, Dan went back into the house and turned on the TV. Football was over, and baseball hadn't started yet. It sucked. He didn't feel like watching basketball. He turned the TV off.

Janet's visit had cheered him up a little. Apple was as bad as he'd been hearing, and Janet was interested in 3Com, too. Maybe they'd both end up there!

When he talked to people from Xerox, no one had ever heard of Analytica, and COMDEX didn't change that. It just didn't have the buzz that hot startups had.

One night that week, he went to hear Phillippe Kahn talk. He was the founder of Borland, which made Turbo Pascal, a hot product making a lot of noise by defying all the rules that software companies were supposed to live by. They sold for $99.95, when serious products like Reflex insisted on a premium price point, like $400 or $500 or even more. Dan was always amused that you had to say *price point* if you wanted to be a serious marketing person and not just *price*.

Even more down-scale, Borland sold through mail order, not via salesmen in computer stores. In the early days of personal computers, that was how software was sold. Furthermore, Phillippe didn't care at all if hotshot marketing guys and their hired-gun PR firms thought he was trailer trash. It was refreshing for Dan to hear.

When Dan arrived at Analytica the next day, he told Miles about it and wasn't surprised to find Miles not interested. He and Clay had built Analytica around a $500 product that you bought in a computer store, and he wasn't going to change now. Dan had the strong feeling that they were going to crash and burn, and he did not want to stick around and be a part of it.

He called up his friend Donald at 3Com, a noted email expert. Donald was in charge of some new electronic office initiative ABC that 3Com was launching, which Dan didn't know much about, but he also owned their email product, 3+Mail, and that was a real thing. Dan thought it would be so cool to work on email!

He offered to send a resume, but Donald told him to just bring it with him to the interview. They already knew him.

Donald had been the *Special Rapporteur* for a multi-year standards committee developing X.400, an international standard for electronic mail. Even at Xerox, people had joked about how they'd be willing just to carry his bags to the meetings because they were always in some exotic-sounding foreign location.

His title was a French word because the committee was under the auspices of the United Nations. X.400 wasn't really in use anywhere, and Donald was pretty vague about 3Com's plans to use it. It was a part of an even bigger standards effort called OSI—Open Systems Interconnection—which would be a complete standard for *everything*, not just email. All the public telephone companies around the world, which were mostly government monopolies, were behind it.

Every government agency had some official statement that they were going to use OSI on all their networks someday. It was just lip service right now, though. No private companies were asking for it, but Donald liked to say that in Europe and most of the world, "OSI isn't just a good idea... it's the law."

Donald had two people working for him, and one, Phil, was a guy Dan knew from Xerox. They both interviewed him. The other guy, Li, had a lot of background on X.25, a public packet-switching network that had been around for years without ever gaining much momentum—maybe because it was slow and expensive. An X.25 connection was actually billed by the packet, probably because telephone companies wrote the standard, and they thought it was just like a long-distance call. When you called someone, you paid by the minute, and in a computer connection, you should pay by the byte. What could be more natural?

Of course, the X.400 standard used X.25, but 3Com wasn't doing much with X.25, either.

Phil had been involved with email for years. He didn't have a lot to ask Dan since it seemed like a foregone conclusion he would receive an offer, so Dan took the opportunity to ask him questions. "So, 3+Mail uses the Xerox protocols, more or less?"

"That's right, XNS. Metcalfe received special permission from Xerox."

"Is anyone else in the industry doing that?"

Phil kept a poker face, "Novell is, from what I've heard, although they don't make a big deal out of it."

He expected Phil to expound on this, but it looked like Dan would have to do all the work. "And the Clearinghouse? Is that the same software we used at Xerox?"

"Well, we have our own implementation, and we don't do all the things that they do. But yeah, pretty much."

Dan thought this was like pulling teeth. Maybe he'd try a more open-ended question. "Can I describe what I think happens when I send a message to a group, and you can help me understand it better?"

"Okay," Phil said grudgingly.

Dan drew five circles on the whiteboard—two for the sender's and recipient's PCs, two for the sender's and recipient's mail servers, and the directory server. The sender was emailing 3Com. Dan started connecting the circles.

The very first network exchange finally excited Phil. The question is, what users are in 3Com? There is a group, 3Com, defined in the Directory, and it has to be expanded to all 250 employees. Furthermore, they belong to subgroups, which belong to larger groups, until you reach the top.

"Well, group expansion really should be done on the server, but right now, it's done on the client," he said disapprovingly.

Dan asked what that meant.

"So first, the client asks, 'Who is in 3Com?' and is told that there are three subgroups. Then, it has to repeat the process for each of those subgroups and continue expanding until it has everybody. It's a mess."

Dan asked, "That's a lot of network traffic."

Phil laughed mirthlessly, "You think?"

"Why was it done that way?"

Phil struggled visibly to be diplomatic, "You'd have to ask Donald that. It was done before I started."

On the way to Analytica in Fremont, Dan thought about it all, and he was excited. He loved the intellectual challenge of networking. In almost all the programming he had ever done, all the data, or really all the "truth," was on one computer. You never had to worry that your code didn't know the whole truth and had to ask someone else on the network. If you did that, you invited all sorts of problems.

Maybe that someone else wasn't even there right now. Or

its own idea of the truth was out of date. Or maybe, you wanted to return the email message as undeliverable, but now, you couldn't do that! Programmers, and especially mathematicians, tended to be on the autistic end of the spectrum and couldn't handle uncertainty. But on a network, everything was uncertain, and you could never be one-hundred-percent positive you were right. Just like in real life.

A couple of days later, he received an offer from 3Com and accepted it. He went to Jacob, his boss at Analytica, and told him he was quitting. Jacob just said, "Well, I can't say I'm surprised."

At his last Engineering meeting, Dan told them he had a trivia question for them. "What song did Johnny Paycheck make famous?"

Everyone knew the answer, so he didn't need to say it... "Take This Job and Shove It."

21

TOGETHER AT LAST

May 21, 1985, and it was Matt's second day and his first 3Com meeting. He and Miriam had driven from Minneapolis to the Bay Area, found an apartment in Palo Alto, and she'd already started studying for her California shrink's license.

The building was like he remembered it from the interview, but the weather was even better. In Minneapolis, the University would virtually shut down if they had a day like this because everyone would be outside enjoying it. Throughout the endless winter, it was gray every day, usually cold, windy, and often with rain, sleet, or snow. A day like this would be precious beyond belief. But here, it was taken for granted.

The receptionist had been nice to him, but she seemed extra nice to certain people who had that indefinable but visible something that said, *"I'm important."* He received his badge, which would let him into the doors with electronic locks.

The morning of his meeting, he arrived at the conference room early and noticed that it looked just like the conference rooms at the University. While waiting for the others, he replayed Miriam's pep talk about his new job. It was a rehash of the one she gave in the car, off and on, all the way out from Minneapolis. He was to strive for World Domination, which were his words when he wanted to annoy her. *Her* words were, "Someone has to run things. Why not you?"

The others arrived, and he shook hands with most of them. He tried classifying everyone as an ally, rival, higher-up, or a tool, as Miriam had encouraged, but it wasn't easy. He knew she would do it for him tonight when he replayed the meeting for her.

Matt was going to inherit something grandly called network services, which simply meant the Clearinghouse for now. Everything depended on this online directory service, most critically, the email service. Every employee on email, meaning everyone, had an entry in the Clearinghouse, along with the name of their mail server. All the mail servers were in there, and all the printers, and all the employee groups. Whenever you did anything online, your software had to query and maybe update the Clearinghouse. It was the nerve center of the network.

They sat in a medium-sized conference room with glass walls and a table big enough for ten people, with whiteboards at the front and back. They went around the table introducing themselves. Donald, a clean-cut guy with a mustache, led the meeting, and he said with a friendly self-assurance, "I'm Donald Haven for those who don't know me. I have the honor of managing email and network services, plus I'm heading up the ABC effort."

"*A higher-up. Gotta cultivate him,*" thought Matt, but then he wondered what ABC was.

To Donald's right was a thirtyish guy with a nice beard and glasses and a plaid long-sleeved shirt. He seemed like a pretty quiet engineer. "I'm Dan Markunas, and I started three weeks ago! I'm going to be working on ABC and email, I guess." Everyone tittered at the "I guess."

Matt thought, *"A tool I can use! The guy who does the work."*

"I'm Phil Robinson, and I work with Donald." Matt had the feeling that Phil would rather not be there. He wasn't sure where Phil fit in his world.

It was Matt's turn, "I'm Matt Finegold, and I started yesterday! I just left the University of Minnesota."

A round of applause and several people said, "Welcome!"

Donald took over for a second, "Matt is reporting to Bob Metcalfe temporarily, but Captain Bob is out goofing off today!"

A very attractive woman with a businesslike air spoke up next, "I'm Janet Saunders, and I also started yesterday. I will be managing the internal network."

More applause and, "Welcome!"

Matt thought, *"A rival? Maybe. Have to see."*

His first impression of Janet was ambivalence. She was very attractive, seemed composed and friendly, and didn't give away much. When they talked about what they had done before coming to 3Com, she spoke in general terms and avoided talking about Apple's legendarily vicious politics. He was imagining describing her to Miriam tonight and wondering what she'd say. Janet clearly had a perch with potential for political power, much more than he did right now, but he had no sense of whether she exploited it.

She added, "Dan and I worked together at Xerox ages ago."

Donald said, "The Xeroids are taking over!"

Matt asked, "So, am I the only one here who's *not* from Xerox?"

Donald looked around and said, "I'm afraid so. But you're one of us now!" Matt simply smiled. Donald continued, "The reason we're here today is to acquaint everyone since we're growing like mad, and we have to start planning the evolution of our network."

He paused, "And of course to welcome Matt and Janet!" Everyone applauded again.

Donald provided a high-level description of how email and directory services worked. Matt and Janet listened raptly and asked lots of questions. Dan knew some of this stuff after a few weeks of work, but he had questions, too. Occasionally, Phil interrupted with corrections, which Donald tried to be graceful about.

Matt forgot to keep assessing people for their strengths and weaknesses, as Miriam had urged. He was too interested in the details of how email and the Clearinghouse worked.

Donald explained that there was a new release of 3+Mail coming out this summer, and Phil and Dan were in charge of making it happen and rolling it out to the entire company. The saying in Silicon Valley was "we're eating our own dog food," meaning "before we ask you, our customer, to use something, we use it ourselves."

Janet straightened up. Now, they were talking about her—using something internally was her department. She'd met the staff she had to rely on to pull this off, but she hadn't seen them work yet. Were they really up to the task? She'd find out.

Her stomach tightened. This dog food bit sounded great to engineers and executives, but to her, it simply meant she was the test dog. The engineers would give her software that was barely tested and expect her to deal directly with the regular 3Com employees, most of whom only wanted it to work. *"Okay, this is management!"*

She'd worked with Dan before, so he was no problem. But this Phil guy seemed pretty standoffish, and his boss Donald had a certain reserve about him, too. And the other new guy, Matt—she didn't know what to think about him. He was fresh out of a university.

She used to be a programmer way back when. But even at Xerox, what she did, building the system and integrating the software, was not the same as writing code. Now, she was definitely not writing code. She'd noticed that a lot of the other managers at Apple were almost proud, in a perverse way, that they hadn't written any code in years. Many in the industry seemed to encourage that attitude, as though once you turned thirty, you'd outgrown programming. And now, you had to manage programmers, and then manage the managers, and so on until you reached your level of incompetence.

Xerox hadn't been that way, though. Plenty of senior people who still wrote code, considered that part of their identity, and didn't want to spend their days in meetings. But out here in the real world, many people thought managing was what you did when you grew up. And now, she had a grown-up job where she had to get people working together smoothly.

ON HIS PART, Dan left the meeting understanding the network a little bit better, although he knew most of the stuff already. He thought Janet seemed more distant than at Xerox. Back then, they'd been buddies, more or less. They'd sneak sarcastic glances at each other during meetings like nothing was too serious. But now, she wouldn't even meet his eyes. After the meeting, they talked briefly, but she pleaded a need to meet with her team and broke it off.

He went back to his cube. Phil was listening to opera as usual. Dan went back to reading the listings he'd printed out and printing out new ones and punching holes in them with the three-hole punch. He was filling up binders with the email code. Sometimes, he'd find a ream of paper that was already three-hole punched and load it into the printer, but he never needed to print out that much all at once, so most of it would go to waste.

After work, he drove down to the Computer Literacy bookstore in Sunnyvale, on Lawrence near 101, not far from Intel and the very heart of Silicon Valley. This was so awesome—a bookstore that *only* had computer books! No longer did you need to mail away or special-order them at a regular bookstore. Stacy's in Palo Alto had some of the more popular computer books. He'd bought the Kernighan & Ritchie book on C there, but Computer Literacy had *everything.* *"Only in Silicon Valley!"* It was a very small bookstore hidden in the back of a strip mall, with only one door in and out. It was way smaller than a real bookstore because it didn't have sections on Fiction, History, Travel, or Cooking—simply computers.

Dan had never realized there were so many books about computers. He bought one by Andrew Tanenbaum called *Computer Networks,* despite fearing it would end up unread, like so many of his good intentions. But this promised to explain many of the terms he'd heard people throwing around, such as ring networks, virtual circuits, X.25, datagrams, and more. Maybe this time, he'd read a technical book instead of watching TV when he came home from work and finished dinner. He'd always imagined that's what everyone did, except for him.

One morning after Dan had absorbed some of the book, he tore Phil loose from his headphones, and they started talking about it.

"So, we use the XNS protocols at 3Com?"

"For the most part, as far as I know," Phil replied.

"What's different about them versus SNA, DECnet, and all those others?"

Phil laughed, "Oh, jeez, I don't know. Those are all proprietary."

Dan said, "But XNS assumes Ethernet, right?"

Donald walked by and listened in.

"Well, technically, any local net that has a 48-bit MAC address, but yeah, basically Ethernet."

Dan was learning the acronyms. He was starting to think that networking was nothing but acronyms. "MAC is... Media Access Control?"

"Right," said Donald. "The hardware address, if you will."

"So, eventually, we'll all be using the OSI suite of protocols?"

Phil was silent, poker-faced. Donald said, "In Europe, it's not just a good idea... it's the law!"

Dan thought he'd heard that from Donald before, but he moved on. "What about TCP and the Internet?" TCP stood for Transmission Control Protocol, yet another three-letter acronym. He thought maybe he should make up a cheat sheet of all of them. TCP was what the Internet was using.

Phil brightened a little, "They're doing some good work. I just wish we had more adoption of it."

"So, companies aren't jumping on it yet?"

Phil said, "Not really."

Donald added, "Outside of universities and research labs, you don't even see TCP."

Dan changed the topic, "And what about X.400 email? Should I be studying that?"

Donald said, "Well, you're certainly welcome to, but it's not an immediate concern of ours."

Phil asked him, "Is there anyone actually using it yet?"

"Not commercially, as far as I know. There are some research efforts in Europe."

Dan was a little disappointed. Having 3Com be a leader with a world standard seemed pretty exciting. Maybe this stuff was going to happen more slowly.

Getting into 3+Mail was a slow process. He'd had the overview talks from Phil and Donald, but those were mainly about the mail server. Phil didn't know much about the client, the software that ran on the PC. That was what users interacted with, and Dan just had to read the code and figure it out. He didn't like that much, but that was life in the real world. You always had to take over someone else's code, and it was never something you would have written.

22

DO YOU KNOW THE WAY TO MANDALAY?

Matt was in the same situation as Dan. They'd both been handed some code that someone else wrote and told to fix the bugs and add features. Matt was in charge of the Clearinghouse, the repository for everything on the network, so everyone blamed it for everything. Plus, they invariably had harebrained ideas for enhancing it.

Still, network directories were a hot area in academia and the industry. Matt immersed himself in the literature and started looking for conferences he could go to as a break from being the mandatory attendee whenever anyone had a meeting about almost anything.

Matt and Dan started hanging out together a lot. It started when Dan stopped by Matt's cubicle near the left side of the building after the meeting on Matt's second day. Matt was flipping through a box of floppies when Dan walked up.

"Hi, Matt, I'm Dan Markunas, in case you forgot all the names."

Matt stood up, and they shook hands, "Just looking for the right DOS boot disk. So, you came from Xerox?"

"The job before last. I was at this horrible startup after that, which we won't talk about."

Matt chuckled, "Okay, let's not. What did you do at Xerox?"

"I was in charge of the database… to put a glorified name on it. In reality, it was just a flat file with a fancy interface. How about you? What were you doing at Minnesota?"

"I started in compilers, but I switched over to LANs because it was just more interesting. I ended up running their network."

"Wow, how was that?"

"It was interesting for a while. Then, it started being bureaucratic." Dan sympathized. Matt continued, "So where'd you go to school?"

"I went to the University of Illinois, bachelors and masters. Did you do your undergrad at Minnesota, too?"

"No, I went to SUNY Binghamton. I'm originally from New York."

"Noo Yawk!" said Dan. "From the City proper?"

"Yeah, from Queens!"

Now that they had the obligatory getting-to-know-you out of the way, they moved into work talk. Dan asked, "You have the Clearinghouse, right? I guess you and I are going to be working together a lot!"

Matt said, "Seems that way. Obviously, I don't know much about it yet. Do you? I know it's called 3+Name at least."

Dan replied, "Oh, a little. Mail looks up all the user names and groups and servers in the Clearinghouse when it's routing a message. That's about all I know so far."

"Yeah, should be interesting. I know the Clearinghouses can talk to each other and push updates, but I have no idea how they do it. Anyway… what do you do for fun around here?"

Dan relaxed, "Oh, work on my house a lot. Sometimes, I go on Sierra Club hikes. Occasional cultural events. Not nearly enough, though." He looked at the cardboard box on Matt's floor and saw a bunch of cassettes. "Some interesting stuff here," flipping through them. "I haven't been buying pre-recorded tapes for some reason. Probably should."

"Yeah, Miriam and I fight about what to listen to in the car."

"Herbie Hancock!" remarked Dan, picking up one of his tapes. "I saw him at Illinois."

"Oh, yeah? When was that?"

Dan recollected, "1973 or so…" thumbing some more, "Art Blakey! I love Blakey. I saw him at the Lighthouse in Hermosa Beach!"

"That's Southern California, right? You lived there? I thought PARC was up here."

Dan had to remind himself that everyone thought "Xerox PARC" was one word, so he ought to be used to this by now. "Star wasn't actually done at PARC. It was a different Xerox unit. Half up here, half down south."

Matt replied, "Got it, got it… Anyhow, there was this concert in New York in February, with both of those guys and a *whole bunch* of other guys, *One Night with Blue Note* that I would have killed to go see. Freddie Hubbard, Joe Henderson, McCoy Tyner…" he tried to think of who else. "Ron Carter, of course."

"Who else would you get on bass? Wow. Yeah, I think I read about that. So do you, or I should say, *did* you go to live jazz in New York? Man, everyone plays there."

Matt felt apologetic, "Not as much as I should have. I did go to the Blue Note a couple of times and the Village Vanguard once or twice."

Dan was respectful, "We'll have to talk about all this some more. Anyway, if you need help with anything, feel free to stop by." He returned to his cube.

Matt was pleased. There was at least one person here who could talk about something other than computers and science fiction. He spent the rest of the day reading code and picking people's brains about Clearinghouse. His guess was correct, and everyone had their own dumb ideas for it.

The next day, he dropped by Dan's cube near one of the printers to ask how to build the mail server, and they fell into a general discussion of networking. Dan had been reading his book, and he had lots of questions. Matt had his respect for actually having done it before.

"So, Matt. Do you have time for some ignorant questions?"

"Sure."

"I've been reading *Computer Networks* by Andrew Tanenbaum."

"I don't know that book."

"It seems like the really big deal in networks is whether you have a circuit, or connection, or not, right?"

"I guess so. I haven't thought of it that way, but yeah. We talk about a virtual circuit, which is like setting up a telephone call."

Dan said, "A VC, yeah. Not at all the same as Venture Capitalist!"

Matt laughed, "Not at all. Two-letter acronyms are very prone to conflict!"

"Right. If you don't have a VC, then you just send datagrams?"

"Yeah. On a LAN like Datapoint, which is what I'm familiar with, it's all datagrams. A VC is something you impose on top of them."

Just then, Phil leaned out into the aisle that separated his cubicle from Dan's. "I couldn't help overhearing. Right. If you have a VC, then you put the packets in order. If not, they can arrive out of order. Or maybe not at all."

Dan knew that Phil's headphones weren't completely sound-proof, and opera music has many quiet parts, so he wasn't surprised Phil caught some of their conversation. "Hi, Phil. So as far as I've been able to determine… when you send out a packet, eventually the other side has to acknowledge it. Or, excuse me, ACK. If you had a perfect hardware circuit, you wouldn't need that because you could just assume it all went through."

Phil made a face. He had a reflexive dislike for imprecise language like *it all went through.* "Well, in our world, the other side can *always* go away. Or any of the routers in between them and us. So, we always have to ACK."

Li, the other member of Dan's team, had wandered by and stopped to listen. "ACKing is fundamental. How long you wait for an ACK after you send is a big, big driver of performance."

Everyone seemed to want to give their opinion on this, but Dan still had the floor. "That's the timeout value, right?"

Phil again, "There are lots of different timeouts. You'll learn about those, I'm sure!" he laughed.

Dan said, "But you can't ACK *every* packet because that would take too long."

Bob Metcalfe walked by, and the conversation stopped. "And so, we have Sequenced Packet Protocol, or SPP, from Xerox, of course!"

Phil said, "Yay. What more do we need?"

Bob held his hands, palms up, "Some protocols for filing and printing, and I think we're done!"

Everyone laughed. Dan said, "So, SPP solves the ACK problem?"

Bob gave them a quick lesson on protocol design.

"The performance trick is to ACK more than one packet at a time. How many? Enough to fill the pipeline from sender to receiver. Keep sending packets until you get an ACK. If you don't get an ACK in a round-trip time, start retransmitting unacknowledged packets. ACKs can help by signaling which queued packets do not need to be retransmitted."

Before anyone had a chance to respond, he pointed at Matt. "You, sir! Let's go talk. I apologize that I wasn't here to welcome you yesterday." Bob was nominally Matt's manager, although no one expected that to last very long since Bob was too busy as Chairman. Matt rose and followed Metcalfe to a conference room. The informal meeting broke up.

JANET HAD one-on-one meetings with all three members of her team. She was trying to feel upbeat about it. They were all happy to have her as their boss and eager to explain what they were doing and what they needed. Still, she couldn't imagine any of them being hired by Xerox or Apple.

Larry was first. He was a clean-shaven medium-height guy with short, wiry hair. He looked somehow as though having anyone disapprove of him would be devastating. When asked for an opinion, he nearly always cited someone else's, and often, he added that the majority of people he dealt with felt that way. He seemed to think of himself as their babysitter.

To hear Larry tell it, his users were non-technical people who thought of the network as magic. Maybe they'd memorized a few stories about how the Ethernet worked in case someone asked them, but they pleaded ignorance beyond that. Often, they thought of Tim Field, the chief hardware designer, as a slightly comic nerd. Larry's main desire seemed to be a group where everything runs smoothly, and no one is upset. He stressed his good people skills.

Janet thought, *"Okay, this guy's easy to manage, but don't make him do anything unpopular."*

Mohan was next. He was a short, slightly built Indian guy who always had an eager smile on his face. Her first impression was that he was extremely agreeable, maybe even too much so. Mohan was here on an H1-B visa. He had attached himself to Larry and frequently supplied the technical energy that Larry lacked, so they made a good team—Larry would promise something, and Mohan would carry it out. Often,

Mohan didn't know how to do it, but he was ingratiating enough to find someone willing to tell him. Mohan was happy with his job. Although he didn't say it directly, she figured that above all, he didn't want to lose his work visa and have to go back to India.

Cassidy was the third and last. She was a short woman with curly hair who looked to be in her mid-twenties. Cassie, as everyone called her, seemed a little intimidated by everything. Janet found out in the interview that this was Cassie's first job out of Cal Poly Pomona. Cassie specialized in helping people set up the config.sys and autoexec.bat files on their PCs so that the Ethernet worked.

Janet invited Matt to meet with them all. The Clearinghouse, or Name Service as they called it, was just magic to them. Matt had fantasized that they understood all about replication—how an update to one unit propagates to the others. Maybe they'd thought about the issues he'd face if he tried to expand email groups within the server instead of making the user's PC do it. Maybe they at least had an opinion about how your PC finds the Clearinghouse. However, they didn't even know those were issues.

That night, Miriam asked him about the people he worked with. He'd mentioned some of them casually.

"So, you and this Dan guy got along, huh?"

"Yeah, he's into jazz, which is cool. I didn't know if anyone on the West Coast was into that stuff."

"It *is* kinda a New York thing, I guess."

"He's even heard of the Village Vanguard. Amazing."

Miriam already thought she could classify Dan as a useful tool, but she just wanted to make sure. "Is he married?"

Matt thought for a second. "No, I don't think so. No wedding ring."

"Divorced?"

"Don't know. We didn't dive into personal stuff."

"*Typical guy. Never asks about what really matters.*" Moving on, "How about Janet? Was that her name?"

"Janet!" Matt said. "Nice-looking, I gotta say."

"Should I be jealous?"

"Heh. No. Not my type. A *shiksa*."

Miriam smiled, ignored that, and pressed on. "So, she was a manager at Apple. Is that what you said?"

"Yeah, she was in charge of the Lisa applications. Quite a big managing position."

"Why did she leave?"

Matt laughed, "Why does anyone leave Apple? It's a snake pit."

"Really? How long was she there?"

"Hmm, not sure. Three or four years?"

"Three or four years. She must have been good at surviving, at least."

"I guess. She seems very controlled."

Miriam thought, "*This one might be a rival!*"

She asked the same questions about Janet without expecting an answer. "How about her? Married? Divorced?"

Matt was annoyed, "*She doesn't realize you don't just go asking these things in a corporate setting.*"

"Not married, at least."

"How about your manager, Donald?"

"Donald is a real gentleman. Mild-mannered, very polite. He's on this international committee for email, so he has to be pretty polished."

"What do you think he's doing at 3Com, then?"

Matt wondered that himself, "Good question. A startup like 3Com isn't the obvious place for a guy like him."

"No? Where is?"

"Well, Xerox was a huge international company where you could think big thoughts. Maybe he needs to be a player like that again."

Miriam crossed Donald off her list of people to worry about. "Well, anyway, are you happy so far?"

"I don't know. It's real. 3Com will probably be successful. And at least we're out here in Silicon Valley, right?"

"Yes, we are! I need to go study for the state licensing exam." She went to the counter for her books.

LATER THAT WEEK, Janelle from HR dropped by Dan's cube to invite him to join a corporate committee. He was thrilled, "A committee? What's it for?"

"We're trying to come up with a consistent naming scheme for the conference rooms! Right now, they're just room numbers."

Now he knew why he, in particular, had been invited. Everyone more senior was too smart to waste their time on this. "Oh, boy. At Xerox, I actually ran a poll for that!"

Janelle was amazed, "You had an election? What won?"

"Monopoly streets, I think," said Dan. "Anyhow, when's the next meeting?"

The meeting was held in a small conference room later that day. There were five attendees. Larry said he worked for Janet, so Dan and Larry chatted about her since he'd worked with Janet at Xerox. The others were all young women who worked in Finance, Production, or HR.

Dan tried hard to maintain interest as the discussion went on interminably. "Rivers in California" was popular until they put all the ones they could think of on a board and ran out after four or five. "Streets near here" was also a contender, but it seemed too depressing, plus the geographical correspondence of the street to its location in the building was a problem. Both of those had the issue that visitors from out of state would find them non-intuitive.

Dan came up with "Cities of the World," which became

the favorite for a while. There were so many possibilities that they'd never run out, no matter how big the company became. Several names that were especially pleasing were put up. Larry worried that the word Mandalay was "too hard for people to say." Dan vowed never to be suckered into something like this again.

Later that night when he was giving his cat Nick a bath, something Nick hated, the doorbell rang. He was too busy to answer it, so he waited until he finished and then went to the door. A thick envelope from a law firm leaned against the door. Apparently, they had a courier deliver it.

It contained a letter announcing the sale of Analytica to Borland for forty-seven thousand shares of Borland stock. Since the original investors had given themselves senior status when the new investors were brought on, they took it all, and it came to less money than they'd put in.

Dan received nothing, meaning the $2,000 he'd paid for his stock options was gone. The sardonic joke that he'd heard at the National Computer Conference when the Star was unveiled came true—he'd not only *not* gotten rich from his startup, he'd lost money. As he liked to put it, "Well, it was a shitty experience, but at least I lost some money."

It was especially ironic that the ruling triumvirate sold to Borland and joined them as employees after trashing it so much only a few months before. Their new CEO, whom they had recruited so diligently, was not invited to join Borland.

Phillippe Kahn apparently had big plans for Reflex, which gave Dan a tiny amount of satisfaction since he'd always known it was a great product.[1]

23

WHAT'S IT ALL ABOUT, DAD?

J anet was indeed good at appearing controlled, but she was tiring of needing to. Dan and Phil were busy migrating the entire company to a new email system, and her group was not part of it. Furthermore, they didn't even seem to care. If she allowed herself, she'd become infuriated by this. *"For God's sake, this is something the company sells! Don't you even care how it works?"*

She came to 3Com because she was dying to learn about networking, and now, it was happening all around her, and she was stuck meeting with non-technical people about the applications they wanted to use on the network. They would sometimes ask her about email issues, and she'd usually have to plead ignorance and pass the question on to someone who knew the answer. She'd been there a couple of months now, long enough for the novelty to wear off.

Sometimes, Dan, Phil, or their boss Donald would ask if her group could help with the migration, and she always had to give the corporate response, "We don't have the resources for that." She'd tell herself, *"It sounds managerial, at least."*

She wondered if her dad might have some ideas. This seemed like a different problem than anything he'd ever encountered in the automotive industry, but he was usually a good sounding board, at least. On Saturday, she sat in the kitchen chair near the phone for her regular chat with Len. He was waiting and answered on the first ring.

"Hi, Dad! How are things back there?"

"Oh, the same as usual, sweetie. The question is, how are you? How's the new job working out?"

"Well, that's what I wanted to talk about."

"Uh-oh. Something wrong?"

"Not wrong, exactly. I'm just wondering what I'm doing with my life!"

"Sounds dramatic! You're doing great as far as I'm concerned. I always brag about my Silicon Valley daughter. People are sick of hearing it from me."

"Aw, thanks, Dad."

"Is the new job not what you expected?"

"Not really. I knew it was managing, but now... well, before, I always felt like I was still an engineer. Even if I wasn't writing any code."

"And now?"

"Now, I don't know. It feels like I'm just a bureaucrat."

"A bureaucrat? Oh, come on. Because you have to do a little paperwork? You should see how much I do."

Janet wasn't sure he was going to be much help. "Yeah, but you probably look at *some* financial numbers once in a while, right?"

"Sure, now and then. But you're telling me paperwork is *all* you do?"

She realized he had no idea what an engineering organization did. He was thinking she literally filled out paper forms with a black pen like he did at Chrysler.

"It isn't exactly paperwork. It's more meeting with dumb people all the time and having a bunch of, let's say, average people to manage."

Len was trying to understand. He thought maybe he had a

clue. "So these average people you have. Tell me about them. Do they call in sick all the time, or come in late, or mess up the work you give them, or what?"

"First is Cassie."

"Cassie. Is that short for something?"

"Cassidy is her real name. She's in her early twenties, fresh out of college, not a lot of self-confidence, but she's trying. I have her helping users with their PCs, and she's becoming pretty good at that."

"Okay, Cassie doesn't sound too bad. And?"

"Then there's Mohan, an Indian guy."

"Mohan? Never met a Mohan. What's the story on him?"

She couldn't help smiling, thinking of Mohan's good nature. "He's a pleasant guy. Does whatever you ask of him without complaining. He's just not real bright."

"Not real bright. Got it. In your industry, that's kinda a handicap, I guess. Are there more?"

"I saved the best for last. Larry is a white guy, thirty-ish, real stiff, and serious. He really identifies with the users' problems, but he just doesn't have a lot of technical smarts or much desire to acquire any."

Len didn't absorb this because he was racking his brain, *"Cassidy? What did I learn about that name when we were researching baby names?"*

"So, you have Cassie, Mohan, and Larry. They don't seem so bad to me. Do they give you any lip?"

Janet loved his expressions like "giving lip." No one ever said that anymore. "No, no. They do whatever I ask."

"So, what's the problem? They're not as smart as you? That's why you're their manager, sweetie." She struggled for the words. Len added, "And also why you are paid more."

Finally, she thought of something, "I mean… is this what life is all about? You are promoted until work isn't any fun anymore, and then you retire?"

This time, he laughed for a long time. "Pretty much.

Maybe they give you more money because it *isn't* any fun. You get married, buy a house, have kids, they grow up, and maybe, they give you grandkids. You buy a cabin on the lake and a boat. You've already done most of that."

"No kids, though!"

"Yeah, I'm still waiting for that one. But no pressure, sweetie."

She chuckled but didn't say anything. She mused about how growing up she used to look forward to their two weeks at the lake in northern Michigan every summer. Swimming, hiking, and going fishing with Dad. People in California didn't go to the lake unless it was Tahoe, and then they called it Tahoe, not *the lake*.

He had the back-in-my-day tone in his voice, "You know... you younger folks expect more from work than we did. We thought of it as a steady paycheck, and that was plenty for us. We had our joys outside of work."

"Hmm. Times are different, though, Dad."

"That they are. So, what's the next step at work?"

"I don't know. I feel like I can help some of these people, Cassie at least. That's one thing you can do as a manager that's sorta satisfying... help someone achieve something."

"There you go. What else? Don't you want to be President of the company?"

She laughed ruefully, "I don't think that's in the cards, Dad. Anyhow, it's too much pressure."

"Well, if you set your mind to it... You're right, though. Who needs all that headache?"

"Yeah. Maybe Vice President. I don't know of what, though. Probably not Engineering."

"Why not? You're an engineer. And a damn good one, pardon my Fr-."

She interrupted, "Yeah, but I'm not doing the hardcore engineering work, and I haven't for quite a while."

His volume level went up, "What does it matter? You understand all that stuff, don't you?"

"Well... not as well as some of the other guys. They think of me as the people-skills person, like that's a bad thing."

Len was silent. He didn't have an answer for her on that one. Instead, he changed the subject, "How's the house? What's the next project? Can you hire that guy I met in the hardware store again? What's his name?"

"Walt. I don't know. Haven't talked to him since the bathroom job. Maybe he could do the other bathroom next."

"There you go. Hold on a second." She waited. He came back after a few minutes. "I found it. The baby-names book from when you were born. Here's the name Cassidy. It means clever or curly-haired."

"So?"

"So... your people are Curly, Moe, and Larry!"

She tried unsuccessfully to stifle her laughter, "Oh, Dad! You're terrible!"

He said triumphantly, "On that note, I'll talk to you next week!"

24

THE GREAT GAME

I t was November 1985, and both Dan's manager Donald and colleague Phil had left. It wasn't a surprise since neither seemed like a good fit for a startup like 3Com. Donald had left to become a partner in a consulting firm, whose clients were mostly giant telecommunications companies. His expertise in X.400, the new international standard for email, was gold. They all thought someday they'd be running a global email network, just like how they were running the phone network.

Phil had joined one of the Digital Equipment Corporation (DEC) research labs in Palo Alto. DEC had taken advantage of the exodus of talented people from Xerox to open not one, not two, but three different labs! If you were a research-oriented person looking for a new home, the chances were that DEC had the welcome mat out for you.

Dan now had a new manager, or really just a Team Lead, Terry Franklin. Terry was an engineer through and through, an MIT guy who'd worked at Draper Labs in Cambridge, and a hardcore IBM bigot. Terry was thoroughly versed in IBM's Systems Network Architecture (SNA) and would gladly spend hours instructing you in it, but he didn't force it on you—

happily for Dan, who had no interest in SNA. Periodically, some customer would visit 3Com who was interested in SNA, and Terry would be called in to meet with them.

Terry had a completely pragmatic approach to corporate decisions, feeling that 3Com had hired him and had the right to make all business decisions. His role was just to carry them out without question. This was a radical change for Dan since the engineers felt that *everything* was their business at his previous two companies, Xerox and Analytica. Dan reluctantly realized that Terry's approach was the correct one for an engineer.

Terry was not upset by any software problem, which made him a joy to debug with. No matter how impossible or intermittent the problem, Terry would just laugh and say, "How the hell are we going to find this?" Since Dan also thought debugging was the best part of engineering, they had a good time together. Both felt that solving the problem was more important than adhering to policy, and no solution was off-limits if that was what you had to do.

Once, Dan thought he had tracked a problem on someone's PC to a bad Ethernet connection, and the only fix he could imagine was to swap in a different connector to the main cable. Unfortunately, this required breaking the Ethernet for the entire company for a few seconds by going down into the baseboard and unscrewing the cable from each side of the connector. "*Oh, well!*" thought Dan as he took a deep breath and just did it as fast as he could. No one seemed to notice. Handling errors was just something engineers had to do when they wrote network software, and he decided that the software on people's PCs must have just kept trying until the network came back. It was the high point of his day.

Reading someone else's email was also something they never did if they didn't have to, but occasionally, they had to. They just treated it as a confidential piece of information they'd been entrusted with. The Ethernet had no security, and the email system's security was rudimentary, too. Dan realized as soon as he learned how email worked that he could read any email in the company and even alter them. He also knew that if he did, he'd be fired and would deserve it. This was the same approach Xerox had back in the early days of Ethernet. Security was treated as an HR matter, not a technical one.

Then, the merger happened! They received an email summoning them to a company-wide meeting. Dan asked Terry, "Do you know what this meeting is about?"

Terry acted as if this was old news, and surely Dan must have already heard about it. "Oh, it's probably just that we're merging with Convergent."

Dan was aghast, "Convergent? *Really?*" Convergent Technologies was a PC maker, not a network company. He wasn't surprised that Terry knew about it and hadn't told him because this was the sort of thing he did all the time.

In the aftermath of the PC revolution, the dinosaur computer companies, like Burroughs, NCR, and AT&T, rushed to get in on it. Late adopter was the polite term for them, meaning always the last to the party.

Invariably, the late adopter's executives had concluded that they didn't know how to join the party themselves, so they hired an OEM (Original Equipment Manufacturer) to get them in. They would put their own label on the OEM's computers and sell them to their loyal customers. Convergent Technologies was one of the big OEMs of the mid-80s.

Dan held a low opinion of Convergent. Any company beholden to those very old, very stupid companies would have no choice but to become very stupid themselves, and Convergent certainly had. They would also face severe cost-cutting pressure from their customers, which would make them stingy with their employees.

"That's what I heard," said Terry. "I guess we'll find out more this afternoon." Terry wasn't interested in speculating.

~

THE COMPANY MEETING was held in the parking lot because there was no conference room large enough. It was explained that 3Com's founders thought the company was too small to survive as an independent entity, and they had to become big very quickly or be swallowed by some giant company they didn't like. Convergent was much larger than 3Com and could provide the muscle it needed.

Dan and Terry were standing together at the meeting. Terry had a look on his face that Dan thought was best described as studiously neutral. Going back inside after the meeting, Dan sought out his friend Matt, who seemed dazed. After they were out of earshot of everyone, he asked, "What do you think?"

Matt said, "I was not expecting this. What do you think?"

"Me neither. That was not the company I'd have chosen to merge with."

"No. Convergent always seemed like a bunch of hardasses to me."

Dan sighed, "Well, we'll find out soon enough, I guess. See ya," he said as Matt turned down the corridor to his cubicle.

Terry came by Dan's cube. "Well? Are you excited?" he laughed.

"Excited!" Dan agreed ironically. "So now, what do we do?"

Terry said, "Well… until we hear differently, I guess we just keep on with what we're doing."

There were more meetings and emails about the merger over the next few weeks. It would be finalized in March, so there was a lot of time for everything to be nailed down. There was no mass exodus of people from 3Com, yet.

Terry was often called away for planning meetings. Eventually, it was decided where 3+Mail would fit in the merged company, and Dan and Terry traveled over to the Convergent offices to meet their new manager and his team. The manager was a guy Dan had known from Burroughs, his first job—a button-down corporate guy through and through. He was friendly enough, though. The new manager's old team and the 3Com additions mingled in his office and talked about what they were doing. But nothing more could happen in the way of group cooperation until the merger was finalized.

Matt expected that Miriam would grill him about what this merger meant for them, and he wasn't disappointed. As soon as he came in the door the evening of the announcement, "So, 3Com is being acquired!"

"They're calling it a merger, but yeah. Same thing."

"So, how does this affect you?"

Matt said, "Hard to say. We have to meet with the Convergent people and find out what the plans are."

"Do you have any say in that?"

Matt laughed, "I'm just a peon, Miriam. They tell *me* what they want."

She questioned him about whether Convergent had a name service, and if not, whether they'd be adopting his. He didn't know the answer to either question, so it was a short conversation—for now.

JANET WAS MORE FLUSTERED by the merger announcement than Dan and Matt. Engineers are usually left alone in mergers since they know the technology, but managers like her were always in play. There was intense political jockeying for power, and being from 3Com, the smaller of the two companies, she was at a disadvantage. She sat in meeting after meeting with her Convergent counterparts, and there was always an undercurrent of rivalry and backstabbing. She hated it. Maybe she'd have to change jobs again, less than a year after joining.

She remembered her dad Len suggesting she work on her house some more, which seemed increasingly like a respite. *"You put in the money and the time, and your daily life improves. What's not to like?"* she asked herself.

She called Ida, the decorator, and Walt, the contractor, and arranged for them both to come over and look at the small bathroom attached to the master bedroom. They both paused to admire their previous bathroom job.

Walter examined the *faux* finish on the walls that Ida and Janet had done together. "Pretty nice! You two did this?"

Ida said, "Indeed we did!"

Janet added, "Ida did all the creative work, though."

Ida was examining the paint job on the cabinet that Janet had done. "Nice job, Janet!"

"Oh, thanks. Now all I see are the flaws."

Walt said, "Do you want me to take a Magic Marker and circle them for you?"

She laughed, "That's okay, I remember them all. Shall we look at the other bath?"

They went over to the master bath, which was tiny and had only a shower, no tub. Walt inspected it briefly. He took his tape measure and made some rough measurements.

Ida's mind was busy with ideas. "Walt, what do you think about extending this vanity out a few inches here?" she said, pointing to the sink.

"Okay, but then how will the shower door open?" Now when it opened, it bumped the sink. Janet was wondering the same thing. Walt and Janet exchanged a quizzical look.

"We can put in a narrower door so that you'll still have room to get out." Ida took her tape measure to the existing door. "I think if we make the shower door nineteen inches instead of twenty-four, that'll give us five more inches *here*," pointing to the sink. "That'll make a big difference in such a small room."

Walt asked, "Isn't there a building code that says it has to be twenty-four inches, though?" He looked at Janet again.

"Well, we're not pulling a permit, right? It'll just be up to the next owner if they care."

This was an issue for the client. Janet took it. "I don't care about a permit... as long as I can get out of the shower!"

Walt was relieved, "I *hate* pulling permits. I do all my work to code or better. Except for this, I guess!"

"Then, we're agreed. I'll draw up some plans and send them to you, Walt." Ida looked at her watch, "I have another appointment. Thanks, Walt. Thanks, Janet." She left.

With the two of them alone, Walt asked, "How do you like the new bathroom?"

"I mainly just use this one. My dad was here, and he used the big bathroom. He said it was beautiful! You met him, remember?"

Walt looked up in thought, "Oh, yeah. In the hardware store. What was his name again?"

"Len."

"Oh, right. Len."

She led him to the kitchen, where he sat down. "Can I offer you some coffee?" He declined. She asked, "How are things with you? Staying busy?"

Walt answered, "Oh, you know. Same old shit. Are you still at Apple?"

"No, I switched. I'm at 3Com now."

"I hope you received a big raise to leave Apple!"

She just smiled.

Walt said, "Three Com? There are so many new companies now. What do they do?"

"Ethernet. Do you know what that is?"

"Isn't the ether what they used to think light traveled through in outer space?"

Janet laughed, "Very good! That's where the name came

from. It's a coax cable for the computers in one office to talk to each other."

"Got it. So, you're an engineer for the coax?"

"Not exactly. I manage the group that runs the internal network."

Walt was impressed, "Wow. How do you like that?"

She made a resigned face, "Well… we're being bought by Convergent Technologies. So, things are all up in the air now."

"Another name I don't know. Is your job safe?"

"Hopefully. There are a lot of meetings about that now. I hate it!"

He was surprised by her tone. Weren't the high-tech people the royalty around here, the ones who hired people like him? Putting up with a little BS seemed like a small price to pay for all the money they made.

Walt rose, "I'd better be running along. It was nice chatting with you! I'll be back in touch when Ida sends me the plans."

She walked him to the door, "Okay, it was great seeing you again, Walt! I'm looking forward to this."

25

THE GOOD FRIDAY NON-AGREEMENT

I t was March 1986, and the merger was about to be finalized. The 3Com'ers had already moved into an empty Convergent Technologies building on Patrick Henry Drive in Santa Clara, a short walk from the Great America amusement park. Dan had a cubicle on the end of a block with all the other software engineers. Captain Bob, or Bob Metcalfe, was just across the aisle from him. Bob usually kept his voice down when he was on the phone, and Dan was grateful for that. Otherwise, he would have been listening in constantly. Like before, Matt was in a different section of the building for some reason. Janet and her group were once again near the server rooms.

The new building didn't look much different from the old one. It was a one-story building set back from the street, with parking lots all around, a little berm separating it from the street, and generic landscaping for a few feet around each wall. It was just like everything in Silicon Valley, except sometimes the building was two stories. In the construction trade, these buildings were called tilt-ups because, during construction, the walls would be trucked in, tilted up, and attached to the building skeleton.

Most of the staff was working on the 3+File and 3+Print software and the network drivers, the software that actually talked to the Ethernet. Dan knew everyone now. It seemed that almost everyone could juggle, except him! He wondered how he'd managed to be hired without passing that test and decided that Donald must have interceded for him.

As a brain-clearing device from writing software, they would pick up three bean-bag-like balls and stand outside their cubes juggling them. A couple of the guys worked on a routine where they each juggled three bowling-pin-like objects, and periodically, each would toss one to the other person. This was hard. Juggling *four* objects was considered a huge leap, and no one could do that.

Dan found the Computer Literacy bookstore, which they were now much closer to, carried a little net bag of juggle balls with an instruction booklet. Apparently, juggling was widespread in the engineering community. Dan bought the kit and made it as far as the part where you juggle two balls, throwing a ball from the left hand to the right hand while simultaneously throwing another from right to left. He found that one hand usually threw the ball forward instead of straight up. *"I could probably master this eventually, but who the hell cares? Life is too short."*

Making your own beer was also a popular pastime for the male engineers. Dan was always willing to take home a beer that someone made and try it. Usually, it either had *way* too much head so that it flowed over the rim or no head at all. The beer tasted good, but he couldn't honestly say it was better than the average import. He also passed on this particular hobby because drinking too much beer was not a healthy habit.

He did a little better on the other touchpoint in engineering culture, the book *The Hitchhiker's Guide to the Galaxy*. Everyone had read it and watched the TV adaptation, so Dan did that as well and thought it was hilarious. You couldn't go wrong in a conversation with a Hitchhiker's reference. The Engineering printer was named Slartibartfast, and if someone even mentioned the word answer, you could always get a laugh with forty-two.

At this point, 3Com was selling a file server called the 3Server. It was a machine without a keyboard or display. This was considered *uber*-cool by the tech press. It didn't run all the regular Windows software because that would have been way too slow. Instead, the 3Server had a special file system—the High Performance File System officially or CIOSYS internally —designed and written by Will, a large, round, and loud engineer who almost always wore a T-shirt that didn't reach all the way to his jeans.

Since the email system had to run on the 3Server, Dan often had to ask Will to help him debug. Unfortunately, any time *anyone* had a file-related bug, Will's software was automatically suspected even if it was user error, and Will was not particularly patient about these false positives. Dan had to learn to be very sure that CIOSYS was at fault before he asked Will to help. Even so, Will always suspected that it was not CIOSYS' fault.

3Com was too small to have a cafeteria, so the engineers usually went out for lunch. There were some standard choices, such as the De La Cruz Deli and the falafel place, usually referred to as "feel awful." The Convergent merger was considered similar to death—it's going to happen eventually, but there's no reason to dwell on it. Still, they felt its inexorable approach.

Then on Good Friday, the day when it was supposed to finally happen, it didn't! The merger was called off. It was electrifying. And Captain Bob was clearly not happy about it. He'd been hoping against hope that the thing would go through, and now, it wouldn't.

He told them all in an informal meeting that Robertson, Colman & Stephens, the investment broker representing 3Com, had withdrawn its fairness opinion, the legal opinion that the merger was fair to 3Com stockholders. They had done this at almost literally the last minute. Their ostensible reason was that Convergent was too dependent on one customer, AT&T. In their view, 3Com was a very fast-growing company, and Convergent wasn't. So, the price of one Convergent share for one 3Com share was too low.

No one asked the obvious question, "So why didn't they just negotiate a higher price?" Maybe Robertson didn't feel they were being paid enough for that kind of work? That was too ugly to even say out loud. Anyway, it was a done deal. Or rather, an *undone* deal. The merger was off.

It would have been unseemly to have a celebration, so they didn't. Instead, there were a few meetings on the topic of "what do we do now?" and then everyone resumed what they'd already been doing. The people who handled real estate for 3Com needed to find office space in a hurry since the company clearly couldn't stay in a Convergent building. Only the executives were upset that the merger was off. Dan, Matt, and Janet all felt like they'd been sitting in the electric chair when the governor phoned in a reprieve at one minute to midnight.

A few weeks passed, and then 3Com moved over to Kifer Drive in Sunnyvale on the other side of 101, the side closer to Dan's house. It looked like every other business area in Santa Clara or Sunnyvale except the streets usually changed names when they passed from one city to the other, for no apparent reason. Kifer Road turned into Walsh Avenue, Bowers Avenue turned into Great America Parkway, and you just had to know they were really the same street. Kifer seemed to have larger buildings, but otherwise, it was the same as everywhere else in Silicon Valley.

The Kifer site was a campus of four buildings, so 3Com had plenty of room to grow, and there was a little wading pool in the center. There were no restaurants within easy walking distance, but they now had a company cafeteria. It was beginning to be a real company.

26

SILICON VALLEY PROPER

D an was seeing a different part of the Santa Clara Valley now that 3Com had moved to Sunnyvale. Silicon Valley companies seemed to start in the high-rent districts of Palo Alto and Mountain View to appear trendy because those areas still had traces of Stanford and downtown Palo Alto coolness. South of San Antonio Road, it became generic and ugly, and almost all remnants of the Valley's agricultural past had been erased in the decades after World War II. Parts of it were so techie that you could change jobs just by walking across the parking lot to a different company.

Dan was commuting up the Lawrence Expressway every morning, as was Janet, although they didn't carpool. In Silicon Valley, expressway does not mean the same as in Chicago, where the Dan Ryan Expressway has at least four lanes and no stoplights. In California, a road like that is called a freeway. An expressway in California is a road with fewer stoplights, no houses, and a 45-mph speed limit or higher. Expressways are usually major traffic arteries, and Lawrence certainly was.

On the west side of Lawrence near Homestead was one of the few remaining tracts of agricultural land. Once all of

Santa Clara Valley was called The Valley of Heart's Delight, and it was covered with acre after acre of cherries, apricots, plums, and other fruit trees. Dan's yard had been an apricot grove—well, it was *some* kind of fruit, but he wasn't sure—up until about 1957. The canine protagonist Buck, of Jack London's *The Call of the Wild*, lived not far from there in the sun-kissed Santa Clara Valley. Poor Buck was kidnapped and shipped to the Klondike one night when his owner was at a meeting of the Raisin Growers Association.

He drove past rows and rows of cherry trees, which bloomed gorgeously for a few weeks in the spring. Sometimes on the weekends, he stopped in the C.J. Olson store on El Camino, which sold all kinds of fruit and fruit-related products. The Olson farm had been established in 1889 to grow Bing cherries and Blenheim apricots, and thankfully, it was still there. Most people in the Valley had no idea about this stuff. To them, Lawrence was just the morning and evening rush hours, and this land would surely be houses, office buildings, and strip malls someday.

At El Camino, there was an overpass so that you didn't have to wait interminably at a stoplight. There was the beginnings of a subculture of Indian and Chinese restaurants and groceries along El Camino near Lawrence and southward. Once in a while, Dan exited at Lawrence and drove around or made a special trip there on a weekend. He liked to cook, and you could buy virtually any unusual spice—unusual for Americans—at these stores. The only problem was finding it on the shelf. Several times, he read a recipe and went in search of the ingredients, but he found no one in the store who spoke English well enough to understand what he wanted. At the Asian supermarket, he'd looked for palm sugar, and a clerk assured him they didn't have it. The checkout clerk corrected him and pointed Dan to the right aisle.

A pattern of employment had developed throughout Silicon Valley, where once a company reached a certain size and needed a *lot* of engineers, they hired more and more immigrants. Naturally, restaurants sprang up to feed these people, and more adventurous eaters like Dan were always looking for the best ones, which required asking around. For Indian food, he'd found that Su's Kitchen was the hip place. Their secret was Su, and when she sold the restaurant, "Where is Su now?" was the urgent question.

At Analytica, the group went to the City to have dinner at a restaurant where Paul Prudhomme was a guest chef. They had to wait outside in a three-hour line, providing plenty of time to talk to the natural foodies in line with them. Dan found out from a guy about Chu Lin, a restaurant way out on west Clement Street, which the guy considered the best Chinese food he'd ever had. San Francisco didn't lack Chinese restaurants, so that was saying something. The Bay Area was a great place to eat.

At 3Com, Terry and Dan returned to working on the email system. LAN email was just starting to penetrate the consciousness of corporate executives and the trade press. Unfortunately, 3Com's email product was only available if you bought the rest of the 3Com software, including the file and printer sharing products and their Ethernet adapters. In the meantime, Novell, based in Provo, Utah, dominated the LAN market with their NetWare product and only sold software. This gave them a huge advantage because the customer could buy LAN cards from anyone and still run NetWare. For email, customers could use whatever product they wanted, and many used cc:Mail. Dan and Terry considered this a dorky product that someone had cloned from the old Unix mail systems.

With the merger's failure, the market seemed wide open again. Everyone could see that this networking thing was going to be big. IBM and Microsoft had stomped into it like Godzilla in Tokyo, or so they liked to think. IBM had their Token Ring, which could tie together all the overpriced IBM gear, and tech journalists wrote breathless stories about how Ethernet was doomed.

Even worse, Microsoft, which had a reputation more ruthless than IBM, was making more and more noise about it. Every business leader in the tech industry was terrified of being anywhere near a market Bill Gates was interested in because surely, he would send his minions to offer you a lowball acquisition price. This offer came with a not-so-veiled threat that if you refused, he'd just assign some programmers to reverse-engineer your stuff and put you out of business. Nonetheless, 3Com was rumored to be in discussions with The Devil. No matter how all-seeing and all-knowing Microsoft tried to appear, Dan and all the other engineers could tell that they knew nothing about networking. However, they were good at buying whatever they needed and learning fast, so no one discounted them.

As the market heated up, Terry's wide knowledge of LANs and IBM software came to be in more and more demand, and his managerial portfolio seemed to expand. Dan was left to run 3+Mail on his own for the most part. He'd managed to learn almost the whole system by now, and he found the entire topic hugely interesting. People were constantly approaching him with wild ideas of what email could do.

One of the wild ideas that they followed through on involved UUCP mail. Their marketing person asked if they could create a gateway to it, and Terry and Dan were always happy to learn something new.

UUCP Mail, also called SMTP Mail for Simple Mail Transport Protocol, was a part of the Internet effort, although not many people called it Internet mail. Occasionally, Dan would see an email someone had forwarded from a weird address with exclamation points in it, such as myvax!ucbvax!mark, where the address meant that the message started at the "myvax" machine and then was forwarded to the "ucbvax" machine, presumably in some kind of batch process, and then finally placed in "mark's" inbox. To send something to "mark," you might need to know the path to his machine.

You might also see something like mark@ucbvax.edu. Dan never really understood the difference, and to make things worse, an email address could have both the exclamation point *and* the @ sign. But there was a guy in engineering, Scott, who was into this stuff, and he offered to work on the gateway in his spare time. So, they cobbled something together, and it ran on a dedicated PC in a server room. It never became a product, though. It turned out that there wasn't that much demand for Internet mail or whatever it was called.

There were so many email systems on the market. IBM had at least one (**PROFS**), and DEC had All-In-1. If you were a corporate worker and had a terminal to a big computer, most likely you had email on your terminal.

Clearly, 3Com could not create gateways to all these systems, so Dan was asked to create an API, or Applications Programming Interface, to 3+Mail. This way, outside users and companies could create their own gateways and maybe sell them. He created an API and wrote the manual, and to his amazement, 3Com assigned an actual editor to review it, someone with deep writing credentials. He thought this can't be the normal practice in the industry because programming manuals were so terribly written most of the time. He wasn't insulted—he was thrilled.

Dan had always thought he was a pretty decent writer, at least for an engineer, although that seemed like an announcer saying a baseball player "runs well for a catcher." Virginia, the editor, found all kinds of sloppy English usage for him to fix. He enjoyed the experience immensely because it was so different from his usual engineering work!

∿

THERE WAS A GUY IN ENGINEERING, Dennis, who had a thin little beard and somehow managed to amuse or irritate almost everyone with his radical ideas about LANs. He had been a game developer before joining 3Com. Games were a guilty pleasure for some programmers, while others like Dan thought they were a waste of time. Dan thought that if you were the sort of person who watched *The Gong Show*, video games were just the thing for you.

Oddly, the hatred was all one-way. Dennis respected and admired the graphics inventions that Xerox and Apple had pioneered, but he and his fellow developers wanted to take them *much* further. They liked the mouse as something you could control with your hands, but they turned it upside down into a trackball for Missile Command.

Dennis was a big fan of the Amiga computer, a fringe machine that some engineers thought was interesting, but it was way out of the corporate mainstream. It wasn't a PC. It wasn't a Mac. And, it wasn't Unix. No corporate computing manager would keep his job if he bought one.

Dennis loved the Amiga and pushed for 3Com to make a LAN adapter for it, which was only slightly less likely than Ethernet for the Commodore PET or the Radio Shack TRS-80. Dennis was good at assembler language, which you needed to really push the PC hardware. His nickname was "The Tick" since he had a way of burrowing into you until you searched desperately for some excuse to get away. Dennis needed a home and some love, or he'd surely leave for someplace that appreciated him more.

Dan thought, "*I can get some useful work out of this guy!*" He had hated conformity all his life, and Dennis was anything but a conformist. He actually found Dennis kind of fun. He didn't exactly encourage Dennis' wild ideas, but he wasn't dismissive of them like everyone else either. 3Com was beginning to remind Dan of high school, where conformity was the rule.

If you listened to CEO Bill Krause, as they did at most

company meetings, "getting everyone on the same page" was a key reason for 3Com's success so far. Krause was the quintessential HP manager, and HP was where he had come from and recruited a lot of the executive team from.

HP was a beloved Silicon Valley legend, having been around since World War II and literally born in a garage. It was almost impossible to meet anyone in the Valley who didn't have some HP connection. They pioneered many practices that Silicon Valley became famous for, such as the Friday beer blast and accessible management. HP was engineering-driven long before that was cool, and they were known for building tools that they wanted to use, a custom known as dogfooding. The founders, Bill Hewlett and David Packard, were down-to-earth, approachable, and believed in management by walking around. HP had a very strong corporate culture, and HP alumni tended to believe that it would work anywhere, and Krause certainly believed that.

He had narrow shoulders, a receding chin, and a small but noticeable tummy. He was organized to the last detail and completely confident in everything. He was a great speaker and always said we needed "hard work, smart work, and teamwork." Then after a pause, he added "and shitwork making everyone laugh. He pushed the gospel of MOST, for Mission, Objectives, Strategy, and Tactics for the way you tackled anything, and he inspired everyone to follow it.

Dan learned that it was career-limiting to question this formula, but he still thought it led to groupthink. In the official HP ideology, "we have robust debate, but once a decision is made, everyone gets behind it." In reality, the robust debate often consisted of people watching each other to figure out what the decision would be, to avoid being the last to back it.

Soon, Dan had the perfect project for Dennis. Email was new to many companies, and corporate workers were not used to using it on their PCs. If you were a 3Com marketing person with a customer on 3+Mail, you worried if they didn't check their mail. So Dan and Terry received a request for a popup that said, "You have mail!" In the Microsoft operating system DOS, this was called a terminate and stay resident (TSR) program, meaning something the user didn't have to manually start each time. Initially, TSR programs were always done in assembler language.

Staying resident in memory was the entire point of Mail Minder. It was always there checking if you had any mail. Dan asked Dennis if he wanted to work on Mail Minder, and Dennis jumped at it.

They immediately started designing it. Dennis' first instinct was to start writing code, as he had always done. But Dan insisted on a proper design specification so that Terry, his boss, and everyone else could evaluate what they were doing. Dennis played along willingly and helped write it with Dan's review and assistance. *"Why does everyone think this guy is so impossible? You just have to teach him."*

Mail Minder (MM) was going to be written entirely in assembler. Terry helped Dennis with the code to check for the existence of mail, which turned out to be the easy part. The part they spent the most time on was the user interface, which didn't surprise Dan, but it did Dennis. When "you have mail" came up, the code had to save whatever was on the screen behind it and restore it when the user dismissed the popup.

Furthermore, Dan and Dennis had to make MM not annoying. What if there's new mail, but you already popped up MM once? Should the user be able to dismiss MM and say, "Don't bother me anymore"? How would they do that? What if the user changes their mind later? How do you avoid overwhelming the mail server with—is there any new mail—queries? What if the user leaves MM on the screen? Should it still check for more new mail? What if the user was typing something while MM popped up? Would any of the characters they typed be lost? They spent time discussing these things and writing down what they decided.

They had their biggest argument about those just-typed characters. MM needed a buffer to hold the characters that the user had *aimed* at some other application, but MM had intercepted. How big a buffer should there be? Dennis argued passionately for two-hundred-fifty-six characters. Dan was acutely conscious of memory constraints. He checked with Terry and other engineers and decided that one hundred twenty-eight was the most they could dedicate. Dennis was very tempted to lie down on the railroad tracks over this, but he was finally persuaded to be a team player and accepted it.

They couldn't run to the boss for a decision every time one of these questions came up. That was what a beginning programmer would do. Dan taught Dennis that you had to try to think of all the issues, make decisions about them and document them, and be prepared to discuss them when the time came for a design review. This was a new practice for Dennis, but he adopted it without complaining.

Mail Minder worked well and was considered a success. Very few people within 3Com used it since they *always* had mail, but it was very useful as a selling tool.

Dan thought that helping someone was the best thing about management, and maybe, the *only* good thing about it. But almost no one appreciated what he had accomplished with Dennis. Dennis remained a quirky individual, and 3Com culture valued group consensus and conformity. He found this attitude a little disheartening. Wasn't management supposed to be about developing talent and getting the most out of your human resources?

The sabbatical leave that 3Com offered after four years of service started looming larger and larger. He could take six weeks off with pay, plus additional vacation time! It was not unusual for people to take their sabbatical and then quit. He thought about what he would do with all that time off—start a new business, go to Australia? The possibilities seemed endless.

27

WORKING IS FOR PEOPLE WHO CAN'T FISH

I t was summer 1986, and the failed Convergent merger was just a bad memory, and Janet was completely bored with her job. Her workload was constantly increasing as the company hired more people, which generated numerous problems for her group. On the plus side, as she reminded herself often, she had no difficulty receiving approval to hire new people. If "grow your empire" was the goal of every manager, she was definitely achieving it.

She spent increasingly more time reviewing ads in the Help Wanted section of the San Jose *Mercury* and meeting with the HR people about which resumes should be filtered out before they even reached her. 3Com was becoming well-known enough that the ads attracted hundreds of responses, most of which went straight into the "we'll keep your resume on file" folder. The HR people wanted specific technologies and years of experience to filter on, which she thought was sort of stupid. A resume could say, "I worked with C for two years," and HR might like to filter them out because Janet required three years of C experience. She found these discussions tiresome.

She read the resumes that weren't filtered, set up interview schedules, conducted the interviews, debriefed everyone who'd met with the candidates, and then held meetings to decide. If it was a yes, she had to seek approval for the salary and stock options. Janet and Len commiserated about it every week since this was one part of her job her dad could relate to. She now interviewed people with one overriding question, "Can I look at this person every day?"

The home improvement project loomed larger for her as a break from the tedium. Ida came up with an amazingly creative design for that tiny master bathroom, and Walt started right to work on it. The bathroom was too small for more than one person, so he worked by himself. Sometimes, she had to leave a key in a secret hiding place for him, but usually he tried to arrive before she left for work. He'd tell her in exhaustive detail what he'd done yesterday and what he was doing today. Of course, she could see it all for herself because she still slept in the master bedroom, but it was still nice to hear it from him.

Walt reminded her so much of an engineer that she thought he'd missed his calling. He absolutely loved to explain exactly what his choices had been, how he'd agonized over them, and why he ended up doing what he'd done. Assuming she approved, of course. "*Of course, I approve! What am I going to say, 'No, rip it out and do it again?'*"

After the demolition work, Walt called in his plumber friend, Pete, to start the new shower. A few days later, he showed up. He and Walt obviously went a long way back. The three of them sat at the kitchen table as Walt and Pete talked about the fishing trip they'd taken last summer in the Sierras and when they were going again this summer. Walt had a boat, which he'd never mentioned before, and he'd inherited a cabin on a lake in the mountains where he liked to go every chance he had. It was an ocean-worthy boat, so they could go after salmon, too.

Janet told them about the fishing she'd done every summer

growing up in Michigan. "Different fish, I bet!" said Walt, which launched her into a discussion of walleye pike, a Midwestern delicacy, great for eating, not such great fighting spirit. Pete had heard of walleyes but had never caught one.

They talked more about the fish in Walt's lake and the lures they used to catch them. Walt mentioned how he grilled salmon he'd caught the same day and how it was infinitely better than anything you could buy in a store.

Eventually, Janet tore herself away and left for work. Pete and Walt went back into the master bedroom to look over the job one more time, and then Walt said he'd be back later when Pete was done. Pete asked him about Janet, "So, is she seeing anyone?"

"I have no idea, Pete. She's just a client. We don't talk personal stuff."

"Okay, understood, but nice-looking girl, though."

"You know, Pete, at my very first contracting job, I learned the surest way to be fired was to hit on the female clients."

Pete was ready for that, "But now *you're* the boss! You gonna fire yourself?" Walt just smiled. Pete added, "She probably makes a lot of money, too."

Walt ignored that, "I'll talk to you in a couple of hours."

Janet thought about fishing as she drove up 85. She recalled a bumper sticker she'd seen once on a car in northern Michigan, "The worst day fishing is better than the best day working." It probably wouldn't be a good idea to put that on her car.

Her dad had sold the cabin on the lake when she graduated college. She pleaded with him not to do it, and she swore that she'd come back every summer to go up there with him, but he was immovable. She suspected he just didn't want to spend that much time with Ken, her first husband, since Len never much liked him. He always claimed he was too old for that stuff, and the upkeep was too much for him.

"What upkeep?" she said. "You never go there!" It didn't matter. The cabin was sold.

That talk with Walt and Pete had brought it all back. The days on the lake when she and Dad always packed a lunch in case they didn't catch any fish in the morning, but they always brought the frying pan and cooking supplies out of optimism. Her mom never wanted to go with them and spent the days gossiping with the other fishing widows.

When they were fishing, he told the same stories over and over. During the Depression, he'd drive all his friends up for the weekend because he was the only one who had a car and job. He caught a gigantic Muskie once, and you'd never see one of those nowadays because the lakes were all fished out. He had this big metal tackle box that weighed a ton and some lures that looked like they dated back to the 30s. Sigh.

～

SHE PARKED the car behind the building and carded her way in the door. Mohan was waiting patiently by her cube with a form for her to sign so that he could get a new computer. They chatted a while, then he left, and she read her mail—more meetings on new applications to install on the network and endless questions on how many different passwords users had to remember to get on all the various applications her group supported.

A continuing headache for her and a big source of emails was software that didn't understand networking. Suppose there was this product Digital Data Whack that ten people wanted to use. Did they each have to buy a copy of Digital Data Whack and install it on their own computers? Why couldn't Janet's group buy one master copy and put it on the server and buy ten licenses? Naturally, it should cost more than a single copy, but hopefully, not ten times as much.

She found that a lot of PC software vendors had no idea

how to do this. Sometimes, they'd tell her, "Well, you just install ten copies on the server, and each user has their own!" This cluelessness was slowly going away for the popular applications, but invariably, some 3Com'er would·ask for a new application, and she'd have to go through the entire thing again. She was training Mohan to do this for her. It was boring, but fortunately, Mohan never complained about *anything*.

There was an email from Larry asking for her opinion on the proper procedure for users to follow for bug reports with one particular new application. Larry was always very concerned about process and especially consistency. If he told people to fill out an Action Request in a particular way for a bug in one networked application, it was very important to him that the exact same rules be followed for all future applications. Any innovations caused him grave angst.

In one bright spot, Cassie had been hanging out with Dan and Terry to learn more about how email actually worked, and she was excited to explain what she'd learned about returned mail error messages—when a user had misspelled someone's name or the person quit or moved. Cassie was always eager to learn stuff like that. Janet could see a day coming when Cassie was ready for bigger things, and she'd move into testing or development. She knew she was going to invest in Cassie and then lose her, but that was what managers were supposed to do—develop their talent. She dropped by Cassie's cube to let her explain email failures a little more, drawing diagrams on the whiteboard to illustrate what happens. She gave Cassie more questions to investigate and thought, "*I could do this part of the job all day!*"

But not the Larry part, she thought, when he dropped in on them and listened with a disapproving look.

"Something I can do for you, Larry?" she said, with what she hoped was an exaggerated air of politeness.

He was oblivious to it apparently. "When you are done

here, I have some *actual* email issues to go over with you," with extra emphasis on the word actual while looking at Cassie. She stuck her tongue out at him. Janet excused herself and went off with Larry.

Later, she received an email from Matt asking about building contractors. Word had gotten around that she had one she liked, and Matt and his wife were paranoid about being ripped off by a shady operator. She didn't see Matt much outside of meetings, but apparently, he'd bought an Eichler in Palo Alto. The Eichler was a pretty radical design from the postwar years, with no crawl space and no attic and an almost completely open floor plan. It seemed people bought one and then immediately tried to make it something other than what the architect intended.

That was apparently what Matt and his wife were doing. Janet sent him Walt's phone number but said she didn't know if he did jobs that far north. Matt replied that when you said Palo Alto to a contractor, the price went up by fifty percent since they figured you were rich. She thought, "*Oh, good. Walt can use the money!*"

When she saw Walt the next morning, she told him about Matt. He was wary. "Palo Alto, huh? Well, always willing to go and check out a job! I can't promise anything beyond that."

"Yeah, I haven't seen the house. I don't even know the guy that well."

Walt thought for a while and then said, "I did a job for someone in Palo Alto once. Let's just say... it wasn't my favorite job."

She didn't think this was an invitation to go deeper into the Palo Alto job. Walt could say more if he felt like it. They talked more about her bathroom, and then as she was leaving for work, he said, off-handedly, "Palo Alto people think they're entitled to have everything perfect, and they become upset when it's not. But hey, if he's a friend of yours..."

"Just a work acquaintance. See you tomorrow."

28

PERFECT PALO ALTO

M att had good news for Miriam that night. He found the name of a reliable building contractor! He parked the car in the driveway and opened the side door into the kitchen, where she was sitting with a cup of tea. Their dog, Mookie, stood at the door, wagging his tail. Fortunately, he wasn't a dog that jumped on people much because he was a pretty big Labrador. Miriam hadn't been too enthused about getting a dog, but Matt had insisted.

"The Mookster! How's my doggie?" He frisked Mookie on both sides of his neck, which made his tail wag furiously. Then, turning to Miriam, "Hey, someone gave me the name of a good contractor."

"Oh, good! Someone at work?" He nodded.

She set her cup down, "So, what's the story on this guy, assuming it's a guy? They used him before?"

Matt poured himself a cup from the teapot and sat down. Mookie lay down at his feet. "Yeah, he did a bathroom remodel for Janet Saunders. I don't think you've met her. She found him from an interior designer, so I guess he came highly recommended."

"Great! She was happy with him?"

"She seemed very happy with how it turned out."

Miriam smiled briefly but said, "That was a smaller job than ours, though, right?"

"Just a *wee* bit smaller. One room versus God-knows-what," he looked around the house, envisioning all the things they'd talked about changing. They wanted to knock out the entire back wall, add on two more bedrooms and a bathroom, a hallway between them, plus they wanted a patio outside and a sliding glass door to it. He'd managed to talk Miriam out of totally de-Eichler-izing the place, as he put it. She was dissuaded by his pointing out the historic nature of their house and how her ideas would destroy that. That seemed more persuasive than the sheer cost of the job.

"You haven't talked to him yet, right?" Matt shook his head. "Well, shall we give him a call?"

Walt came to their house the next night. Mookie loved visitors, and Walt loved dogs, so the visit was off to a good start. After some small talk, they walked around the house and pointed out what they wanted. He made a lot of notes and asked a lot of questions. They went outside and looked at the house from the outside, and then they came back in and sat at the kitchen table. Walt spoke first.

"This looks very doable. I'll have to work up a formal estimate if you want, and then you can decide if you want to move forward with it."

Miriam said, "Do you have a rough idea of what it's going to cost?"

Walt was used to this, of course. He knew if he gave them any number, they'd fix on that and compare it to whatever he came up with later, so he'd learned to be careful at this stage. "Well, I have to bring in an electrician, plumber, tile guy, drywall guy, painter, roofer, and probably a few other subcontractors, so it can take a while to line them all up. I don't want to mislead you. We also need to pull permits from the city of Palo Alto, I assume."

Matt appreciated this. Palo Alto could be persnickety about things like building permits. "Yeah, I guess it's complicated, huh?"

Walt nodded. "I can tell you the job always expands after we start. The clients always think of more stuff they want done."

Miriam did not look happy, "Do you have a general idea of the cost, at least?"

He was used to this part, too. He looked down at his notebook and ticked off items with his pen.

"Well, you have an outside wall being moved out. That always costs money. There are two bedrooms, but those don't cost much. You have a bathroom, and those can either be cheap or expensive, depending on your choices. We didn't talk about the hardwood flooring. Do you want it new throughout the house so that it's the same everywhere, or do we just install the new part? There are a lot of things we didn't talk about. With Eichlers, the plumbing and wiring are always tricky. Your pipes and wires are embedded in the concrete slab, so that can be a godawful mess."

She said, "Hmm. Can we make some reasonable guesses on all that?"

He was cornered, "Well... I would hope we can get it done for about $100,000, but that's just a guess at this point."

Matt and Miriam tried not to look shocked. They knew it was probably going to end up being more than that, too. He said, "Well... we'll look forward to seeing your final estimate! Thanks for coming over, Walt."

Miriam echoed that, and they showed him out, Mookie following, and sat back down. She said, "$100,000! Holy shit! Let's get some more estimates."

Matt replied, "We don't have any other recommendations right now."

"So, get some. Do you want me to ask around at work?"

Matt pictured a bunch of therapists with thoughtful opinions on home remodeling. He'd met these people, and they didn't impress him on any level. "Let me ask more people at work. But is this a job you want to give to the lowest bidder?"

She looked annoyed, "No, but shouldn't we at least get more opinions?"

Matt agreed, "I guess. How did you like him, in general?"

She went into therapist mode, "He seems nice. How did you like him?"

"I liked him. He seems like a straightforward guy. Janet said he was honest and diligent. What more can you ask?" He held his hands out, palms up.

Miriam made a mental note, "*There's that Janet person again!*" She said, "Where does she live?"

Matt didn't see the relevance of this. "I don't know. San Jose, I think, or Cupertino. Why?"

"Oh, I don't know. I just wonder if he's ever worked in *this* neighborhood."

"You mean Palo Alto?" She nodded. "I don't know. Does it matter?"

"Maybe not. You're right," she said, beating a strategic retreat.

Matt felt like he'd won, "I mean, the building materials are the same, right?"

"It seems more suburban down there, but you're right," clearing the tea things away. "There's big house construction going on in the next block. Maybe I'll talk to the owners there."

Matt had seen that project, too, so they talked about that and then turned on the TV.

∾

WHEN WALT ARRIVED HOME, he called Janet to thank her for recommending him. She was watching TV in the family room with Rocky, her cat, in his usual perch on her shoulders.

She asked, "How'd it go?"

Walt was always careful what he told one of his clients about another client. "Well, they have pretty ambitious plans. I think now they're going to think hard about what it all costs."

She didn't think she'd get any more out of him than that. He wasn't the gossipy type. "Well, anyway, how's everything going with you?"

"Same old shit. Just thinking about that first day when I thought your cat got out, and I made you drive all the way home from work!"

She laughed, "That's okay. I probably needed the break anyway."

"Well, I was just glad you didn't fire me on the spot!"

"Nah. It happens. Anyhow, I hope this job with Matt works out."

They hung up. Janet thought about Walt and Matt. Would they get along? Walt was very engineer-like, she remembered. He'd tell you exactly how he did things, and he didn't leave out any of the details or fudge over his indecision about it. Sometimes if the work had turned out exceptionally well, he was so pleased with himself that he just had to show it to her. It was endearing.

But would Matt and his wife like that in him? Sometimes, people wanted a more distant managerial type, who didn't tell you anything unless you asked, with an exaggerated attitude of deference to you as Owner and Client. She'd noticed that some of the people she'd known at Apple seemed to talk that way about their gardeners and house cleaners like they're not real people. *"Maybe they've been watching too much 'Upstairs, Downstairs!'"*

When she was growing up, her dad did all the yard work,

and her mom did the housework. If there was home repair work to do, her dad did that, too. She couldn't remember any tradespeople ever coming to the house. These upper-class people probably had different upbringings.

She wondered what her next project with Walt should be. Probably a new drainage system to get the water out of the backyard instead of it going under the house. That had to be the most unsexy project she could imagine, but Walt had said there was some water in her crawl space, so she'd better do it. She could do some of the digging and save herself some money, and Walt could plan it out to ensure the water drained out toward the street. Oh boy. Maybe they could do that before Matt's gigantic project, assuming they chose him.

29

HEAVY IS THE HEAD THAT WEARS THE CROWN

J anet was sitting in the family room watching L.A. Law. *"These lawyers lead such exciting lives. How come every lawyer I meet hates their job?"* she asked her cat, Rocky. The phone rang.

She turned down the TV, walked over to the phone, and picked it up. It was Keith, a guy Janet had been going out with. He'd also worked at Apple and left shortly after she did. At first, they spent their time talking about what a snake pit Apple was and the backstabbing they'd personally witnessed, and that was cathartic. When they were working there, they were too afraid to speak openly, even to close friends, but now, they were free to dump on everyone! It was exhilarating.

Keith lived in Menlo Park, not far from the Sunset Magazine offices. They'd eaten at Late for the Train a couple of times and ended the evening browsing at Kepler's bookstore. They often went to some cultural event in the Palo Alto area —TheatreWorks, movies at the various independent theaters, or Stanford events. She could never come up with a good reason for him to come down to her neighborhood, so she always drove up to his.

He grew up in Southern California, went to Stanford, and stayed in the area. He joined Apple fairly early and was one of the many millionaires minted by the IPO, so his house was paid for, and he liked to say about his departure from Apple, "What's the point of having fuck-you money if you never say fuck you?" Now, he was working at Sun, where he didn't have to manage anyone and could do pretty much whatever he wanted. Janet's ex-husband, Ken, would have said Keith was living the dream.

The Apple bitching was starting to wear thin, though. Keith obviously wanted a real relationship and to get married and have a family. He'd seen several of his fellow Apple millionaires do that—hire a nanny to raise the children, send them to private schools, and drive them to school in a large BMW. He alluded to this frequently. The fact that Janet had a real career before she met him was an essential part of his idea of a quality wife.

Last Saturday, she kissed him goodnight as usual, and he got a little handsy. She thought it might be time for the "I just want to be friends with you" speech, and she was dreading it. He had a lot more money than almost anyone she'd ever gone out with, and she could see marrying him meant she would be minor royalty in Silicon Valley. How many girls in her old neighborhood would kill for that? *"Well, they're welcome to it."*

Keith seemed to have turned object-oriented programming into object-oriented life. She picked up the phone and delivered the bad news.

He didn't take the "let's just be friends" speech well at all. She had the feeling he'd received it before and was tired of it. He must have read one of those interviews with successful urban women claiming that their husband was their best friend, and he really didn't see anything wrong with that. He pretended that they were still going to go to cultural events together, but she suspected that might happen once, at most, or more likely never.

She turned the volume back up on the TV and thought, *"Another empty Silicon Valley guy."* At least in Southern California, people didn't all work at the same thing as they did here. If you watched the movies, everyone in LA was in music or movies or TV—or now, they could be a glamorous lawyer!— and absolutely everyone was writing a screenplay. That was not reality, though. Many normal people worked in aerospace, but it wasn't a one-industry town for that, either. Up here, it seemed like women were a scarce commodity because engineers were mostly young men.

Up here on the street, at the stores, or in the parks, she'd sometimes see people who were obviously not in computers. Where she lived, which was a more affluent part of San Jose but still *in San Jose*, you'd see lots of people driving old American cars or Toyotas, wearing clothes from Kmart, and smoking cigarettes. On the other hand, in Palo Alto or Menlo Park, it seemed like everyone on the street was white, well-dressed, and well off, and you could lay 10-1 odds they were college graduates.

There was even an urban legend at Apple, which she suspected was true, that when an Apple manager was promoted to VP, they came under heavy pressure to move to one of the approved zip codes—Los Altos Hills, Portola Valley, Woodside, and the like. It just would not do for an Apple VP to live in Santa Clara.

She'd discovered that your politics were prescribed here, too. You had to be against land development and in favor of open space in every controversy. You had to be against Reagan. And if you were old enough, you had to have opposed Vietnam back in the day. Maybe some of the older executives were still allowed to be Republicans, but they would retire soon enough, and the ones coming up would all be Democrats.

She found it all tiresome, and Keith was just the latest example of it. He seemed to think he'd won the race already.

And while he'd never say so, she should be grateful for the chance to join him in the winner's circle.

"Sigh!" she said to Rocky, who had moved to the couch when she got up. She picked him up and put him on her lap, where he went back to sleep. She thought more about this latest guy.

She really could jump to the winning team here in Silicon Valley and marry one of those guys. Why didn't she just do it? Maybe because she'd already been married and didn't have that life goal to check off. Did she really want to have kids? Not all that much. So, why do it? Dad would probably love to have grandkids, but he never nagged her about it.

Maybe there was some normal guy out there. She wasn't going to move back to Detroit to find one, that's for sure. That was the trouble with moving to California—you couldn't face the thought of moving back to that horrible weather in the Midwest, even if you grew up in it. And, there were no tech jobs there.

Today's *Mercury News* was next to her on the couch. She picked up the business section to see that Apple's quarterly profits were up forty-seven percent. The *Merc* considered Apple the hometown hero. When Steve Jobs was fired, it was front-page news. "I am but 30 and want still to contribute and achieve," was the line she remembered from his farewell letter. "*My God, the self-importance!*" she thought at the time. She didn't miss being there.

AT WORK THE NEXT DAY, her curiosity got the better of her, and she had to ask Matt what he thought of Walt. He had brought his dog Mookie to work, and the dog was sleeping on his dog bed. No one had ever tried having a dog at work before at 3Com, so there was no rule against it. She thought there probably would be one soon, given how the HR people felt they should run everything. The dog was a large, friendly Labrador who greeted her enthusiastically.

"So, you had Walt over last night? How'd it go?" she said, stroking Mookie, who gazed raptly into her eyes.

Matt was surprised she knew about his visit. "Oh, he called you or something? He seems like a very nice guy. We're still gathering estimates and talking to other contractors."

"Yeah, it's a big step. Did he give you any idea what it's going to cost?"

"A lot! More than we were thinking. You said he was pretty reasonable when he worked for you?"

She smiled, remembering how she always paid him immediately. "Oh, yeah. Those guys are in business just like we are. Many of them are skating right on the edge, so if you pay them without any hassles, it goes a lot smoother."

Matt's New York instincts always made him suspect a scam. "You hear these horror stories about them taking your deposit, knocking down a wall, and then disappearing for a month."

"Well, he didn't have any walls to knock down for me!"

He thought this part of the conversation was over, but while she was in his cube, he might as well ask. "Hey, different topic. Have you heard anything about discussions with Microsoft?"

She had heard about that, but it was supposed to be strictly confidential. How did he hear about it, and what did he know?

"Microsoft? No. Like what? They're going to acquire us or something?"

Matt had always believed the best way to find out something is to pretend you already know it. This was tricky now because she might figure out he was bluffing. "I heard they wanted to create a new standard for network APIs, and they wanted us to endorse it. Or something like that."

"*Uh-oh. He does know something.*" She said, "A new standard?

Interesting. But Novell pretty much owns LAN software, don't they?"

"*Nice try, but you were just a tad slow responding there!*" Matt continued, "Well, Microsoft pretty much gets whatever they want. Should be interesting!"

Janet pleaded she had another meeting, nuzzled Mookie one last time, and left. Mookie started following her, but Matt called him back.

Matt figured he had his answer. They were talking to Microsoft. Now, what to do with this information? Miriam would have ideas. It had to be worth something. But he couldn't just go blabbing it around. At the very least, he had to seem like the sort of person who knows everything but also keeps his mouth shut.

Janet thought about Matt while walking back to her cube. Was he some kind of power player, despite lacking any formal title? Someone had to have told him about Microsoft, but why would they? Larry was waiting for her with some questions about bug reporting procedures, so she forgot about Matt.

Dan was waiting in the hallway, and he came over as soon as Larry left. "Hey, Cassie's been hanging out with us lately. She seems very sharp!"

She wondered what he really wanted. "Yeah, she is. I hope she's not being a bother."

"No, no. She makes us think about stuff we just take for granted."

"So, is there something you wanted? I have a lot to do."

Dan said, "Not really. I'm just thinking about the next generation of Mail client and wondered if your group had any ideas."

Janet sighed silently, "*Once upon a time, I would have ideas on something exciting like that. Now, it's just managing.*"

"New client! Sounds good. Keep us informed. Gotta run!" she said, heading down the hall.

Janet actually didn't have a place she had to be, but she

tried to walk briskly anyway so that she'd look busy. She thought back to the times at Xerox when she could just drop in on Gwen and seek her advice on anything. Now as a mucky-muck, a word she now realized applied to her, she had no one to confide in. Everyone had their own agenda, and anything she said could be used in some way she wouldn't like.

Her dad wasn't too sympathetic when she told him this, either. "Heavy is the head that wears the crown," he'd said. She didn't feel like the ruler of a kingdom, though—more like a well-paid princeling governing an unruly province so that the far-off king didn't have to.

What was the goal anymore? To become a Vice President of something or other? You still wouldn't have any real power, and the politics would be exponentially more vicious. Still, it was nice to be someone who mattered at 3Com, even if it didn't come with any absolute power. You found out about stuff like the Microsoft talks before other people did. Well, *most* other people, anyway. Somehow, this Matt guy found it out.

One time, she'd wandered by his cube when he and Dan were talking, and Matt had been fantasizing about his dream of giving up all this shit and opening a hardware store. "It's a cash business! You just report enough income to keep the IRS off your back." Somehow, leaving high-tech completely didn't seem so weird anymore, although a hardware store wouldn't be her choice for a retirement career.

She found herself at the back door of the building, so she went through the parking lot to the front of the complex and found herself on the sidewalk. There was a Caltrain station not too far from 3Com, and some people actually commuted down from San Francisco or somewhere north and walked to work. You could theoretically walk to a restaurant over on Lawrence, although she couldn't remember ever doing it. Now that 3Com had a cafeteria, she probably never would.

Walking didn't fully clear her head, though. She kept

thinking about the performance reviews she had to write and the software vendors' calls she had to return.

30

THE MARCH OF SCIENCE

At 9:30 on a morning in April 1987, Dan saw yet another car being ticketed at the intersection of Kifer and Lawrence for turning right in the bike lane. Since he rode a bike himself, he was well versed on what cars were and were not allowed to do in that situation. They had to get into the bike lane well before the stop light (changing lanes safely, of course), so they didn't suddenly cut off a poor biker. The cops were using that to fill their ticket quotas, rather than protecting actual bikers, since there were rarely any bicycles in the lane.

When Dan arrived at the office, Terry was already there. He usually came in early, and he was avidly reading the recent IBM announcements. "Hey, IBM finally announced the PS/2 and OS/2!"

"Oh, boy," said Dan. "What's special about the PS/2?"

"Well," Terry said happily. "It has the Micro Channel Architecture, which is a new bus that should finally get rid of the clones!"

Dan just smiled at the thought of IBM trying one more time to put the genie back in the bottle. The PC market had gotten away from them a long time ago. But they had just loved that old mainframe industry where they made all the rules, and they kept trying to recreate it.

Frowning, "And it has a new hardware interface for the keyboard and mouse."

"Great. So, our old ones won't work?"

"Looks like it. And our Ethernet cards won't, either."

At that point, Will wandered by and stopped to listen. "Well, actually…" he stopped himself. "I guess I should wait for Howard's announcement. I think it's this afternoon."

"Howard" was Howard Charney, a Founder and Vice-President, Metcalfe's fraternity brother, and beloved by everyone. Whereas Metcalfe could be extremely charming when he wanted to be, Howard was effortlessly charming all the time. Dan vividly remembered one of his early company meetings when the entire crowd chanted, "How-EE! How-EE! How-EE!"

Dan and Terry both looked at Will. Terry always knew everything, so Dan figured he must know what Will was talking about. He also didn't think just asking directly would work, but maybe a wild guess would. "Is IBM paying us to develop for it?"

Bingo. Will was caught. "Something like that. Howard's going to announce it all today, I hope."

This was too much for Terry. The cat was out of the bag now. He chuckled contentedly, "Not only an Ethernet card but a Token Ring one, too!"

Will looked crossly at him. He didn't like spilling secrets, even if they wouldn't be secrets much longer. Terry received the message and changed the subject. "And then there's OS/2… the DOS killer."

Dan and Will both laughed. They'd been reading stories about OS/2, the new PC operating system, in *PC Week* for months now. Dan said, "Well, that one might have a chance."

Will agreed, "We can always use the DOS compatibility box."

Dan and Terry had both read that the thousands of old PC applications would still work with OS/2 in a special compatibility box, which was not an actual box but just a special programming mode. IBM had to do that, or no one would take it seriously. The PC software industry was huge, so IBM couldn't just destroy it.

Terry said, "But then, we can't take advantage of all the neat features the new O/S has."

They both held back from deriding IBM because it still had a reputation for knowing how to build a real operating system, and Microsoft certainly did not.

Dan said, "So is Microsoft supporting all that stuff, too?"

Will answered, "What choice do they have? IBM's still calling the shots." He despised Microsoft as they all did.[1]

Terry agreed, "Well, it's going to be interesting!" Dan and Will both went back to their cubes.

Dan read his mail and then dropped by Matt's cube as he often did in the morning. Matt hadn't read about the IBM announcements and wasn't much interested. Dan asked him if he'd seen the recent public TV show about Steve Reich.

"Mr. Minimalist? No, we missed that. How was it?"

"Kinda boring. Why do people think this stuff is worthwhile music?"

Matt had a more expansive attitude toward culture than Dan. "Yeah, I saw him in New York. Not really my cup of tea, but Miriam liked it."

"Everyone performs in New York," Dan said, looking around the cube for the dog, "No Mookie today?"

"No, an HR lady told me that dogs are no longer allowed."

Dan smirked, "So which HR lady was it? Miss Smarmy?" Dan hated the HR people, and he had a new word to apply to them!

Matt laughed, "Smarmy! What a great word. It sounds like..." He pantomimed wiping his hands on the carpet with a look of disgust on his face, "I assume you're talking about Kristen?"

Thus encouraged, Dan went on. "Any of them, but yes, her in particular. The way they adopt this pose of earnest corpiness. It makes me vomit."

Matt laughed some more, "At most companies, HR is there to hire and fire people and arrange the benefits. But here…"

Dan was wound up now, "Here, they think they should have a voice in everything. It's like this is high school, and they're the popular girls deciding who's up and who's down."

Matt encouraged him, "How about unctuous? Would that word work as well?"

"I also like oleaginous," replied Dan.

"Smarmy. Unctuous. Oleaginous," Matt chuckled. "The Tres Amigos."

"Four more, and we can have The Seven Dwarves."

Eventually, Matt steered the conversation around to what they were paid for, and today's topic was the relationship of Directory services to Mail. Dan expected that 3+Mail would eventually become X.400-compatible, whatever that meant. X.400 was an international email standard created by the CCITT, Consultative Committee for International Telephony and Telegraphy, an arm of the United Nations and dominated by the big telephone monopolies of the world. Their standards process took place over years, and the first version of X.400 was released in 1984. It was immensely complex, but it seemed to people in the industry that X.400 would eventually take over—after all, how could it not? The telecoms and governments of the countries they operated in were all behind it.

Dan couldn't just tweak a few settings on 3+Mail and say, "Okay, it's X.400-compatible!" Ironically, Dan's original boss at 3Com, Donald, had been the *Special Rapporteur* of the X.400 standards group and also the original architect of 3+Mail. So naively, you might think the conversion would be easy. But no! X.400 was way too raw back then.

To really use it, one had to buy into the complete OSI, Open Systems Interconnection, model, which covered your network from top to bottom. Almost no one in the world ran OSI on a working network, except maybe a few test labs deep within the telecoms. Nonetheless, OSI was still the official gospel, which someday everyone would be running. Until that glorious day arrived, there was something called ISODE, ISO Development Environment, which let people experiment with higher-level protocols like X.400 on a real network.

An email system needed a directory of users, mail servers, and other online resources. 3Com had 3+Name, which was modeled on the Xerox Clearinghouse. None of the competing LAN email systems had anything close to it. Dan and Matt always found that handy whenever they had to fend off threats from 3Com marketing people who wanted to acquire someone else's software, a regular occurrence. It seemed like the first thing every new product manager with a fresh MBA did was read the trade press, talk to two customers, and propose a big acquisition. This way, they would be in control, not the engineers. It was an article of faith to them that everyone in another company could do things better than anyone on the inside.

When a new product manager talked to an engineering manager on the inside, within 3Com, that person had a long list of tasks queued up and was always cautious about committing to anything new. No such annoying problems came up with a fellow marketer at another company. Everything was possible, everything was easy, or even better, it was already done! It was always appealing to an MBA to just make a deal and leave it to the engineers to clean up.

Matt and Dan were cynical about this. They knew they just had to ask, "But what about the name service? How would we migrate that?" and they would receive blank stares.

The new MBA would slink off and eventually move on to some easier target.

Oddly enough for an email standard, there was no directory standard to go with X.400. That was coming next year, and it would be called X.500. Dan's old manager was an architect of that, too.

Dan and Matt had both read the draft documents and spent endless hours debating what it meant and which vendors might be supporting the standard. In particular, they debated how to represent an email address like 3Com's within the Distinguished Name (DN) construct in X.500. The notion of DN was that it was a series of attributes, which might be defined by each country and weren't necessarily the same everywhere. A DN for you might have an organizational unit as one of its attributes, which would be the company you worked for. Or you might be a residential person where only your postal address was given. What if both of those were given? Who knew? Apparently, the committee thought it would work like the postal system, where it first went to some giant system in each country and then routed to an individual server.

More to the point, the massive draft documents still left a zillion practical questions unanswered. Was there a standard character representation of a DN? Was there a standard Applications Programming Interface (API)? Was there a reference set of code that a developer could download to make it easier to get started? And even more basic, if you had a question about it, whom did you ask? The representatives to the CCITT were governments, not private companies. A private citizen could go to a meeting but couldn't vote. Dan and Matt discussed these topics endlessly and tried to make practical decisions. If nothing else, it was an intellectual challenge.

Today was another of those discussions. As he walked back to his cube, Dan passed Will and Terry, who were engaged in another discussion with lowered voices. They stopped talking when Dan walked by. That afternoon, Dan and everyone else found out the real story about the IBM PS/2 and its unique Micro Channel Adapter. IBM had paid 3Com to develop both an Ethernet and a Token Ring adapter for it. IBM felt they required a story about LANs when they announced the PS/2, and being able to say that 3Com was already supporting it was valuable to them. Howard led a tour of the building where the work had taken place, which had been restricted to people with a need to know.

Ethernet cards were the source of almost all the company's revenue, so this was a big, big deal. Dan didn't much care about them, but since his boss, Terry, knew all about IBM and Token Ring, he was increasingly called into meetings with customers and other companies. Dan saw him less and less, and when he did, Terry made noises about mail not being strategic. Bridget, one of the engineers, used to say, "Strategic means you don't make any money."

A COUPLE OF WEEKS LATER, Dean Corman from The Wollongong Group (TWG), a consultancy and software vendor headquartered in Palo Alto, visited Dan, Matt, and some other engineers. Three or four of the Internet architects worked for TWG. Their name was a nod to Wollongong University in Australia, which gave them a core software release, but it was not an Australian company.

Someone in 3Com management had read that the Internet Engineering Task Force (IETF) had developed the specifications for an entire suite of protocols, including TCP/IP and related systems, for something called the Internet, and thought 3Com should look into it. It seemed to be gaining support in universities and research labs, especially among Unix users. Occasionally, a customer would ask about it, a marketing bigwig would delegate it to an eager junior product manager, and now, here was Dean! The Wollongong Group could supply you with working TCP code if you decided you wanted it.

Matt was familiar with TCP and the IETF group from his time at the University of Minnesota, but he hadn't kept up with it. In the meantime, IETF had been very busy. Dan had only a vague idea of how it all worked. He'd read some of the Request for Comment (RFC) documents produced by the IETF and was always struck by how down-to-earth they were. They were plain text documents you could just download, and if you wanted to join the email list and participate in the discussions, you could.

Dean started, "Usually when people ask for TCP, they really mean the entire suite of Internet protocols... DNS, FTP, Telnet, routing, email, and all the rest."

Elaine Simmons, the marketing person who had arranged the meeting, interrupted him, "Dean, can you please explain what those acronyms mean for those of us who aren't familiar?"

Dean answered, "Sure, sorry. DNS is Domain Name Service for mapping system names to their network address. FTP is File Transfer Protocol, which most of you have probably used. Telnet is the terminal protocol you use when connecting to a remote system as if you dialed into it. Shall I go on?"

"Thanks. That's great for now."

Dan and Matt perked up when he said Name Service, but they decided to hold off on those questions for now.

Dean continued, "The IETF works on a rough consensus and running code basis, not by voting. There's a path for something to become a standard, and it always involves two or more implementations that interoperate."

Elaine was unwittingly playing Straight Man here. She said, "Aren't all standards done that way?"

Dan and Matt burst out laughing, but Dean was too diplomatic to insult his host. Finally, he said, "One would wish. In reality, some of the larger companies just announce something and call it a standard. Or maybe, an international committee designs something on paper, without any actual testing, and calls that a standard."

Dan chimed in, "As Bob Metcalfe always says, the nice thing about standards is that there are so many of them."

Elaine could have felt chastened by this, but it was her meeting, so she pressed on, "So, we have these technologies that have been adopted via rough consensus and running code and the universities and research labs who use them. Are there any commercial businesses adopting them?"

Dean was used to this question. Marketing people at commercial companies were always eager to dismiss the Internet as something only non-profit institutions would ever care about. Real businesses would always use their own vendors' networks, such as IBM's Systems Network Architecture, DEC's DECnet, or Novell's NetWare. Or maybe, eventually, the telecom companies' OSI.

He'd noticed that there was a slow but noticeable shift in the types of people who called him. It had been almost all geeks initially, as Elaine implied, but increasingly the business people were becoming curious, too. He answered, "I can point you to a number of them. Usually, they're companies who do a lot of business with the universities and research labs, as you said, but it's spreading out from there."

Elaine said she'd like to get those names from him offline, meaning after this meeting. She pleaded another meeting and thanked Dean for coming in.

Dan and Matt took over and asked about the other systems he'd mentioned—FTP, Telnet, and DNS. Dean was in his element now, explaining how work with IETF specifications was branching out since meetings a few times a year were not enough. There was also a company running an Interop conference where networking equipment vendors met to actually test with each other. According to salesmen, customers had become wary of gadgets that "should just work"—they wanted to actually see it work. Interop became a way to do that.

Dean explained in more detail how an internet standard was developed and resulted in an RFC. A senior member of the IETF, Dean was one of those, was assigned to each working group to inculcate them in the history and practices of the IETF. Most technical issues were settled over email, but they held in-person meetings three times a year. Dan and Matt were welcome to join any currently active group, and Dean mentioned several that might be of interest.

Dean had other meetings on his calendar, but he gave them each a business card and invited them to call him if they had questions.

Dan and Matt left the meeting dazed. A bunch of working engineers meeting without a lot of pretension and getting standards done—so different from the stiff, formal CCITT and the giant computer companies who only cared about account control!

For now, though, it was just a curiosity.

31

LEAVE 'EM SMILING

I t was May 1987, and Matt and Miriam were busy planning their house remodel. Walt Campbell, Janet's contractor, had come, looked around, and given them a back-of-the-envelope estimate of $100,000. They had been shocked. They held off on signing with him until they received more estimates, but everyone else came in as high or higher. They signed, and Walt and his helpers started the work.

Their house was an Eichler, a house plan popular in northern California in the 40s and 50s. It had high ceilings, no crawl space, no attic, and all the plumbing was embedded in the concrete slab. This gave the house a wide-open, airy look but made it a bitch to work on. Eichlers were more prevalent in the south end of Palo Alto, the less fashionable side. Miriam hated being there. But once they had kids, they would go to some of the best public schools in the country. However, she always felt that people from the tonier areas near downtown and Stanford looked down on anyone from south of Page Mill.

She had a counseling job in a small private clinic of psychologists, whose clients all seemed to be from those tonier areas. Her clients were often high school kids, who were generally overwhelmed by the pressure to make good grades, take Advanced Placement classes, and be accepted into an Ivy League school. Sometimes, their mothers came in for help, too. She never saw the fathers unless it was for marriage counseling. The fathers were almost all executives in high-tech companies, which meant working very late hours and weekends and leaving the child-rearing duties to the moms.

And, these people had a lot of money! Paying for the shrink was never their problem. The moms all drove the kids to their appointments in a BMW or a Mercedes, and the kids played soccer or took ballet and generally tried to be the well-rounded individual that Ivy League admissions officers looked for. The psychologists had to dress the part if they were going to work with upscale people like that. So, Miriam had spent a lot of money on clothes since she moved to Palo Alto.

She'd been talking about her home remodeling plans with her colleagues and occasionally with the clients' mothers. Everyone had a horror story of a job that stretched on for years, cost five times the original estimate, and sometimes ended up in court. During the endless work, they always grew sick of having to eat out because their kitchens were torn up and having workmen around the house from dawn to dusk with the radios blaring. The consensus of her friends seemed to be "put everything in writing, and don't let those slimy contractors get away with anything."

But once in a while, she visited a house where the remodel was just a fading memory. She was green with envy and came home to Matt with a long list of ideas. They had to have an island in the middle of the kitchen with a sink and a wine refrigerator! They had to have granite countertops! They had to have a professional stove! The head of the clinic Abigail Johns and her husband Bernard had all those.

Abigail and Bernard lived near Lucie Stern Theater, a little complex of theater, studios, and classrooms on Middlefield near Embarcadero. They had two children, a boy and a girl, who both went to Palo Alto High and took all the Advanced Placement classes the school offered. Abigail and Bernard donated generously to TheatreWorks and West Bay Opera, two arts companies that performed at Lucie Stern, and occasionally, they hosted fundraisers for them. Miriam and Matt visited during one fundraiser, and Matt felt enough social pressure to give $100. Miriam aspired to be like them.

They were also involved with efforts to keep non-Palo Alto people out of "their" parks, mainly people from East Palo Alto (EPA). EPA was a separate city and heavily minority with a very high crime rate. The people from there didn't have nice parks of their own and liked to come over and picnic in Palo Alto. The City Council's public meetings often featured speakers demanding they do something about those outsiders taking over their parks. Abigail and Bernard, who had attended several of these meetings, insisted this had nothing to do with race—it was just about the safety of the children and the parks' capacity. Matt thought it was better to change the subject whenever Miriam brought this up.

WALT WAS FINISHING the drainage system at Janet's house when the job with Matt started. Janet and Walt chatted every morning when he arrived, although there wasn't much to talk about on this job. It was much more straightforward than the bathrooms had been. There weren't as many construction decisions for Walt to make or cool tricks he just had to show her. Janet was curious about Matt's remodel, but it took a while to overcome Walt's reticence about other clients. The fact that she and Matt knew each other and she had put them in touch in the first place made him a little more forthcoming.

The Finegolds' job included a simple kitchen remodel, without changing the basic layout—just new appliances, fixtures, cabinets, and countertops. That was enough work, but he figured he wouldn't have to change any plumbing, at least. He had his plumber friend Pete look it over, and Pete thought the original plumbing had at least ten years of life left. That should be plenty, he thought. They'll probably move before then.

Janet started looking at her ancient kitchen from the late 50s and wished she could upgrade it, too. She asked Walt a lot of questions about cabinets and countertops, and his practical knowledge always impressed her.

Walt had had a few conversations with Miriam that made him nervous. She was visiting other houses in Palo Alto whose owners had spent a *lot* of money on their kitchens, probably way more than Matt and Miriam were budgeting. It was normal for a client to have second thoughts once they signed, and change orders were a regular occurrence. He told Janet he tried to be accommodating rather than being a hardass like some of his competitors. "You want to leave the client smiling and recommending you to other people," he said.

Of course, there was always more demand for contractors than trained people, so it wasn't like he'd starve if someone badmouthed him. Still, you don't want to be fighting with clients. "Life is too short," he said in conclusion. "I'd rather enjoy what I do and go fishing a lot than always fight with people. Knock on wood… I have enough money that I don't have to worry."

She thought about him on the way to work. How many middle managers in high-tech have his attitude? She wondered if she did! Did she think of herself as giving satisfaction to customers? "*Only by accident!*" she thought ruefully. Walt was not working for The Man like she was—he was an independent businessman who had some control over his life.

She resisted the urge to talk to Matt about his remodeling job. He'd probably be annoyed that Walt was telling her about his private business. Most likely, Matt would bring it up on his own.

Her ace bureaucrat-in-training, Larry, wanted to talk about 3Com's new product, the 3Station. This was an exciting new product, a diskless PC that got all its storage from the network! It didn't even have a floppy drive. So if you were an IT manager for a giant corporation and worried about employees stealing information, this would solve your problem. Plus, you wouldn't have any more hassle installing network hardware and software on people's PCs because the 3Stations would already have Ethernet.

As the internal network manager, Janet was expected to be a good citizen and encourage employees to at least try out the 3Station and maybe even migrate to it completely. This was what dogfooding meant—you demonstrate to the customers that they should feed it to their dogs because we're giving it to our own dogs! Or did it mean you were eating the dog food yourself? Yuck!

Eventually, Matt dropped by to talk about Walt. "Hi, Janet. We're using your contractor guy, Walt, for our remodel. He's deep into demolition right now!"

"Oh, boy! Lucky you. Everything going okay?"

Matt pointed to her guest chair and looked inquiringly, and she held out her hand as if to say, "Have a seat."

"That's what I wanted to talk to you about. Did you have any changes to the plans after he started?"

She thought for a second, "Yeah, I guess so. It's hard to remember it all now. Why?"

He looked pained, "Well, Miriam is getting all sorts of ideas about kitchens from her rich friends. She keeps taking them to him, and he keeps putting her off. Or so she says."

Janet thought about Walt and what he'd said about Palo Alto people. She felt guilty that she might have given him yet another headache by sending Matt to him. "Hmm… does she want him to do more work than you already agreed to?"

Matt felt slightly irritated. Was she taking Walt's side in this? "Well, maybe so. But I would have thought we could have a Change Order and negotiate additional money. Or something like that. That's why I asked."

Janet thought about the times Walt had told her how her own job was going and the problems he was running into. Finally, "I don't think I ever had any big changes after he started. Sorry. I don't know what's normal in a case like that."

"Yeah… we're supposed to pay him $10,000 this week for the work so far," he said as he rose to leave.

Now she felt panic. Why did he bring that up? Did he want her to lean on Walt? That was not going to happen. It was his business, not hers.

"Oh, well. Not my problem."

She walked over to Cassie's cube. Dan was standing there at her whiteboard, explaining something. They both smiled at her.

"Dan's explaining how Mail talks to the Name Service," said Cassie.

"Oh, good. I've never quite understood that," she said, sitting back on Cassie's desk.

Dan continued drawing boxes and lines and explaining each one, with Cassie interrupting occasionally. Janet didn't want to make him start at the beginning again, but he could tell she was lost, so he stopped.

"Cassie, how about you explain how we keep track of what mail servers all the recipients are on?"

She said, "Oh, boy. I'll try." She took the marker and recapped what she'd learned so far, this time with Janet asking a lot of questions. They were laughing and having a good time, and people walking by stopped and listened in.

After fifteen minutes or so, Larry came by and pointed at his watch. Janet said, "Oops, we have a meeting about the 3Station," and left. The crowd dispersed.

32

WHAT DOES 'STRATEGIC' MEAN, AGAIN?

3 Com had gone and done it. They made a deal with the Devil—Microsoft. Except that when you sell your soul to the Devil, weren't you supposed to get something for it? 3Com thought they would get a piece of the enormous PC business, but Bill Gates wasn't into giving *anyone* a piece of his business. As soon as you reached a certain size, he told his minions, "Okay, that's ours now. Go and make it so," and they did.

3Com was going to develop something called LAN Manager with Microsoft and IBM. IBM hoped that it would principally run on OS/2, IBM's new operating system, and DOS. Dan read up on OS/2, which at least was a real operating system, unlike DOS.

Engineers were repeatedly told that this deal was strategic. The founders were convinced that a small player in the networking space stood no chance once the giant companies jumped in, and they had to merge with a larger player. This fear was largely what drove the failed Convergent merger— you had to become big in a hurry. Dan accepted that as conventional wisdom, although his feeling was, "*Lots of small companies find a growing market, dominate it, and become large, so why can't we?*" He remembered what Bridget, one of the other engineers, always said, about "strategic" projects—you never actually make money.

It was indeed hard to see how this was a good deal financially for 3Com. They were allowed to market LAN Manager themselves, calling it 3+Open, but Microsoft had all the rights to 3+Open after the 2.0 release. A very large segment of 3Com's engineers were devoted to implementing a Microsoft-defined software interface called NetBIOS, a name intended to sound like BIOS, the Basic Input Output System on every IBM-compatible PC. The hope was that NetBIOS would eventually drive Novell out of its leading position because it would be a standard they could not control.

Fortunately, Dan was exempt from the NetBIOS effort. It was largely a task for the specialists in lower-level software. He was left to run 3+Mail mostly on his own since it was not strategic. Of course, that made it an easy target for any 3Com'er looking to prove their mettle by killing it. At one large product meeting, Dan witnessed one of these attempts. The finance guy patiently explained that 3+Mail was actually one of the most profitable products since 3Com owned all the technology, unlike 3+Open.

3Com engineers hated their Microsoft counterparts, and the feeling was reciprocated. This was really no different from any joint project of two or more companies—the engineers always hated each other unless one of them was Hewlett-Packard. HP's engineers were some of the nicest and easiest-to-work-with on the planet.

Microsoft's engineers were not like HP's. A leading engineer in networking at Microsoft had said semi-publicly, "My two-year-old can write better code than 3Com engineers." The NetBIOS project dragged on and on and became known as Viet BIOS after the long, bloody, and unsuccessful Vietnam War.

At the same time, in July 1987, 3Com announced they

were acquiring a smaller company, Bridge Communications. It was with the same get-big-or-go-home mentality, except this time, 3Com was the big player. Bridge was not a teensy startup. They had been around for six years and were a pioneer in a new category of network product, the router. Their founders had the insight that once a company had many local area networks, they needed a way to tie them together. There weren't too many companies ready for that, though, which was a problem. Customers didn't even know what a router or bridge was. But if they did know, as some cutting-edge institutions did, Bridge was their go-to supplier. There was also a very small competitor called Cisco, but Bridge was the biggest player in this tiny market.

Regular companies had minicomputers and lots of plain old dumb terminals, and they wanted to connect them. That was a more mature market, and Bridge made terminal servers for those people. They had good success with that and managed to go public in 1986.

The acquisition was called a merger of equals officially, although everyone below the rank of CEO regarded it as 3Com acquiring Bridge. Detailed planning began at once. Dan's boss, Terry, was called in to help compare 3Com's products and Bridge's to look for overlap. There really wasn't much. 3Com was trying to be a computer company, and Bridge was a pure networking company. The arrangement was that Bill Carrico, the Bridge president, would be President of the combined company, and Bill Krause, the 3Com president, would be CEO. No one knew how this was going to work out, but Krause told a story at the company meeting about how at The Citadel, his alma mater, they had a successful arrangement of "Mr. Inside and Mr. Outside" for their football team. In his version, Mr. Inside attended to the running of the team, and Mr. Outside handled the press, the alumni, the league, and other outside duties. Carrico and Krause would attempt something similar, with Carrico being "inside" and Krause "outside." Krause was a great speaker, so him being Mr. Outside made sense.

After the initial excitement of the announcement, Dan never heard much more about it. Some of the other engineers had meetings occasionally at Bridge, but he never did. The 3Com engineers brought back tales of unhappy people there, but since he didn't know any of them, he didn't think much about it. The two companies did not seem to be planning to move into a single building. He asked various managers, including Terry, if that would ever happen, and their answers were disturbingly vague.

As head of 3Com's internal network, Janet was often gone for meetings with her counterparts at Bridge, presumably to connect the two companies' internal networks. Janet and Miss Smarmy, as Dan called the HR head, frequently reported on their progress at the company meetings. He remembered the Convergent merger and all the engineering-level meetings they'd had before the thing even happened, but this one somehow lacked that same urgency.

In late August, his curiosity finally got the better of him, and he wandered over to Janet's cube. Matt was sitting there, and they seemed to be having an intense conversation. Both of them seemed worried.

"Am I interrupting something?"

Matt looked like he'd been caught red-handed and was trying to hide it, "Oh, hi, Dan. No, we were just talking about contractors. What's up?"

Dan said, "Contractors! I need to talk to Janet about that." She smiled, and Matt looked embarrassed. He continued, "So, what's happening with the Bridge merger? I hear you and Kristen talking about your meetings, and yet, we never hear anything about it in engineering."

Matt silently mouthed Miss Smarmy when he said Kristen's name. With an effort, Dan ignored him.

Janet adopted her managerial I-can't-tell-you face. "Oh,

we're just being sure the company cultures are harmonized before we move in together… you know, things like that."

"*Okay, you're not going to tell me.*"

Matt said, "Don't they have private offices for their executives? I heard that was becoming a problem."

Janet became even more remote, "You'd have to ask Kristen about that. I'm just dealing with the network."

Dan knew he should probably drop the subject, but he just couldn't help himself. "Uh-oh! Everyone here has a cubicle, even Krause and Metcalfe."

She looked annoyed and said nothing. Matt jumped to her defense, "I'm sure Kristen's going to work it out, somehow. She's good at being diplomatic."

"That she is," said Janet. Then glancing at her watch, she said, "If you'll excuse me."

Dan asked Matt, "So, what do you think is going on?" as they walked toward Matt's cube.

"Beats me. I heard they didn't like being forced to give up their private offices."

"I don't blame them. I had one at Xerox, and it was wonderful."

"Yeah. Anyway, how's it going?"

Dan said, "Oh, you know. Terry's always off on some kind of management thing, so I never see him. How about you?"

They arrived at Matt's cube, and Dan sat in the guest chair. Matt said, "So, you know we're doing this big house remodel, and we're using Janet's contractor, right?"

"Oh, boy. Lucky you. How's it going?"

Matt had that "this is going to be a long story" look on his face. "What kind of floor covering do you have in your kitchen?"

Dan said, "It's just linoleum. Someday, I'll upgrade my 1950s kitchen. Sigh."

"Same as Janet. Well, ours is marble tile or actually travertine. Something expensive."

"Okay."

"After we started, Miriam became absolutely fixated on a free-standing island in the middle of the kitchen floor, even though that wasn't in the original plans."

Dan thought of houses he'd seen that had those. He didn't have room for one in his kitchen, so he'd never thought much about them. "Wow, that sounds like a major change, but what do I know?"

Matt was just warming up, "Yeah, I guess. But don't engineers *always* have to make major changes during development? It's just part of the job."

Dan wasn't so sure, "I don't know. The physical world is less forgiving than our world. They call what we do software because it's *soft*."

"Well, whatever. Anyway, this guy Walt says he'd send us a revised estimate, and we think, 'Alright, a day or two and then back to work.' But it takes him a week, and then, the cost comes back almost doubled! And meanwhile, we have no kitchen, and we're eating in the backyard."

Dan winced, "Ow! Maybe you should forget about this island thing."

Matt was reliving the anguished discussions with Miriam about all this, "Well, she really insists, and by now, we're hip-deep into this fucking job."

"So what happened? You swallowed hard and went ahead with it?"

"What else could we do? These fucking guys know that once your house is torn up, they have you over a barrel."

"So... now it's in progress at least? But I'm guessing the answer is no."

Matt looked *really* annoyed, "I wish. He keeps coming up with more stuff he didn't estimate. The foundation has to be jackhammered to make room for the drain pipe from the island. That one he should have seen coming and included it, right?"

Dan said, "You would think."

Matt continued, "The latest one is, the kitchen tiles have to be torn up to reach the foundation. And now, the new tiles will not match the old ones because you can't buy the old ones anymore. So basically, we have to replace the entire kitchen floor. All this was stuff he should have planned for."

"And of course, all this is extra money."

Matt just simmered, "I don't know how we're going to pay for all this. I'm applying for a construction loan, and these fucking loan officers don't like to come in during the middle of a job. They want to be in it from the beginning. It never ends."

"Ugh. I don't even want to think about all this!"

"I wish I didn't have to. So now you know." Matt's phone rang, and he held up his palm to signal that this would be a while. Dan was grateful for an excuse to return to his cube.

Dan thought about the two big things going on—the Microsoft deal and the Bridge merger. Neither augured well for the future. Believing anything Microsoft said when real money was on the table was like believing Lucy's, "I'll hold the ball, Charlie Brown, and you come running up and kick it." Unless it didn't matter to them, but networking definitely did matter.

Still, there was that sabbatical 3Com gave you after four years—six weeks off with pay! And, he was over halfway to earning it. You could tack on regular vacation time you'd accrued, too. *"What would I do with all that time off? Go to Australia, for one thing."* But the possibilities were endless. Lots of older companies offered sabbaticals to their employees, but the practice was dying out. He might never have another chance.

He turned his attention to the 3+Mail software that ran on people's PCs, the client software. It had a limit of a hundred and ten messages in an inbox because when it was developed, that was the number that fit on a floppy disk. There was no way to search the inbox, assign messages to folders, or mark messages so that you could operate on them in bulk. Message bodies were limited to twenty-thousand characters because it could only use an in-house-developed editor called Mail Editor (MED), which kept the entire message in memory. Twenty thousand was its buffer size. MED had its own idiosyncratic command keys, unlike any other PC software. The mail screen took up the entire display, and there was no way to change that.

The client was showing its age. But everyone at 3Com was used to it and liked it just the way it was. There was also the phenomenon in all high-tech companies that "the second you leave, all your code turns to shit." If the author of something still worked there, people were reluctant to replace the work, but as soon as they left the company, all problems were blamed on them. At 3Com, the original 3+Mail authors were still there.

Customers never complained because they were thrilled to have email at all. And email was not strategic, as Terry kept reminding him, so rewriting it was a low priority. In this situation, an engineer like Dan had two options—being a good citizen and accepting the judgment or quitting. Most engineers would do the latter if they wanted to work on something and their company didn't want it. There would be no hard feelings on anyone's part, *"You wanted to work on email, the company didn't want to invest in it, but that's life. See ya."*

Dan took a different tack. He knew from experience that most companies do not really follow the military model of decision making—the commander gives the orders, and everyone carries them out. In theory, it's that way. But in practice, it's often more like mob rule, except at Xerox after the Star came out. Everyone told the management they were blowing the opportunity of a lifetime—those executives really did believe in the top-down model, and they were wrong. Hence everyone quit, including Dan. And now, here he was.

Sometimes, you have to whip up support for your preferred course of action from people with influence. In a small- to medium-sized company like 3Com, it was not hard to get to know virtually all the influencers. Dan had always believed nothing beats the power of working code, so he wrote a simple demo of a new email client and went around showing it to them. Of course, people were excited, and he had the freedom to keep developing it, at least for now.

33

WHEN THINGS GO SOUTH

Walt dropped by Janet's house one morning in early September 1987 to pick up his final check for the drainage system work. She invited him in. "Can I make you some coffee? I'll get my checkbook."

Walt was grateful. He looked like he needed the caffeine. "Coffee sounds great, thanks." He sat down at the kitchen table.

With her checkbook in hand, she returned to the kitchen. "So, how's it going?"

"Oh, you know, same old, same old. How are things at 3Com?"

"The same." She hesitated for a second, and then feeling some responsibility for the Matt fiasco, she said, "I was talking to Matt Finegold the other day."

He tried to remain impassive, "Yeah, that's a fun job." She sat down but didn't say anything.

He looked like he wanted to say more. "They're kinda, let's say, unhappy right now."

"Matt told me a little, but I don't know much about it."

Walt drank some coffee. "Wow, that's good. Anyway, Matt. Or maybe I should say *Miriam*."

"I've never met his wife."

"Consider yourself... well, no, scratch that. Anyhow, Miriam decided she wanted a free-standing island in the kitchen after we had the job all costed out and were into demo."

"That's demolition?"

"Right, sorry, demolition. Anyhow, I always try to accommodate the clients' requests even when they're ridiculous."

Janet poured them both more coffee. "I don't know anything about construction, but that sounds like a big change."

He looked pained, "You think? Yeah, you have extra plumbing, extra wiring, need to jackhammer into the concrete foundation, tear up the kitchen floor... it goes on and on."

She looked around at her kitchen. "Well, there's no room for that in here! When you do this place, which I hope you will, we're keeping the same layout."

"You're smart. Anyway, these big jobs always become more complicated, and you always discover more stuff *after* you get into it. Especially with an older house. Big stuff. *Expensive* stuff."

Matt had told her about all that, but she didn't want to betray too much of what she knew. "So, is that what's going on there?"

Walt rose, "Do you mind if I use your restroom?" He knew where it was, of course.

He came back and sat down again, looking at his watch. "My guys are probably arriving there right about now. Not looking forward to this."

She took their cups to the sink. "Walt, I'm so sorry I got you into this!"

"Oh, don't apologize, Janet. It's not your fault. I try and appreciate all the jobs, even the ones that end up like this. Thanks for the coffee."

As she put the cups into the dishwasher, she thought about

him. The adult men she knew growing up in Michigan were like him—stoic was the word that came to mind. They preferred not to share their feelings, especially about other people. There were so few of those guys out here in California.

She drove to work. It seemed the traffic on the Lawrence Expressway was worse every month—like a parking lot. She also noticed that the 3Com parking lot now resembled the ones at TRW and Xerox—big. The buildings had lobbies, staircases, potted plants, couches, and glass coffee tables with *The Wall Street Journal* for visitors. She found her way to her cube and scanned her mail.

Kristen, the HR person, had been hinting that big changes were coming in the company now that they'd made the Bridge merger. She sent Janet another message about that, expanding on her theme that 3Com-Bridge would be a billion-dollar company real soon, and everyone in management had to up their game. She suggested a one-on-one meeting soon. "*Whatever 'up your game' means.*"

The phone's message light was always blinking these days. Voicemail seemed to be the communication medium of choice for a certain class of people who just picked up the phone and blathered endlessly, requiring way more time on your part than an email. She listened to today's messages with a sigh, but one was her old friend from Xerox, Grant Avery! She hadn't heard from him in almost six years.

Grant had been on the corporate side for Star in Palo Alto, and then he transferred down to El Segundo to work on the 5700 printers. This marked him as unusual since people almost always moved in the other direction.

Once he was in LA, he was drafted into being the 5700 representative to his previous group in Palo Alto and was then "asked" to move to Japan to be a liaison for all the advanced technology Xerox was doing. That was in 1981, and she'd lost track of him.

Grant had clearly wanted to be much more than friends, asking her out repeatedly. She finally went out with him once, but she didn't want to pursue it any further. He was too much of a conservative corporate-type for her, and he'd probably spend his entire career at Xerox, moving up the ladder to a VP-ship.

He was still in Japan, but he was coming back to Palo Alto for a business trip next week, and he wanted to see her. He hinted at some very big news that he'd tell her when he saw her. She checked her watch, and it was the middle of the night there, so she didn't call back, instead putting a sticky note on her phone. She wondered how Walt was surviving his morning with Matt's wife.

WHEN WALT ARRIVED at the Finegold house, his workers were standing around in front waiting for him. Miriam was looking out the front window every minute or so, also waiting. When she saw him, she came to the door with a frozen smile. Mookie, tail wagging furiously, tried to edge past her to greet Walt. She shooed him back into the house.

He greeted her, "Morning, Miriam. How are you today?"

"Good morning, Walt. We're doing great. Can we talk for a minute?"

"Sure," he said, trying not to look apprehensive. His workers looked at their feet. They went inside, and she said, "Have a seat. Would you like some coffee?"

He sat down on the couch and said, "Thanks, I've already had plenty today."

She sat down in a chair opposite him, which felt like her job as a therapist. "Matt and I are concerned about how this job is expanding, both in time and cost. I know we gave you some extra work after you started, but I thought we had that all ironed out."

He started to answer, but she continued, "We've been eating out in the backyard or going to restaurants for what seems like forever."

He waited a little longer before starting to speak, but she cut in again. "I mean, when does it end? It seems like every week, there is a new expense we weren't counting on or a new set of bad choices. Either pay a whole bunch extra or leave our house looking like shit."

This time he waited to see if she had still more. Finally, he decided she didn't. "I know, Miriam, and I'm sorry. My guys and I feel bad about all the extra work, too. It seems like every time we dig into something, we hit some new work we weren't counting on. Like the old wiring we had to replace. Like this bit with the kitchen floor tiles…"

That last one seemed to set her off, "Right, so now we have to replace the entire floor. We didn't budget for that at all. And how do we know that won't create even more work when it's done?"

"*You don't!*" But he couldn't just say that. He sometimes reached this point with a client, where the job just keeps growing and growing. Sometimes, they were understanding about it and recognized how their own choices got them to that point. Janet had been that way on the jobs he'd done for her.

At other times, it could become ugly. He wished he could figure out how to capture all the job requirements on paper, cost it out, and agree on everything before the work started, but somehow, it never happened that way. He often ended up doing extra work for free and losing money on the job, just to avoid a Better Business Bureau complaint or something even worse. He fought with his first wife all the time about that. She was infuriated at him for caving in to the unreasonable clients. He was trying not to do that anymore.

"I can't promise you there isn't even more work lurking in

there, but right now, I don't see it. I think when we finish up this kitchen floor work, we'll be back on the original plan."

Miriam tried to look relieved and started to get up. Walt had one more item, though, "I know this isn't the best time for this, but you're a couple of weeks behind in the payments now. Can you write a check today?"

Miriam said, "Oh, Walt, we don't have that much money in our checking account. Can we pay you next week after Matt's payday?"

This was the sort of excuse Walt was used to hearing. His ex-wife used to berate him for falling for it. Not anymore.

"Yeah, it's tough. I know. But I have to pay for the new flooring, and my account with the supplier is about tapped out. My guys need to be paid. I'm afraid we can't do any more work without a payment."

"So... what? We're just supposed to keep living with no kitchen?"

"*And why is that my problem?*" But Walt knew "I can't" and a plea for sympathy were always better answers than "I won't."

"I know, believe me, I know. But I'm in a hard place, too. Those suppliers just run and hide when they see me coming!"

She smiled weakly and said, "Okay, let me call Matt," and went into the bedroom. Walt sat and waited, and finally, she came back. He could tell this was not going to be good news.

"Your invoice was for $4,000, right?" He nodded. She handed him a check. "This is for $2,000, and we'll pay the rest next week. Will that be okay for now?"

She was hoping this would do it, but Walt wouldn't budge. "Thank you. I really appreciate the effort, Miriam. But I'm afraid I need the balance."

Miriam and Matt had planned for this scenario. "Okay, then Matt and I have decided to stop the work now. We're going to have other contractors look over the job."

Walt stood up, "If that's what you want to do. I'm real sorry we couldn't come to an agreement."

Miriam said, "We'll be in touch about closing this out."

Walt thought of reminding her that they still owed for the work he'd already done, but somehow, he didn't think now was the time. He went out and told the workers they were off for the day, and of course, he'd pay them for the lost time.

Driving home, he thought about how this job had gone south. What should he have done when they made it a much bigger job than they bargained for? Janet had recommended him, so at least he must have managed that client relationship properly. Now, she apparently felt bad about how it turned out. He wondered when he'd have a chance to tell her not to take it on herself, and he was a big boy.

34

MOSHI, MOSHI

For a change, Janet had no meetings this morning in late September and no crises to resolve. She thought about Walt and felt nothing but guilt for putting Matt in touch with him. Walt was such a decent guy, and his reluctance to say anything about the job spoke louder than anything he could say.

It was too soon to ask Matt about it, and that might not be a good idea in any case. Both Matt and Walt would probably resent her for being involved. But Dan and Matt hung out a lot. Maybe she could wait a while and worm it out of Dan! Now she had a plan.

Regarding Dan, it turned out Cassie had been learning a lot from him. She told Janet about this cool new user interface for 3+Mail that Dan was working on. It had windows, used a mouse, and everything! *"Oh, great, just what we need!"* she thought but tried to sound interested. As far as she was concerned, email finally worked, and everyone knew how to use it, so leave it alone. Larry had also been out trash-talking this new threat to his serenity, so she'd already heard about it.

Dan had explained the intricacies of envelopes in 3+Mail,

the part of the network message outside of the message itself, and she finally understood it. He stressed that having too much information in the envelope was just as bad as not having enough. Finding the correct balance was the art of protocol design.

Dan was pleased that he got the concept across. He thought Cassie should be in Testing or Development, but coming out of college, she'd been slotted into network support, and it was hard as hell to get out of a job like that, no matter who you were.

That sort of thing might happen to a man, too, but it was probably more likely to happen to a woman—no matter what anyone said about equal opportunity. Dan felt that helping one person at a time was more his style than making a big noise about it, and that was one thing you could do as a manager that you couldn't otherwise.

He headed over to Matt's cube to shoot the shit. Matt had just ended a phone call and had a resolute look on his face like he'd just made a tough but necessary decision. He turned to Dan and said, in a flat tone, "Hey. What's going on?"

"Nothing much. What about you?"

Matt said, "I just got off the phone with a lawyer."

"Uh-oh. Are you acquiring Cisco or something?"

Matt laughed and pretended to make a note for himself. "Good idea, but no. We're expecting to be sued by our contractor, if we don't sue him first. Thank God, the initial lawyer consultation is at least free."

"Oh, no. That was Janet's contractor, wasn't it?" Dan really didn't want to hear the details.

This was awkward for Matt. "Yeah, what can I say? Our job was different from hers, I guess. This fuckin' guy just keeps discovering new stuff he didn't figure on, and all of it *super* expensive stuff. Miriam can't stand him anymore."

Dan wanted to escape. What was he going to say about

that? Finally, "It's the home remodeling job from hell, huh? You hear about these things from time to time."

"I'd settle for hell at this point... actually, I think he's a pretty decent guy. I can see why Janet gets along with him. But he and Miriam are not best buds, let's put it that way."

"I haven't met him. I was actually thinking I'd hire him if I ever need a contractor. Before this, I mean!"

Matt laughed, "Well, maybe don't listen to me. He comes with good references, not just from Janet."

He turned back to his computer and pointed to some news story up on his screen. "Hey, changing topics for a sec... have you heard of this new Apple thing, HyperCard?"

Dan hated new Apple cutesy-pie names like HyperCard. "No, can't say as I have. Should I?"

Matt laughed, "When I worked for the summer at Data-Point..." He stopped, "Did I tell you about that?"

Dan shook his head, "DataPoint... didn't they have fancy terminals or something?"

"And ARCnet, which is why they hired me here. It was a summer internship when I was in grad school. Anyway, they had this famous guy, Ted Nelson, at the time."

"I think I've heard of him."

"Yeah, he's been pushing his Project Xanadu forever. I don't think DataPoint was the right place for a guy like him. Anyway, he invented this term hypertext back in the 60s, and now Apple's glommed onto it."

"So, it's one of those 'this text links to that' thingies? Instead of a bunch of boring old linear documents, now everything links to everything?"

"Now, you've got it. Apparently, Apple has some product that does that, sort of. I don't have a Mac, so I can't show it to you."

Dan was a little interested, "Well, maybe we can have someone here with a Mac show it to us."

Matt was excited, "And PowerPoint. We have to see that, too!"

"Another name I don't know. What's PowerPoint?"

"Dan, Dan, you're so far behind the times. PowerPoint is this new product for creating presentations. Microsoft just bought it from some company called Forethought down here."

Dan looked puzzled, "Forethought? I knew a guy at Xerox who was going to work there if I remember correctly. But I thought it was some kind of database."

Matt shrugged, "I don't know about that. All I know is, they developed this thing called Presenter, and now, they're all going to be rich. That's the way you do it."

Dan said, "I thought you had to play your git-tar on your MTV!"

Matt turned back to his computer, humming "Money For Nothing," and Dan left.

He hadn't been back in his cube for more than five minutes when Janet stopped by. "Well, to what do I owe the pleasure? I hardly ever see you anymore!"

Janet replied, "Yeah, I spend my life in meetings these days. I'm sorry. I saw you in Matt's cube. Did he say anything about Walt, the contractor I referred?"

"Well, as a matter of fact… I guess they're not too happy with him because Matt was just talking to a lawyer."

Janet looked alarmed, "Oh, my God. Oh, my God."

Dan had that feeling that he'd said too much, "Uh-oh. Maybe I should have let Matt tell you. Me and my big mouth."

Janet had guessed Dan would tell her, and she was right. But if she left now, Dan might suspect the real purpose of her visit. So, she forced herself to make small talk for a while, telling him of Grant's phone call. Dan hadn't known Grant all that well at Xerox, but "what are the former Xeroids doing now?" was always a good topic with anyone else from Xerox.

It was just assumed that everyone had left by now. They discussed the current employment of all their former acquaintances, and she told him she was now the proud owner of a Macintosh II since 3Com was going to sell Ethernet cards for them. Then, she excused herself.

Should she call Walt? He might be annoyed. She'd already apologized this morning, and he was pretty emphatic that there was nothing to apologize for. Matt would probably be annoyed at her for poking her head into it, too. Sigh.

"Matt's wife must be a godawful bitch." Matt and Janet each decided to avoid talking to one another until things cooled off.

Later in the day, she figured it must be late enough in Japan to call Grant.

"Moshi, Moshi," Grant answered.

"Grant, it's me, Janet Saunders!"

"Oh, my God. Janet, thanks for calling back! How the hell are you?"

"Oh, just great, Grant. How about you? So, you're coming out here?"

They made plans to meet for dinner the next week. Grant refused to tell her what the big surprise was. *"He was probably promoted to Deputy Assistant General Manager or something."* But still, keeping up with the gossip was always a worthwhile thing to do. She hadn't heard much about what Xerox was up to since all the Star developers left.

The next Monday night, she met Grant for dinner at the Fish Market in Palo Alto. It was a pretty safe choice since everyone could find something they like there. It wasn't too noisy, and the parking was easy. Also, it wasn't too far from Xerox.

He was waiting in the lobby, and he stood up and hugged her. Her eyes were drawn to the ring finger on his left hand— he had a wedding ring! He noticed and held up his hand.

"Cat's out of the bag now! I got married!"

"Oh my God, Grant! That was your surprise? Congratulations! Who's the lucky girl?"

"Her name's Jun, which means obedient in Japanese. I think her parents were hoping that would be a hint for her, but it didn't work." Janet laughed.

The waiter came out and led them to their table. They sat down, and he handed them menus and put a bowl of sourdough bread on the table. They studied the menus and then set them aside.

"So, where did you meet Jun? Does she work at Xerox?"

"She actually does. Jun is one of the coders, as they call them over there. We've been married for a little over a year now."

"And no kids yet?"

He smiled broadly, "Soon! Late March 1988 looks like Baby Day."

Janet remembered how much he had yearned for a wife and family, and he'd clearly hoped it would be with her. She just didn't see him that way, but he'd always been decent and helpful to her. She was really happy that he now had what he always wanted.

"So, are you speaking Japanese a lot now?"

He said something in Japanese, but she had no idea what it was. "That was 'Yes, I am learning a lot, but I will always sound like a *gaijin*.'"

"Well, you could have fooled me anyway."

He was happy to report that Jun spoke good English. She had gone to graduate school at the University of Utah, so she had to. Utah had Ivan Sutherland, one of the fathers of modern computer graphics, and Alan Kay, so it was a good place to have gone. And, speaking English in Japan was a big advantage for getting hired at an American company like Xerox.

The waiter returned and stood holding his pen and pad, "Have you decided?"

Janet ordered the grilled mahi-mahi and Grant the broiled salmon. They both ordered a beer as well.

Grant was originally supposed to guide Fuji Xerox's development of a special VLSI chip for Mesa, the language used at Xerox, but Fuji's enthusiasm waned as soon as they realized Xerox was not going to take over the computer market. The production volumes would never justify the investment. As the liaison from the U.S. for Office Information Systems products, he had plenty of work. The Japanese version of the Star had full support for typing and editing Japanese characters, and Fuji had made sure of that by sending a number of their engineers to help with Star development.

Janet remembered the Japanese engineers when she was working on Star. She didn't remember too many details of what they were doing, but the fact that Star had a reasonably efficient way of typing *Kanji* characters—of which there were almost 50,000—was a huge source of pride for everyone at Xerox, American and Japanese. Of course, Star could also type *hiragana* and *katakana*, the two phonetic alphabets also used in Japan. Grant could talk about this topic for hours on end if he needed to, and quite often over there, he did need to! Everyone had tons of questions about how to type on the Star, and they frequently had problems that no one back in the States had anticipated.

Besides the Star, which was sexy but didn't sell a whole lot, there was the new generation of copier/printers, like the 5700 Grant had worked on, and those also kept him busy. His staff had grown and grown over the past five years, and now, he'd become an important person in the Xerox organization there.

The food came. It was excellent, and they were silent for a while as they dug in. You could always count on the Fish Market for solid, dependable food.

Janet wondered if he was planning to stay in Japan or move back here, but she thought it was too early to ask him that. And, he wanted to hear about her life after Xerox. She told him briefly about her experiences on the Apple Lisa, which were not all that great, and now she was at 3Com.

"Do you remember the big lightning strike in Palo Alto that took down the Ethernet?"

"How could I forget? And you were the hero!"

She said modestly, "Oh, come on, I just found a wrench and figured someone left it up there. Tim Field was the person who figured out that was it!"

"As I said at the start."

Grant was still bitter about how he'd suggested that the lightning storm might be the culprit, and they'd laughed at him. She doubted that he'd had any clue at all about how lightning might have fried all those transceivers. It took a genius like Tim to figure that out. But they left that topic and moved on to her job at 3Com, how she was in charge of all their internal networking, and what a big job that was growing into.

It appeared that both of them had done a great job of climbing the corporate ladder. But Janet's mind was elsewhere, "I bought a house!"

"You bought a house? That's wonderful! Tell me all about it."

She went through all the details of finding the realtor, looking in different neighborhoods, buying the house, going to show houses to find her decorator, Ida, and Ida getting Walt, the contractor, to do the work on her bathroom.

Grant said without much interest, "So, he did a good job, did he?"

She beamed, "He did *such* a great job. I've used him for two jobs since then. He's like an engineer."

Grant smirked, "And that's a good thing?"

She smiled briefly and said, "In a good way, I mean. He loves to tell you everything he's doing and how difficult it was. And then, he's just so proud of himself sometimes."

"Yep, that's an engineer for you." Grant finished the last

of his beer. "So what else is going on? Are you seeing anyone?"

Janet frowned resignedly, "No, these Silicon Valley types are all the same. I don't know what I want, but it's definitely not them. And the fact that I make more money than most of them doesn't help, either."

Grant couldn't think of anything to say about that, so he wisely remained silent. They talked about Xerox people they knew and what they were doing now, but her mind was clearly elsewhere. Finally, out with it, "Can I ask your advice on something?" Grant nodded. She told him how she'd given Matt a referral to Walt, and now, the job was going horribly, horribly wrong, with talk of lawyers, and she felt so bad for Walt. And Matt, of course.

"I just don't know if I should even try to get involved or if that would make matters worse."

"*You* get involved? How? What would you even do?"

"That's what I can't figure out. Maybe try to mediate? I mean, I'm the one who put them together."

Grant felt like something wasn't quite right here, but he wasn't sure what. "This must happen to contractors all the time, though. Walt doesn't blame you, does he?"

Janet looked anxious, "No, he *says* he doesn't. But I still worry."

The waiter brought the check, and Janet reached for it. "Consider this an advance baby gift or maybe a delayed wedding gift, Grant!" He graciously let her pay.

"I don't know, Janet. It sounds to me like you like this guy Walt. Is he married?"

She was shocked, "I don't think so, but what does it matter? He's a contractor, for God's sake."

Grant said to himself, "*So the fuck what?*"

"Well, all I can tell you, Janet, is you're a friend. I want to see you happy."

She checked her watch, "I appreciate it, Grant, I really do.

It was great seeing you, and be sure to send me a baby picture!" She turned and walked toward her car.

"*They laughed when I said lightning might have brought down the Ethernet! Now, she's laughing about this great contractor guy. We'll see.*"

35

LIFE GOES ONLINE

Dan needed a plumber. His house had a gas water heater, but that was in the garage. And, he wanted a gas line to the kitchen so that he could cook like a civilized person. Electric ranges were for apartment dwellers.

Fortunately, Janet had the names of many good crafts-people from her work with Walt, so Dan asked her, and she recommended Pete, the plumber who'd worked on her bathroom. Pete thought it would be a quick job, so he could squeeze it in on Tuesday, September 29. Dan left work early in the afternoon to be home for him.

Pete was about six feet tall and stocky. He had graying hair, a reddish mottled face, and wore a baseball cap and old worn jeans. He was friendly, and Dan liked him immediately. He checked out the job, said he'd done hundreds of similar ones, and set to work. Dan sat in the family room, out of his way, and read some documents from the Internet Engineering Task Force working group on Directory Services.

In a few hours, Pete was finished. Dan didn't have a gas stovetop yet, so Pete just capped off the gas pipe underneath where the stovetop would go. They sat at the kitchen table as

Dan wrote out the check. "So, you worked on Janet Saunders' house, huh?"

He searched his memory, "Saunders, Saunders... that's near here, isn't it? It's hard to remember all the houses."

Then it came back to him, "Oh, right, nice-looking girl. Do you work with her?"

Dan reminded Pete that Janet recommended him, and Walt Campbell had done a bunch of jobs for her. Now he remembered the details.

Dan continued, "Speaking of Walt, Janet seemed very worried that Walt's job with Matt Finegold was going south. Lawyers and everything."

Pete was always reluctant to talk about other clients, and especially those of other contractors. Still, this seemed to make him thoughtful, "Worried? Why should *she* be worried? It's Walt's problem, isn't it?"

"You would think. I guess because she was the one who put them together."

"Yeah, maybe," said Pete. He rose, "Thanks for the check. Call me anytime!" He paused, "You know... Walt chewed me out for even hinting at this, but what the hell. He's single, she's single, they get along... you know? None of us are getting any younger. I'm getting married again myself. Maybe I can finally get it right this time!"

Dan laughed, "Congratulations! I was wondering about Janet and Walt, too. But for sure, I don't want to be involved in *that* one!"

Pete laughed, agreed, and left.

It was dinner time, so Dan put a pot of water on for pasta. He cursed the electric burners more than ever, now that gas was finally possible.

This new TV show was on, *thirtysomething*. The success of the movie *The Big Chill* had apparently convinced Hollywood that there was still good money to be made from the Baby Boomers, even though the 60s and even the 70s were long gone. *"Hey, now they're grown up and married, maybe, and having babies, maybe. We can milk that."*

He watched it. It all seemed so contrived. But it was TV, and hey, it was still better than *Married... with Children* or laugh-tracked garbage like that.

He thought about what Pete said. Janet had been married when they first met, and then she divorced. He'd seen her giving her phone number to guys at Sierra Club hikes when they lived down in LA, but as far as he knew, it never became very serious. Grant Avery had the hots for her, but she clearly didn't return the feeling. And she'd never given Dan the slightest signal that they could be other than friends, so he'd never even asked her out. She was pretty distant at times, now that she was a big manager and everything was a public performance.

So, what *did* she want? He'd met her husband, Ken, once or twice in LA, and he was a typical aerospace dork. Maybe she just didn't want a husband again. There had to be lots of VPs and CEOs asking her out, so if that's what she wanted, she'd have it by now. Oh, well. Not his problem.

THE NEXT DAY, he was showing Cassie how the mail server stored messages in people's inboxes and how they were *encrypted* on the server. He and Terry always chuckled about that since the encryption was nothing but an exclusive-or with 1s, meaning if the bit is 0, change it to 1, and if it's 1, change it to 0. If you do that twice, you end up with the original bits. So, you could practically break the encryption in your head— you didn't even need a computer. He made her promise not to tell anyone. He told her that this knowledge would let you read the email of anyone in the company, but if you were caught, you'd be fired and deserve to be.

She swore her lips were sealed. To break the solemnity, she

asked him if he'd watched *thirtysomething* last night. He had, of course, so she asked what he thought of it.

"*Uh-oh. What can I say that won't land me in trouble?*" He decided to go for bland, "Well, it was better than yet another cop show, anyway. What did you think?"

"I thought of these older friends of mine who just had a baby. My God that gives me the creeps!"

Dan smiled, "Which part? The baby getting Hope and Michael out of bed, or the scene with Hope and the screaming baby and her single friend at the restaurant, or what?"

"All of it! Especially the part about houses with kids are always sticky!"

Dan laughed, "Yeah, I have noticed that, but I usually try to pretend I don't."

Matt stopped by his cube, "Oh, you're talking about *thirtysomething*? Yeah, that was a riot."

Cassie said, "You and your wife don't have any kids, right?"

"Not yet. It's good to know what's involved!" Matt joked.

"Oh, it's *much* worse than that!" she said.

"Much worse!" Dan agreed.

"Wait, how would either of you know?"

"I saw a movie about it once," offered Dan. All three laughed.

They were in a silly mood now. Matt asked Cassie, "So, your boss Janet… we never see *her* with a guy at the company parties. What's up with her?"

Cassie said, "I don't know. She never talks about that."

Dan said, "This plumber who worked on her house is trying to fix her up with her contractor!"

Matt said, "Who, Walt?" Dan nodded.

He said with a conspiratorial tone, "She does seem a little concerned about our troubles with him. Maybe *too* concerned!"

That caught Cassie's attention, "Wait, what? Who's Walt?"

Matt brought her up to speed on the remodeling job from hell and how they originally found the contractor through Janet. She was intrigued and asked a lot of questions.

Suddenly, Larry was standing there. Apparently, he was looking for Cassie, but when he saw she was busy, he just said, "When you have a second," and walked off.

When he was out of earshot, Cassie said in a low voice, "It's Leisure Suit Larry! I wonder how much he heard."

Matt looked blank, but Dan understood the reference and helpfully explained that it was a new video game. Finally, Matt said, "I'd hate to break up a budding romance. Maybe I'll meet with him! He seems like a decent enough guy. But my wife will kill me."

Cassie said, "Your wife doesn't like him?" He shook his head.

Dan said, "That's kinda like saying Lady Macbeth doesn't like Duncan."

Matt replied, "Or maybe Medea doesn't like… who was it again?"

They both looked puzzled. Dan said, "Wasn't it Jason or something? Eumenides? Euripides? Eucalyptus?"

Matt could hardly stand up, "Eucalyptus! I think you meant Pyracanthus, the Greek god of fire."

Cassie interjected, "Jason and the Argonauts! That skeleton sword fight was so cool."

Dan said, "That movie came out before you were even born, didn't it?"

She said, "I don't know. My parents rented a Betamax of it last time I was home."

Dan and Matt mouthed the word Betamax silently to each other. Dan made a note, saying in a low voice to himself. "Plant some Pyracanthus in the backyard."

Cassie stood up to leave, "You guys. Okay, let me work on this!"

Matt wiped his eyes, "Eucalyptus... Oh, man! Dan, you're too much."

"That's what they all say," Dan said modestly.

They sat silently for a while. Finally, Matt said, "Speaking of Janet, I think she has a Macintosh for testing Ethernet on the Mac. Should we have her show us HyperCard and Power-Point and all the sexy new stuff on it?"

Dan said, "I'm sure we'd have to get on her calendar or something, being that she's a big mucky-muck and all."

"Before we leave the subject of TV altogether, did you see the new *Star Trek* series the other night?"

"*The Next Generation?*" replied Dan. "No, thanks. I liked the old generation just fine."

"You're a fuddy-duddy, Dan. The march of progress and all that."

"'Fraid so," said Dan, "I've seen all the original *Star Trek* episodes at least three times."

"Never gets old. Anyhow, I came by to ask if you guys had the pre-release of OS/2 yet."

"As a matter of fact, yes. Do you want it?"

"Depends. How many floppies is it?"

Dan turned back to his desk and opened a drawer. It looks like four for the basic thing. You know it only runs in text mode, right? And IBM insisted it had to run on a 286."

Matt winced, "Fucking IBM. Always stuck in the past, forever."

"And, how long has the 386 been out now?"

"A couple of years, at least. Do you have enough memory in your machine?"

"I have 2 meg. Is that enough?"

Dan looked skeptical, "It should be. Supposedly."

"So, do I have to dedicate a machine to this?"

"You mean, can you boot it as DOS so that you can do

your work?" Matt nodded. "You can always stick in a DOS boot floppy. If you mean, can the hard disk boot either one, the answer is no."

Matt looked resigned, "Oh, well. I guess that isn't too bad. Are they going to have dual-boot eventually?"

"Who knows? One would hope."

Matt took the floppies, thanked Dan, and left. Dan went back to his email. A controversy was raging. Some people apparently had too much time on their hands.

DAN HAD STARTED a mailing list called WantAds in imitation of the one at Xerox. Xerox had dozens of non-work-related lists, and he didn't want to go that far with time-wasting, but this seemed like a fairly harmless one. It was definitely useful to buy or sell stuff, find someone to house sit for you while you were on sabbatical, or ask for a good realtor.

It turned out that WantAds filled a gaping hole in 3Com'er lives that no one knew was there. Xerox had had a thriving culture of non-work-related email, going all the way back to the 70s. Dan had an officemate there who would sit by his computer waiting for the next reply to some political post so that he could jump in and answer it. He had no desire to replicate that, but he figured Xerox was a special case, and 3Com'ers couldn't possibly be that way. Classified ads in the newspaper were expensive, and you had to deal with all sorts of yucky people, but an ad within your company—well, that was safe and free.

He was wrong about the response, though. Someone would advertise something, and then everyone would argue about it all day. A parent would advertise a child's bike for sale, and people would talk about children's bikes in general, which ones were the best, how they used to ride on the streets without helmets when they were kids, and on and on.

He also noticed a phenomenon similar to people's behavior in cars—much more aggressive than they'd ever be in real life. Someone who was always circumspect and polite in person would turn into a curt little jerk on email. If they were talking about a work issue with colleagues they saw every day, they'd still be reserved and formal, but in a larger company, as 3Com was becoming, it became more common that you only knew someone from WantAds. Your entire picture of their personality came from their online behavior.

Dan felt like how Victor Frankenstein must have felt when his monster behaved badly. He could say, "I started this list, and it isn't for general discussions!" but it didn't help at all. They just kept right on while also explaining why it was okay to discuss this, and he should please shut up. Finally, he gave up.

Right now, there was a message on WantAds from Cassie. She was asking if anyone knew a good contractor. He wondered what that was about since she lived in an apartment. Oh, well. It would be interesting to see if Janet or Matt responded if they were even on WantAds

36

MUM'S THE WORD

C assie's WantAds message about contractors was an endless source of entertainment on an otherwise slow day. As usual, there were a few messages actually answering the question, followed by endless debates and stories about contractors.

As it turned out, neither Matt nor Janet said anything about it. Dan found out that neither belonged to WantAds, but Cassie didn't know that. However, she still got what she was after. When the initial flurry of replies had died down, she prodded the beast a little:

Interestingly enough, I have a good friend in high tech who's dating a contractor. She says it's a completely different experience than dating a boring old enginerd, no offense to you nerds out there!

Oh, my God. You would have thought she'd insulted the Pope or something. Dan laughed as the number of replies passed fifty. Male engineers objected to the term nerd. Women extolled the virtues of their engineer husbands. Eventually, it became more political as a few women asked why a woman couldn't earn more than her boyfriend.

Kristen, as the responsible HR person, finally became involved, telling everyone to cool it. Larry, or "Leisure Suit Larry" as Cassie called him, seemed to think some humor was called for to wrap things up:

I can't imagine why this is even an issue, anyway. Most contractors I've seen are too dumb and uneducated to even cover up their butt crack when they squat down.

A few people thought this was too inflammatory—or funny to some—to leave unanswered, but finally, the email storm died out.

Janet had to get involved, and she hated stuff like this. Kristen left her a politely worded voicemail asking her to chat with Cassie and Larry since they both reported to her. She returned the call and asked Kristen to forward the offending email traffic since she wasn't on WantAds. She knew Kristen would hate this because she had to bring up every single "RE: RE: RE: [etc.]" message and forward it, and there were a lot of them.

After a whole bunch of FWD: RE: emails, she finally sent the "that's the last of them" message. Janet called Cassie and asked her to stop by. She decided that since Cassie was in her first job out of school, she received a pass. Janet just asked her not to provoke people with hot-button issues in the future, she apologized, and that was that.

Larry was a more challenging case. He was thirtyish and should have known better. Lately, he'd been acting like *he* was going to take Janet's job when she was promoted, although she often said to herself, "*Not if I have anything to say about it.*"

She'd reserved a conference room for this since her cube didn't offer enough privacy. He sat down with a sheepish look on his face.

"So, Kristen asked me to talk to you. You probably know what this is about." He nodded. "You can't use expressions like butt crack on the corporate email system. It might not be legally obscene, but still, we have to adhere to a higher standard."

"Okay," he said. After a pause, "It *was* pretty funny, though, you have to admit."

"Actually, no, I don't," she said frostily. "I don't like making fun of people for their social class."

Larry looked chastened for a second, but then some resentment took over. "You know, I heard Dan, Matt, and Cassie talking about you in relation to some contractor."

"Me? A contractor?" Janet was shocked, but she stalled for time.

"I just caught the tail end of it. Some guy named Walt?"

Janet tried to remain impassive. She thought, "*This Larry guy really is a little snitch.*"

Finally, she was as severe as she could manage and said, "I will talk to them separately. In the meantime, my private life is not any of your business or anyone else's. Is that clear?"

"Sure. I'm sorry," standing up to leave.

She hated 3Com for its high schoolish gossip. All the little signs of it came back to her, like the time she overheard Larry and his crony, Paul, talking about some party Larry went to. Paul said, "Yeah, I heard there was a lot of boinking."

"*Boinking. Is that what they call sex now? Little adolescents!*"

People were gossiping about her romantic life or lack of one. Maybe it came with the territory of being a manager, but she still hated it. Maybe she should go back to being an engineer. Her dad, Len, would be a big help on this. He always had a calm, rational take on things. She usually talked to him on Saturday, so that would be Topic A this week.

She and Cassie had a pretty good relationship. Maybe she could just ask her what Larry might have heard. She arranged to take her to lunch tomorrow, assuring her that she wasn't in any trouble.

Cassie was in a panic even so. Why was Janet asking her to lunch *now*? Larry was missing his usual air of smoothness after meeting with Janet, so she knew something must have happened. But what? Larry probably wouldn't tell her anything, so there was no point in even asking him.

Whether to talk to Dan was another hard call. He obviously knew that Cassie had some agenda for sending those messages on WantAds because she'd done it right after leaving his cube. He didn't have the kind of relationship with either Janet or Larry that would give him any special insight. What to do?

Finally, she realized that she, Dan, and Matt had a conspiracy going, but the aim was just to make Janet happy! What the hell was wrong with that? Maybe some deception was totally justified for such a good cause. She decided just to plead ignorance if Janet asked her. She walked over to Matt's cube.

"Hey, guess who asked me to lunch tomorrow?"

Matt replied, "Who? Bill Krause?"

"Close. Janet."

Matt stood up and said, "Let's go take a walk outside." They went out and sat down by the fountain. When they were settled, he said, "So, Janet. What's all that about, do you think?"

Cassie smiled, "Well, I can guess it had something to do with Larry's message, based on him acting all upset after talking to her."

Matt thought for a long time, and then a sly smile appeared, "You planned all this, didn't you, young lady?"

Cassie was caught. She put both hands over her mouth, "*Moi?* How would I plan something like this?"

"Well, let's see," said Matt, looking up. "There was the message on WantAds asking for a contractor. Why would you need a contractor anyway? You don't own a house."

"I was asking for a friend!" she protested.

"Uh-huh. And then, there was the message about your, um, friend who's dating a contractor."

"It's true! I can give you her name if you want."

"Right. How convenient when we were just talking about Janet and *her* contractor!"

Cassie giggled, "I have no idea what you're talking about!"

"Okey-dokey, then! So if Janet asks if you know what's going on, you don't have any clue, right?"

"I really don't!" she insisted. "And if you and this Walt guy just *happened* to reach some kind of understanding, that would be just good business for both of you."

"I *always* aim for a win-win solution!" he agreed.

They both chuckled and walked back inside. Matt called Walt, who was suspicious but agreed to meet Matt tomorrow one-on-one, away from the house. The fact that Miriam would not be there gave Walt some encouragement.

THAT NIGHT, Matt told Miriam he was meeting Walt tomorrow. She was intensely interested, "What time tomorrow?"

"Around 9:30."

"You know that's my weekly staff meeting! Can't you move it?"

Matt looked apologetic, "No, Walt called and said that was the only time he had free all week! I asked if there wasn't some way you could be there, too, but he was pretty firm on that."

Miriam looked suspicious and said, "Shouldn't we have our lawyer there?"

Matt could tell Miriam was in one of her combative moods. She'd been the one who talked up the idea of going to court. Once it was settled, she'd be pissed for a while, but then, she'd accept it and move on, especially if a different contractor finished the job.

"Oh, then we *know* nothing will get done! Don't worry… I'm just going to see if we can't save us both a whole lot of time and money."

Miriam argued and argued but to no avail. Matt and Walt were going to meet, and that was that. She told him multiple times not to give away the farm. He promised he wouldn't.

The next morning, Matt met Walt at the Hobee's on Central in Mountain View. They both ordered a slice of coffee cake and talked about the weather, dogs, and other neutral topics. Then Matt got down to business.

"So, this dispute about the remodeling job."

Walt said, "Matt, I'm sorry as hell it's reached this point. I always try to leave the client happy, and if there's something I can do to make all this right…"

Matt interrupted, being careful not to mention Miriam. "I know, Walt. I'm sorry, too. I think you've always been straight with us. You told us remodeling an Eichler was always iffy. What can we do?"

Walt thought for a long time. Was he dealing with Matt and Miriam here or just Matt? And did he really want to finish the job, or would he rather take the money and say goodbye forever?

"Well… if you'd like me to finish what we started, that would be my preference. But if you and Miriam would rather go with a different contractor, I certainly understand." He didn't mention, "And pay what you owe" on the second option. He figured that was *probably* understood already.

Matt said, "Understood. I know we changed the job after

you started, and you've bent over backwards to accommodate us."

"*You got that right!*" But instead, he just said, "Oh, it happens all the time. Don't worry about it. No one knows exactly what they want when they start."

Matt smiled, "That's a relief! We've never done anything like this remodeling before." Walt waited. Matt said, taking out his checkbook, "So, how much do we owe for the work so far?"

Walt reached into his briefcase for a folder labeled Feingold. He opened it and slid an invoice over to Matt.

"$4,134.75," said Matt as he wrote out the check. He tore it off and handed it over to Walt. Walt put it in the folder and reached out his hand. They shook.

"Pleasure doing business with you, sir!" said Walt.

The waitress came by with the pot of coffee and refilled their cups.

"Can I bring you gentlemen anything else?"

Matt thanked her and asked her to give them a few more minutes.

"I'm glad we can get rid of the lawyers!" he said as Walt smiled. "If you have a few minutes, I have something totally unrelated to bring up." Walt looked surprised. "Janet Saunders."

"Yeah, I told her not to blame herself for this, but she won't listen!" Walt said, laughing.

"One of your friends thinks you should ask her out!" he exhaled. "There, I said it!"

"Who? Pete? I'll kill him!"

Matt said, "I don't know who Pete is, but maybe that's his name."

"Pete needs to learn to mind his own business. I don't date clients," said Walt without any sense of anger. "He's getting married himself, and I'm his best man. He must want everyone to be as miserable as he is."

Matt didn't think arguing was going to accomplish anything right now. Instead, he motioned to the waitress for the check, and she directed him to pay at the counter.

"Well, I've been married for a while, so I can't say I'm current with things anymore. But what would be your reaction if *she* asked *you* out? Women do that nowadays."

Walt had never experienced that himself and wasn't sure he liked the idea.

"Hmm. Not sure I'd go for that!" he said as they stood up.

They walked out the door and shook hands again. Walt thanked Matt for the check.

While driving to work, Matt thought about the last part of their conversation. *"At least I planted the seed!"* Now, Walt would be thinking Janet was going to ask him out, even though Matt didn't say that, and most likely she wouldn't. He patted himself on the back for that.

As for Miriam, she would be pissed, no doubt about that. When he reached his desk, the message light on the phone was blinking. It had to be her, checking up on him. He didn't listen to the message right away.

37

PROBLEMS SOLVED

M iriam was indeed pissed at Matt—*royally* pissed. She screamed when he told her he'd given Walt the check. He let her go on, and on, and on. Hadn't they discussed this endlessly? Hadn't they agreed that this guy had to be made to pay? Why did Matt do this without checking with her first?

Finally, he shifted the conversation to finding a new contractor. She refused to discuss this right away and said they could talk about it more when he came home. He had a feeling that by then, she would have thrown herself into finding someone else and made Walt a bad memory. Mission accomplished, maybe.

Meantime, he dropped by Dan's cube to tell him the good news. "Hey, I did my part on the Walt bit! It's all settled."

Dan was puzzled, "Walt? Remind me."

"You know, the contractor Janet likes, and we're trying to play *yenta* with."

"Oh, *that* Walt! It all comes back. Good work there, buddy!" They slapped hands.

Matt said, "Now what do we do?"

"You're asking *me*, the life-long bachelor?"

"Don't undersell yourself. Anyhow, I thought maybe we should ask Janet to show us HyperCard and PowerPoint on her Mac, so at least we have an excuse for talking to her."

"Oh, yeah, I forgot about those things. Okay, I'll send her an email."

Matt left, and Dan sent an email to Janet. She set up a meeting for the next week with all her group as well. Meanwhile, Dan did what research he could.

The Computer Chronicles was a show on PBS about computers, and they had done a show on HyperCard recently. He usually didn't watch it, but he watched this episode. As a guest, it featured Bill Atkinson, the famous Macintosh graphics expert and inventor of HyperCard. You made these cards, and you could set up all kinds of links from card to card so that you could go through the material in non-linear ways. Supposedly, a non-programmer could create a HyperCard stack, although Dan felt like he'd heard that one before. A new application was suitable for non-programmers, but somehow a programmer always ended up being required anyway.

Apple was always creating these cutesy things that made Mac users feel immensely superior to mere Windows people. Meantime, Bill Gates and Microsoft ended up getting all the users and making all the money. Apple considered itself too morally pure to be compatible with Windows in anything. Dan was sure HyperCard was just another instance of this. But still, Apple sometimes had good ideas, so it was worth at least learning about this.

PowerPoint was something else again. Microsoft had acquired the company, which meant that it would be on Windows, not just Mac. Dan couldn't remember how many times he'd given a presentation by printing out the hard copies and then loading blank transparencies in the paper tray of the copier and copying the material onto them. At the talk, you'd put the transparencies onto an overhead projector one by one. The transparencies were always heavy and awkward and stuck together, and afterward, you might need to save them for later. Maybe you had 3-hole-punched holders to keep the slides in so that you could put them in a binder. But then the slides stuck in the holders. It sucked.

If you were a hotshot executive, you could pay for a service to make 35mm slides, which were gorgeous, but that was super-expensive, and Dan had never done it. So at least, this was a real need they were addressing.

But going from the computer onto a screen—how would you do that? He was dying to know if they'd solved that problem. Next week he would find out.

Janet kept thinking about people gossiping about her. She couldn't wait for Saturday for her regular call with her dad. Finally, it came.

After the usual news and status checks, she told him the situation. He said, "So, this Larry guy said that your friends, if that's the word, were scheming to fix you up with someone?"

"Yeah, something like that."

"Why is he telling you this? He sounds like a little brown-noser to me!"

She laughed, "That's what I'm thinking, too. But he's the type who goes around and gossips with everyone. That's the part I can't stand."

"Yeah, I don't blame you. Can you talk to Personnel about him?"

"We call it Human Resources, Dad."

"Oh, right. HR. Anyhow, he has no business gossiping about your private life. That should earn him a stiff warning at least."

"Yeah. And the other people, too. I'm sorry I ever gave Matt the name of my contractor!"

"Wait a second! Is that the guy I met that time in the hardware store?"

"Right. Walt," she confirmed.

"Walt. Right. Nice guy!"

"Yeah, we get along, but he and Matt's wife… let's just say they did not!"

"That's not your problem, though," said Len.

"I *guess* not, but I still feel responsible."

Len thought for a while. Something didn't add up here. "Okay, let's assume you talk to HR, and they tell Larry if he gossips about you, there will be consequences. Problem solved?"

"Yeah… I guess so."

"But there's something else?"

Dad could always tell when she was holding back. He went on, "Honey, don't kill me for this, but would you want Walt to ask you out?"

"Oh, Dad, He's a contractor!"

"So he's beneath you. Is that what you're saying?"

"No, of course not!" she said quickly. She didn't like how that sounded. "I probably make three times what he makes!"

"So, he'll let you pay for dinner occasionally! Anyway, this is 1987. I've heard this happens sometimes."

"It has seemed to be a problem with some of the guys I've met since Ken. They never say it, but I can tell it's there. They can't accept that I have a more responsible job than they do."

"Well… nothing you can do for them, right? You've been very successful, and you're not going to give that up."

"No."

"No. Maybe Walt's business has good years and bad years. Maybe some years, he makes more than you do! Those guys sure charge enough." She laughed. "Let me ask you this, sweetie. Do you like Walt?"

Janet stopped herself from answering yes too quickly. She knew he meant, "Do you like him *that* way?" She hadn't thought about it. "I don't know. You met him. He's handsome."

"Yes, he is," agreed Len.

"He's not like the guys I usually meet."

"Yeah, I'm sure he's not! Is that a good thing?"

"It would be interesting to go out with him, let's say that. I just never really thought about him that way."

"Interesting. Now, there's a good word," said Len. "So, what do you have to lose? He has my blessing if that's worth anything."

"Oh, Dad. This is like high school when my dates had to come in and meet you!"

Len laughed, "That was as awkward for me as it was for them. Poor guys!"

"Do you remember Ernie Lett, the skinny guy with the pimples?"

"You'll have to narrow it down for me. That was all of them!" They both laughed and laughed and recalled all the geeky guys she'd gone out with.

Len didn't push on the topic of Walt. He thought he'd done enough for now.

Janet thought about Walt off and on all weekend. When she was growing up, the tough guys used to make fun of other guys they considered pussies. Or worse names. She was pretty sure no one would have said that about Walt. He wouldn't have been one of the name-callers, but he wouldn't be their target, either.

He went to college for a while, but he dropped out. He never said much about that. Janet gathered that he just valued his independence and didn't like being bossed around. Maybe if he'd had a lower draft number, he'd have gone into the military, but he was safe, so he went to work in construction.

But she'd feel weird about asking *him* out! Would he think, *"Here's this rich lady who can marry a CEO and live in Atherton if she wants. What does she want with a guy like me? I didn't even finish college."*

So, somehow it had to be Walt's idea. But how was that going to happen? She didn't even see him regularly to drop a hint. Did they know anyone in common? She racked her brain all weekend.

THAT SAME WEEKEND, Matt and Miriam asked everyone they knew, including their neighbors, for contractor recommendations. Miriam seemed driven, just as Matt had hoped. Now that she had a goal to work toward, she concentrated on that instead of her grievances with Walt.

They discovered a lot of the neighbors had similar horror stories. All of them seemed to look down on the contractors and their helpers and considered them a very unfortunate necessity. One had even written into the contract that they couldn't have a radio playing while they worked.

Their next-door neighbors, Jessie and Kate, told Miriam their own stories. Matt couldn't stand them, so he made a point to be busy whenever they were around. Jessie and Kate were former hippies in their forties who both taught at Gunn High School. They had been in their house for twenty years and ranted at every opportunity about these techies ruining Palo Alto and how two teachers like them couldn't afford to buy a house there anymore. They wore tie-dyed t-shirts and would happily tell you how Kate had taken guitar lessons from Jerry Garcia back in the early 60s before the Grateful Dead started.

Jessie had been the most insistent of all the neighbors in complaining about Mookie's occasional barking. He would leave little notes in their mailbox whenever it happened, full of passive-aggressive hints of hassles he'd prefer to avoid, so would they please deal with this problem? Since Mookie was *in* the house at the time and it was during the day, Matt didn't quite see why it was a problem at all.

Jessie's own banjo playing in the yard used to annoy Matt and Miriam, especially since his playing was terrible. But somehow, that didn't enter into Jessie's calculations of neighborliness. They were full of stories about bad contractors who had tried to take advantage of them. Miriam had asked them before if they had any *good* recommendations, and they didn't then and still didn't.

She tried the other neighbors. Some she had tried before and a few new ones. Finally, she heard about a guy named Bill who lived in Menlo Park and had been around for thirty years. The fact that he was a local seemed to factor heavily in the good estimations. They were warned Bill was very busy, so they would be lucky to get time on his calendar. Nonetheless, Miriam called him, and Bill came over on Monday night, declined to comment on the work so far, and gave them an estimate for what it would cost to finish the job. It was actually *more* than Walt had been estimating, but Miriam thought it was a good deal anyway.

"*One problem solved,*" thought Matt. But how the hell were they going to get Walt and Janet together? He still had no clue about that one. Maybe they should have a party and invite them both? But Miriam would never go for that.

Miriam stayed pissed off about Walt, unbeknownst to Matt, who assumed they had moved on. But no. She was still fuming about how Matt had settled their dispute with Walt without asking her. In her mind, Walt had condescended to her and failed to be honest about how much all her changes would cost. He'd surprised them with big bills that seemed way out of line, and he'd failed to return her phone calls for days. She was ready to stiff him and force *him* to sue. But Matt just gave him his check, and she never saw him again.

Her boss at the clinic, Abigail, was a good sounding board in all this. Abigail had been through a divorce a long time ago, and most of their clients in the clinic were divorced or about to be, so she was well acquainted with marital troubles. Palo Alto was full of divorced women with children, who formed the bulk of their practice. Some were well-off after the divorce, and usually, they had kept the house. For some, that was all they had. Abigail had definite ideas about how that came about.

Miriam decided to talk to her. She began by recounting the Walt story. Abigail asked a few questions and then said, "So, Miriam, how are you feeling about the marriage now?"

"Well, I'm not sure. He seems to be more full of himself now that he's becoming a Silicon Valley bigshot. I don't feel like my opinions count anymore."

"Is he, though? Does he have a lot of stock options in… what company is it again? 3Com?"

"He does, but when I look in the paper, the stock is never doing much. So, I don't know how much we're going to get out of it."

"No, 3Com kinda blew it," said Abigail. Almost everyone in the Valley kept tabs on all the local companies, so she knew what the stock was doing as well as Miriam did.

"How long has he been there?"

"It's going on three years now," said Miriam.

"Three years. So, three-fourths vested?" Miriam nodded. "It might be time for him to look around a little."

"Yeah, I try to tell him that."

"He doesn't listen?" Miriam shook her head. Abigail paused, and then, "I'll tell you, and this is hard to hear. In California, which is a community property state, if he makes a lot of money while you're married, you're entitled to half. Whatever he makes *after* a divorce, *if* you went ahead and did that, he'd keep all of it."

"And so?"

"And so, you want him to make the money *now*. I have clients where the guy became a VP at some startup that

IPO'ed, and he was set for life. And so was she after the divorce. You met Suzanne Maris?" Miriam nodded. Suzanne always drove her kids to the office in a big black BMW. "Her husband was a founder of Quibex Technology or something like that. It's so hard to keep track of all these names. Anyway, they IPO'ed, the lockup came off..."

"Lockup?" interrupted Miriam.

"That's what keeps everyone on the inside from selling all their shares immediately. It's usually six months or so. Anyway, he cashed in, and then he divorced her. Half of all that money was hers. You notice she dresses pretty well?"

"I'll say. Those shoes of hers..." Miriam thought again of Suzanne's Manolo Blahniks, that time she was dressed for a charity affair.

"Right," she said, glancing at her watch, "I have a client in a few minutes. Think about it!"

Miriam did. She *had* to get Matt out of 3Com and into some company that would make her rich, whether they stayed married or not. 3Com wasn't going to do it. If he did stay there, he'd have to start climbing the corporate ladder.

ON MONDAY MORNING, Cassie dropped by Dan's cube for their regular email and networking tutorial. She was also dying to tell him about her lunch with Janet. "So, did Matt tell you Janet asked me to lunch last week?"

"How nice for you!" said Dan, who was inordinately fond of that expression.

She smirked, "How *very* nice for me. She heard something from Leisure Suit Larry about our *yenta* plans for her and her contractor."

"Larry? How would he know about it unless you told him?"

"Yeah, like I'm going to tell *him* anything. I think he overheard us talking."

Dan absorbed that. Finally, he asked, "So anyway, what did she say? And what did *you* say?"

Cassie was thoughtful, "It wasn't what I was expecting."

"No?"

"No. She said she likes Walt. I felt like I was back in high school again!"

Dan laughed, remembering how a girl's girlfriends would do the dirty work of telling some guy that she liked him, in case he hadn't already figured it out.

"Oh, boy. Do you have to go and tell Walt now?"

She laughed, "I don't even know the guy! How would I do that?"

"I don't know him either, just his friend Pete, the plumber."

They both pondered the problem. She said, "As I recall, this all started with you telling us what Pete said about it."

"Yeah... I don't suppose she can just ask him out? I've heard that happens nowadays."

Cassie said, "Yeah, I don't think she wants to do that."

Dan admitted that a contractor asking his client out might seem a little weird. Of course, this was California.

Cassie finally said, "Fine. We have to get them together somehow without either one of them thinking it's a fixup."

"I'm glad you're handling this!" said Dan with a smirk.

"*We're* handling it, along with Matt. Anyway, how was your weekend?"

Dan looked pained, "Well... I went to Cubberley Auditorium on Saturday night for dancing lessons. Have you ever been?"

Cassie brightened, "Cubberley? I used to go there all the time! Are you into dancing?"

"No, but it *is* a way to meet women. My parents actually

met while dancing, so you would think I'd inherit some of that. But no, I don't really like it."

"Yeah, typical guy. A lot of times, the girls have to dance with each other!"

"So, you're into it?"

"Am I? I have a bunch of girlfriends, and we all go up to the Avenue Ballroom in the City every week to jitterbug!"

Dan searched his memory. "Oh yeah, I think they taught jitterbug one night at Cubberley. Usually, I can remember the basic step of each dance, but I forget all the variations, and then I feel stupid in the open dancing."

"Do you have a good lead?"

Dan looked embarrassed, "Probably not. The problem with those lessons is, the girl already knows what you're going to do, so you don't have to lead her."

"Yeah. It's easier for the girl. You just have to follow his lead."

"Anyway... let's talk about connection-oriented protocols like email," he said, changing the topic back to networking— the thing they were paid for.

He thought about Pete, his only connection to Walt. He'd have to call Pete.

38

SOMETHING NEW AND SOMETHING OLD

Matt and Dan sat down in the small conference room where Janet was giving her Mac presentation. She was going to show them some sexy new Apple technology, if that term wasn't a redundancy. Her entire group was coming, plus a couple of the technical writers.

She and Cassie had wheeled in a special cart with the Mac on the lower shelf and a large monitor on top. This would have been too small for a very large group to see, but for this audience, it was okay.

Cassie took the keyboard and mouse, and soon, there was color on the screen! She beamed and sat down. When everyone arrived, Janet spoke. "Welcome, everyone. Matt and Dan asked me to demo some of the new Mac stuff, and of course, you know that 3Com is developing for the Mac, too."

Cassie knew her lines, "So, Janet, where's the overhead projector?"

"I'm glad you asked, Cassie! We don't need one to show PowerPoint, although it helps."

"What's PowerPoint, Janet?" This was becoming too scripted, Dan thought.

"Another great question! How *do* you manage to keep coming up with those?"

"Just talented that way," said Cassie modestly.

"PowerPoint is one of the applications we're going to demo today. If you follow the news, you know that Microsoft acquired a company called Forethought, which has a new tool for giving presentations. It's only for the Mac right now, but you know if Microsoft bought it, it'll be on Windows. Here's the first slide." She nodded to Cassie and narrated, "You notice that the presentation file is stored on a 3Server. This is old hat for us PC people, but now, the Mac is also going to have Ethernet."

It was underwhelming—a black-and-white "page" filled the screen with a heading and some bullet points under it that summarized what Janet was going to say. "*Wait, what happened to the color?*"

"I'm giving this presentation without using an overhead projector because we have a small group. Maybe someday, we'll have video directly from the computer," she said.

"So right now, you still have to make transparencies, right?" asked Larry.

"Unfortunately, Larry, that's correct. Although, you can preview the presentation on the screen like we're doing now."

The next slide came up without Janet or Cassie doing anything. "You also notice it advances from slide to slide automatically. Of course, you can do it manually like this." Cassie hit a button. "I don't have a clicker, but you can use a remote control. And notice each slide has the same header."

A dialog appeared, allowing you to control the interval between slides or to make it manual. Janet pointed out the features. So far, the response was tepid.

Larry said, "So, right now we use Word or some other application to make a bunch of pages and print them and then copy them to transparencies. How is this better? I can see for a small audience like this where you don't have to project."

Cassie said, "But if you imagine a decent video projector, someday…"

Larry echoed the "someday."

Janet said, "I think this might grow into something big someday. Right now, you're right. It's not that impressive, but maybe we're not the best audience for it."

Dan asked who the best audience was.

"People who routinely give talks, such as marketers or salespeople. Sometimes, it *is* only to a few people like if they're rehearsing or showing it to a customer."

Everyone seemed satisfied with that. She moved on, "And now, we have HyperCard!"

Dan assumed the voice of Stewart Cheifet, the host of *The Computer Chronicles*, "HyperCard? What *is* it? It's not hyper. It's not even a card!" Everyone laughed.

"Thanks for that, Dan!" said Janet. "You're right. It's not quite system software. It's not quite application software!" More laughter. Cassie was annoyed that she wasn't assigned those lines.

Janet brought up *The Complete Car Cost Guide* since that was the example featured on *The Computer Chronicles*. She showed how you could click on the Ford logo, and it brought up the card for Fords. Hypertext was a concept that Ted Nelson had coined years and years ago, and Matt mentioned that he met Ted that summer when he worked at DataPoint.

Cassie showed how a user, potentially a non-programmer, could create a HyperCard stack. She had gotten deep into it and would have happily worked on it full-time if Janet let her. There were many questions about the "programming" you had to do to create a card stack.

Not everyone had seen the show on *The Computer Chronicles* about HyperCard, so Janet went through some of the graphical things it could do. For example, you could click on the wheel of a carriage, and it showed you the other cards that had a wheel on them. On the show, Bill Atkinson said there were several hundred card stacks already on the public networks, and the term public networks was itself interesting. Apparently, Cassie had gone onto CompuServe at home, which Dan had heard of but never tried. Someone had once asked him if they could build an email gateway for CompuServe mail, and he thought it might be fun, but Marketing didn't think anyone would buy it.

It was all quite interesting. Larry didn't see how HyperCard was relevant to his job, and Janet agreed and said he was free to go if he had something else to do. He took her up on that and left.

Dan asked Barb, the lead technical writer, if they would be creating HyperCard stacks for the Mac Ethernet instead of distributing printed manuals. She ducked the question and said they'd have to look into it.

AFTER THE MEETING, Dan, Matt, and Cassie went out for a walk around the complex to conspire together, an activity they enjoyed immensely. Cassie told Matt that Janet was surprisingly open to the idea of going out with Walt, and Matt told them both that he had brought it up with Walt and was stonewalled. But he definitely had the feeling that Walt might have some attraction, at least in some universe.

Cassie said, "Okay, we have a problem here in *this* universe, guys. How are we going to solve it? I don't even know Walt."

Dan and Matt both stroked their chins and pondered. Matt said he didn't have any reason to call Walt again since they'd settled their business. He'd feel like a pimp if he pushed Janet on him again.

Dan said, "Well, I know his friend Pete. He said Walt's going to be the best man at his wedding."

Matt said, "Maybe he should invite Janet as well!"

"Why would he do that? He barely knows her."

Dan agreed and was silent again. He thought maybe Janet could jump out of a cake at the bachelor party but restrained himself from suggesting it.

Finally, Cassie had an inspiration, "A wedding? What do they have at every wedding reception?"

Matt answered, "Food?"

"Besides food?"

Dan saw where she was going, although he still didn't quite see how it helped. "Dancing? But we already said Janet wouldn't be at the wedding!"

Cassie was impatient, "But Pete could tell Walt he has to brush up on his ballroom dancing! They could go to Cubberley, and Janet could be there!"

"Genius, assuming Walt goes for it!" said Dan. "But does Janet even go dancing? And how do you know she'd be there the same night?"

"Leave that to me," said Cassie triumphantly.

Matt said, "I think we have a plan. Dan, you must get Walt to Cubberley, and Cassie, you have to get Janet. And I have nothing to do!"

Dan said, "We'll think of something for you. Maybe you and your wife can go there that night, too."

Cassie said, "It'll be a dance party! Thanks, everyone."

39

THE PLOT IS IN MOTION

D an took a vacation in October, and it was his first trip to Seattle. He went on an organized bike trip in the San Juan Islands, and it was definitely not a bare-bones backpacking trip. They were staying in nice Bed & Breakfasts and eating in good restaurants every night. A van with lunch, spare parts, snacks, and their luggage followed them.

There were nine people on the trip. Some of them brought their own bikes, but he thought it was way too much hassle to package up his bike as baggage. So, he simply rented one of the tour company's bikes. They were nice bikes, and the best thing was, if you had a flat, the van had spare wheels for them. The van driver could just swap one in, so you were on your way again in no time. And Dan had two flats during the week.

On Orcas Island, six of the nine riders, including Dan, rode to the top of Mount Constitution, twenty-four-hundred-feet high. The guide said that was the strongest group he'd ever led. They reached the top in the late afternoon, and it was windy and cold up there. The view was spectacular, however.

He flew back on Monday morning and went straight to work from the airport. It was October 19, and the stock market crashed that day by an astounding twenty-two percent, the worst day ever on Wall Street, with $500 billion in paper losses. Dan realized again that you could be right on the fundamentals but wrong on the timing. He'd bought a put option on the S&P 500 so that if the market went down, he'd make money. Unfortunately, this was a few months before the crash, and he lost money on it. Had he just waited until last week, he'd have made a ton of money. Sigh.

Matt and Cassie put the Janet-Walt plot on hold while Dan was away. His action item had been to talk to Pete and get him to drag Walt to the dance lessons. So until then, the others couldn't do much.

When he arrived at 3Com, everyone was freaking out about the stock market. Matt dropped by his cube, "Hey, have you seen the stock market?"

"Um, yeah, hard to miss. I hope you're not too heavily invested."

"Me? I have no money. 3Com stock is tanking. Down over four points."

Dan winced, "Ow! Anyway, I guess you and Cassie are waiting for me to talk to Pete?" Matt nodded. "Okay. Let me think of some plumbing task for him to do at my house. What else is going on?"

"Oh, let's see. You might be visiting Wang Labs! They were here, and we told them you were the person they really wanted."

"Wang? How nice for me. What do they want?"

"Email, I think."

"And, they have their own stupid email system, I suppose?"

"Presumably. We didn't go into much detail with them."

Dan absorbed all this. Wang was in Lowell, Massachusetts, a decaying factory town whose best days had been a century ago. But 3Com's marketing people would probably make Wang come to California again to be sure there was a possible business deal. Jeff, his Product Manager *du jour*, would handle it.

"I'll talk to Jeff. What else?"

They talked for a long time about the latest activity in the Internet Engineering Task Force, IETF. There was always a lot going on in IETF, whereas the official international standards bodies that produced X.400 and X.500, run by the telephone companies, moved at a more stately pace suitable for international diplomacy. Nonetheless, the official standards were still given lip service by many in the IETF, who always had groups figuring out how the Internet would work with them, assuming it ever needed to. Dan and Matt were nominally concerned with all this, but they found almost no one else at 3Com was. This gave a slightly surrealistic tinge to their discussions. They knew the company didn't really care, but it wasn't ready to just stop it either.

There had been a lot of IETF activity about domain names and how to keep track of addresses—this was a hot topic. The top-level names, like .COM, .MIL, .EDU, and the others had been defined for several years now. Universities had a domain name ending in .EDU, companies like 3Com were in .COM, non-profit institutions were in .ORG, and so on. This was enough formality to start things moving, which was the operative philosophy in the IETF—rough consensus and running code. The official standards groups debated endlessly about the *proper* way to do everything for the next one hundred years, while the IETF just went ahead and did something for *right now*. The phone companies figured everyone would just wait for them to create the rules, but unfortunately, many people didn't want to wait.

Dan felt vaguely depressed, and he'd only been back from vacation for an hour. The Internet was happening. Besides the official IETF, there had been an Interop conference in

Monterey, California, where the various companies and universities met and tested their TCP implementations against each other. This procedure was sometimes called a "bakeoff." It sounded like fun.

He felt the Interop enthusiasm every time he read about it. It was a club, the Internet Club, where you were closer to your colleagues from other companies than to most people at your own. Dan wanted into the club. 3Com executives didn't share the excitement, however. The executives they talked to at other companies all thought of the Internet as just something for a bunch of grad students with their Unix machines.

For 3Com, the world was all about PCs and the software that got you on the network, not about the network itself. The deal with Microsoft was a prime example. People at Bridge were quitting steadily since the merger had clearly failed. Cisco hired a lot of them and was booming. 3Com was selling Ethernet adapter cards by the trainload and filling up their four-building campus with new hires. Yet inside the company, people were whispering, "What happens when PCs come with Ethernet already built-in?" The executives scoffed and claimed they'd already planned for that.

Dan and Matt had covered all this before. Dan said, "So, nothing much new, huh?"

"Nope. Same shit, different day. The economy is going to hell."

"Nah, it's just the stock market," said Dan. Matt tended to a more apocalyptic view of things, he knew. Matt left.

He thought of the kitchen faucet at his house that he wanted replaced and called Pete. There was no answer, but Dan left a message. Then, he went by Cassie's cube, and finding her out, he walked around until he saw her head over the walls of someone's cube. He drew her attention and went back to his cube. A few minutes later, she came by.

"Hey, how was your trip?"

"It was great! Have you ever been to the San Juan Islands?"

"No, where are they?"

"Seattle area. Just beautiful. And almost no rain!"

"No rain in Seattle? You *did* have a good trip!"

"Yeah. Anyway, I just called Walt's friend, Pete, so we can advance our little scheme!"

Cassie giggled, "Our little scheme... I've been telling Janet about ballroom dancing every chance I can."

"Yeah? How's that going?"

"It's a tough sell, but I think I'm making progress. She said she always loved the Fred Astaire movies, especially *Shall We Dance.*"

"Great movies. They make every guy feel clumsy."

"And badly dressed!" said Cassie, looking pointedly at his shoes.

"Yeah, all the old movies do that. Only tramps and hobos dressed like we do now."

"I want her to go up to him and say, 'Shall we dance, Mr. Campbell?'"

Dan laughed out loud, "We can hope. Anyhow, keep working on her."

Cassie left. A few days later, Pete was at Dan's house to install the new faucet Dan had bought. It was straightforward, and Pete finished it in less than half an hour. They sat down at his kitchen table while Dan wrote out the check.

"So, Pete, a bunch of us at work are taking your idea to heart!"

"My idea? Which idea is that?"

"About Walt and Janet."

Pete paused, "Yeah, well, you know what they say about 'you can lead a horse to water.' If he's afraid to ask her out..." He shook his head.

"We have a plan!"

"I'm all ears."

"Well, he's going to be the best man at your wedding, right?" Pete nodded. "And you will have to dance at the reception, right?"

Pete thought he knew where this was going. "I can't invite her to the wedding. You can't believe how carefully her mother is going over the guest list. I barely know Janet."

"That's what we figured. But what if you told him he needs to learn some dance steps so that he doesn't make a fool of himself?"

Pete guffawed, "Which he will. But what's the plan?"

Dan explained that there was a weekly dance at Cubberley Auditorium in Palo Alto with lessons. If Pete could take Walt to it, they'd get Janet there as well. Then the magic would happen!

"Well… I suppose that *might* work. So, I have to ask Walt to go dancing with me?"

Dan chuckled, "Don't put it like that! Just say you both need to brush up, and it'll be less painful if you go together."

"My God, is he ever going to owe me *if* this works out!"

Pete and Dan agreed on a possible date when this could happen and agreed to keep each other posted.

40

AT THE DANCE

The monumental Saturday night had arrived. Pete had cajoled Walt into going to the dance lessons at Cubberley with him, probably with the aid of threats and blackmail, but Dan preferred not to think about the means.

Cassie had convinced Janet that she should go too, and Cassie would be there for moral support. Dan went. Cassie's boyfriend hated dancing and could not be coerced by any means, and Dan thought she could maybe teach *him* something about dancing. He and Cassie had gamed out how on that enchanted evening Janet would see Walt across a crowded room during Ladies' Choice, cross over, and ask him to dance. Dan had started trying to write a song about it. He found that this songwriting business was harder than it looked.

Matt wanted to go, but he'd need to take Miriam, who hated Walt. Bad idea! He told Dan to call him afterward and tell him how it went.

Cubberley was on Middlefield Road in southern Palo Alto. It had been a high school from the 1950s until 1979, a period when Palo Alto had a lot of Baby Boomers with children. The population grew older, and richer and new young families did not move in, so they didn't need the school anymore. Rather than bulldoze it and build houses and strip malls, the city turned it into a community center, and the gymnasium was now home to ballroom dancing. You could still see the folded-up wooden bleachers along the walls, and it had hardwood floors, ideal for dancing. The floors still had lines painted on them for basketball, backboards retracted up out of the way, and a railing around what had been the upper deck of seats.

The school had an enormous parking lot, which it might have needed when it was a school. When Dan arrived at the gym, he could see Cassie out on the dance floor, but she didn't see him. He paid his money at the door and picked up a copy of *The Ballroom Dancer's Rag*, a little newsletter that covered all the dance news in the Bay Area, of which there was a lot. You could go dancing every night of the week if you wanted, and some of these people probably did. He sat down in one of the chairs along the wall.

The serious dancers, who were invariably dressed up, had special shoes for dancing, too flimsy to wear outside. They sat down and put them on as soon as they entered. Dan didn't own any of those, but he knew not to wear rubber-soled shoes at least.

Pete and Walt came in shortly after Dan. Walt had that "going to the dentist" look on his face. They sat down near Dan. Pete said, "Dan! You made it."

"Yeah, it never gets any easier. Hi, I'm Dan," he said, reaching over to shake hands with Walt.

Walt said, "I see you got the lecture on shoes." He was wearing a pair of black wingtips, which looked like he wore them only to weddings and funerals.

Pete said, "You two are going to be cutting the rug like Fred Astaire by the end of the night! Do they still use that expression?"

Cassie overheard that last part as she came over to greet them. She was wearing a pair of thin leather dance shoes with low heels. "Me, I say it all the time! With my parents, anyway." She introduced herself. They chatted for a few minutes, and then the music stopped, and Rob, the teacher, said over the loudspeakers, "Tonight, we're going to learn the foxtrot! Will all the men line up here and the ladies over there, and we can begin?" About thirty men and many more women, at least forty, dutifully lined up, and Rob stood in between them.

"Which lucky lady wants to be my partner?" He chose one from the lineup. Frank Sinatra's version of "The Way You Look Tonight" came on.

Dan mouthed, "Where is she?" to Cassie. Janet had not arrived. Cassie held her hands out palm up in bewilderment. Pete looked at her inquiringly, too.

Rob demonstrated the basic step for the gentleman's part —starting with the left foot, walk, walk, side, together. Then, he demonstrated the lady's part by grabbing his volunteer and leading her through it. He had all the couples try it.

Dan thought, "Okay, 4/4 time," and remembered the time he'd danced with his parents in his living room. Just to mess with his dad, he put on "Jive" by Michael Franks, which is in 5/4 time. Dad didn't care and did the foxtrot anyway. He realized that dancers are not musicians. Once, he asked a dance instructor if waltzes were in 3/4, and the instructor looked confused.

He did the basic step with his partner, and then Rob stopped the music and asked the men to move down to the next lady and do it again. He danced successively with each lady who didn't have a partner because there were not enough men, as usual.

Rob had everyone do the basic step with one more partner, and then he demonstrated the first variation, the rock step turning left. Dan's anxiety ticked up a little. He did the variation with his partner and remembered his conversation with Cassie, *"She knows what we're going to do! I don't have to lead her."*

There were more variations, and Dan kept moving down the line. When he reached Cassie, she motioned him to move on to the next lady because she was staying with Walt. Every week, some couples who didn't feel like dancing with total strangers did that, which he thought defeated the purpose of going to a public dance. But he realized that maybe in this case, Cassie had her own agenda with Walt!

Walt seemed to have relaxed a little, and Dan wished he could relax, too. With each new variation, his dance anxiety grew. Finally, the lesson was over, and Rob said there was a special exhibition tonight by an organized dance team. The women came from one end of the gym and the men from the other, all in costumes. The men wore black pants that came all the way up to their belly buttons, with black vests, white shirts, and black neckties. Dan thought they looked like a bunch of sissies.

After the team's rhumba exhibition, it was open dancing, which always started with the step they'd been taught that night. Another Sinatra tune came on, "I've Got You Under My Skin." Dan, Cassie, Pete, and Walt all gathered near the wall. Cassie went up to Walt and said, "Shall we dance, Mr. Campbell?" They headed out to the floor, Cassie holding his hand.

"*Well, at least someone used that line!*" thought Dan.

When Walt was out of earshot, Pete said, "So, where's your friend Janet?"

"Beats the hell out of me. That was Cassie's department."

Pete just shook his head, "If you knew what I had to do to get him here…"

"He's dancing with a pretty girl. It doesn't look like he hates it!"

"No," agreed Pete. "It doesn't, does it?"

One of the women Dan had danced with at the lesson came over and asked him to dance, so he left Pete alone. When he finished dancing with her, Walt and Pete had left. He was about to do the same when Cassie came over. "I'll kill her, I swear. She said she was coming."

"You're sure she knew it was tonight and not some other Saturday?" he asked.

She gave Dan a dirty look and grabbed his hand, "Come on... I'll show you something about leading."

Out on the dance floor, she instructed Dan to think of her, for the moment, as a sack of potatoes to move around. It took him a while to get the hang of it, and then when she was satisfied, she started responding more easily. He remembered the time at his house when his parents were demonstrating dancing, and Mom reacted to the stiff-armed stance he'd been taught with, "That's how you dance with someone you don't like!" She encouraged him to get belly to belly with her, but he didn't think Cassie would appreciate that level of familiarity.

In his parents' day, the dance halls employed special monitors to keep the dancers in line. Whereas in the old movies, you'd see wild dancing where the man flung the woman around in circles. Dad said if you tried something like that back then, a monitor would tap you on the shoulder. The halls also paid some men who were good dancers to informally teach people and dance with the single ladies, and Dad had been one of those guys. Dan thought he must not have inherited whatever genes those were.

He never stayed very late at these things, and after a few dances with Cassie, he excused himself and left. She stayed.

MATT AND MIRIAM stayed home that night. Matt was noticeably anxious, waiting to hear how it went. He didn't want to tell her they were trying to get Walt and Janet together, so he had to invent some excuse, which she didn't buy at all. She decided to just let it go for now and went into their brand-new kitchen to make popcorn.

She had to watch *The Golden Girls*. He thought the old ladies must remind Miriam of her mother and her friends. Matt took Mookie out for one last walk before bed.

On Monday, Cassie accosted Janet, "Where were you?"

"I was going to ask you the same thing. I went to the YWCA on Alma, just like you said!"

Cassie looked horrified, "Oh no! I did mention that, didn't I?"

"You did. I went there and, of course, didn't see you."

"It was supposed to be Cubberley on Saturday night!"

"Oh, well, I learned to cha-cha, anyway." She demonstrated. "How was Cubberley?"

Cassie didn't want to give away the plot, but something in her face made Janet suspicious.

"It was fine. We learned the foxtrot, which I already knew."

"Well, we'll have to try again sometime." Cassie agreed and left.

"Damn! We'll never get Walt there again. But wow, he is sexy. Janet should definitely go out with him."

41

THE TRUTH COMES OUT

D an and Matt were shooting the shit one morning in late November 1987. The scheme to bring Janet and Walt together had fallen apart when she went to the wrong dance lesson, and Cassie had to accept the blame for that. Walt had been inveigled into showing up by his friend Pete, ostensibly so that Walt could make a good showing at Pete's wedding, which was only a week away. Walt was the best man, so he wasn't in a position to say no.

The topic was too depressing to tackle straight off. But there was always work to talk about. Matt asked, "So, what's the news on Wang? Are you going out to Lowell now that it's turning colder?"

"Heh. We have to meet with them here first. And with the holidays coming up, who knows when that will happen."

Matt was simply making conversation, so he didn't pursue this. "I've been keeping up with the Internet boys. Now they have this new thing called Simple Gateway Monitoring Protocol."

"What does that do?"

"Well, if you want to check on the health of a device in the middle of the network or, God forbid, fix it, you can't just open a connection to it because the net itself might be dying. You need some way to send just one packet and hope it goes through."

"Makes sense to me. These Internet guys are really serious, aren't they?"

"They are. And what the hell are we doing here?"

Matt was always inclined to rile Dan up so that he would bring up the issue via some inflammatory email and absorb all the flak, and Matt could stay above the fray. Occasionally, Dan would catch on to what Matt was doing, and today was one of those days.

"Working with OS/2 and Microsoft, I guess. What, you don't think that's the right course?"

"Have you heard how many Bridge people are leaving?"

Dan had. "This Mr. Inside and Mr. Outside setup didn't work out, I guess," referring to Bill Krause's pollyanna-ish prediction of how he and Bill Carrico, the head of Bridge, were going to divide up the work. "Now they're all going to Cisco!"

"Cisco! I had a headhunter from there call me last week."

Dan said, "Damn! They're not calling me."

Matt smiled but ignored that, "Internetworking! That's where it's at."

Dan wasn't sure, "Yeah, maybe. But how many PCs are there and how many routers?"

"The question is… how much money can we make off those PCs before Bill Gates takes it away?"

He had a point. No one made money in PCs for long without the beast from Redmond swooping in. This was a depressing topic they'd covered before, and Dan didn't feel like going there again. He was about to change the topic when Cassie dropped in.

"Hope I'm not interrupting anything! Guess who was invited to Pete's wedding?"

Both looked surprised. Dan said, "I assume that would be you. By whom?"

"By Walt! I guess I made an impression on him at the dance."

Matt laughed, "Oh, God. You haven't told Janet, have you?"

She made the shush gesture, "No, and don't you tell her! I told Walt I have plans for that day."

Dan said, "Wow, great work, Cassie. You tell Janet the wrong place on the wrong night, and then you steal her boyfriend! What's your next trick?"

They all laughed for a long time. No one had any ideas of how to get Janet and Walt together now. Cassie wandered off.

Matt said, "Did you see where Mayor Washington in Chicago died?" He knew Dan was from Chicago.

Dan was unimpressed, "Another Daley successor bites the dust. What did he die of?"

"He had a heart attack. Haven't they had a bunch of mayors since Daley?"

Dan laughed, "Let's see… there was Bilandic. Then there was Jane Byrne. Then Harold Washington, the first black mayor. I miss all that political comedy. Chicago politics is simply entertainment for the locals."

"And then they always go to prison unless they die, right?"

"No, you're thinking of the governors." They both laughed.

"There was Governor Walker, who was anti-corruption and anti-Daley. He walked across the entire state. Get it… Walker, who walks? You can guess how that turned out."

"He went to prison?"

"Not yet. He was sentenced for bank fraud. But Daley got rid of him a long time ago."

Matt said, "Good times. But New York politics is pretty brass knuckle, too."

"Nah, they're only mean to each other."

That topic having died off, Matt wandered away. Dan checked online on the Mayor Washington story and then went back to studying the OS/2 specs. He'd be eligible for 3Com's sabbatical in only... he calculated the months until May 1989. Not that far from now. Then, he'd come back and quit. It was pretty common practice to come back from sabbatical and resign. No one wanted to give up their sabbatical, but 3Com stock wasn't doing much, so that wasn't a reason to stay. Six weeks off with pay—now *that* was a reason.

JANET HAD DECIDED WEEKS AGO, actually months ago, that she would go out with Walt if he asked. Something told her that he'd never been asked out by a woman, let alone one who made way more money than he did. "*So what am I now, a blue-collar sex toy for a rich lady?*" she envisioned him thinking. It had to be his idea.

But he never called. What to do? Her daydreaming was interrupted by Mohan knocking politely on her cubicle entrance.

"Hi, Mohan, what's up?"

"I'm sorry to bother you. Larry said he's receiving more questions from users about IBM Token Ring. He asked me, and I didn't know what to say."

She tried to hide her annoyance but realized it probably wasn't working. "Why was he asking you?"

Mohan said, "I think he thinks you're mad at him."

"Of course, I'm not mad at him! Thanks, I'll talk to him. While you're here, how is everything going?"

Mohan didn't like to talk about himself. "Oh, the same as usual. Keeping 3+Name and everything in sync with the hiring, which is becoming more all the time."

She'd heard regular complaints about new employees not receiving all the required permissions fast enough to do their jobs. More people were hired every week, and the number of applications they had to use was changing all the time, too. This was getting old, but Mohan didn't mind it at all.

"Any problems you need help with?" Mohan would never come right out and admit needing help. Janet had learned to probe to find out how things were going. They had a long conversation where she ferreted out that he really needed some programming help to automate all the work he was doing. She made a note and thanked him.

Back to Walt. She was sure Cassie knew more than she was telling her. What was up with this dance lesson thing, for instance? After that one weekend when they'd had the scheduling mixup, Cassie had been oddly silent. She decided to ask her to lunch and worm it out of her. They went to the company cafeteria. When they sat down, Janet said, "Are you still going dancing?"

"Oh yeah, jitterbugging at the Avenue Ballroom most weeks. It's pretty fun."

"I bet. Not at Cubberley anymore, though?"

Cassie tried to be casual, "Not lately. I'll probably be going again one of these days."

"Yeah, sorry about that one night."

"Yeah, well, these things happen," Cassie was becoming nervous. She tried changing the subject, "Can we talk about work for a second?"

"*She's ducking! She knows I can't say no to that,*" she thought. "Sure."

Cassie brought up the new twisted-pair Ethernet adapter since some of her users were asking about it. They talked about that for a while.

Twisted pair meant the telephone wires builders had installed for generations, whereas coax, for coaxial cable, was usually not found in offices. Up to then, the Ethernet had required coax, although it had not needed the old-fashioned thick variety for years. Opponents of Ethernet loved to allege that it required stringing coax through your office's ceiling, whereas Token Ring did not.

Somehow, this was not making Token Ring win in the market, though. Ethernet had a huge industry of suppliers and users because it was open, meaning 3Com really did not control it, so they weren't going to yank the rug out from under everyone. No one believed that IBM would ever make Token Ring as open. It just wasn't in the company's character to give up control.

Janet was more than adequately informed about all this since she heard it at almost every high-level management meeting. She held forth on the topic until Cassie's eyes glazed over. Then, she came back to what she wanted to know. "Was there anything special about that night at Cubberley? Other than my big chance to learn the foxtrot, I mean!"

Cassie said, "No, nothing special!" but it was too quick.

"Really, Cassie?"

She was caught. She thought for a long time while Janet waited. Finally, "Okay, the truth comes out."

"Mmm-hmm."

"Pete... you know Pete, right?" Janet nodded. "Pete made Walt Campbell, your contractor, go there that night to brush up on his dancing for his wedding next month."

Janet was alarmed, "Whose wedding? Walt's?"

"No, no. Pete's. Walt is his best man."

"Ah, I see. So, you were trying to fix us up?"

"Janet, we love you! We only want you to be happy."

Janet said, "I *am* happy. It's sweet of you, but I don't need people fixing me up."

Cassie thought that actually she did but simply said, "Understood, and I'm sorry. I'll stay out of your private life from now on."

"No harm done. Thanks for thinking of me. At least I learned to cha-cha!"

Cassie laughed, "One-two, cha-cha-cha!" She felt some

relief that she hadn't confessed that Walt asked her to the wedding.

Janet asked, "Anyway, how did Walt do at the wedding? Did Pete tell you?"

In reality, Walt told her how his dancing went, but Cassie didn't want to tell Janet that part.

"Yeah, Pete told me he did fine. Well, for a guy, I mean!" They both laughed. Cassie told her they went to Hawaii on their honeymoon and stayed at the Coco Palms in Kauai. Barbara was a big Elvis fan, and she had to see the lagoon where he'd been married in the movie *Blue Hawaii.* They laughed about all the bad Elvis movies they'd seen and what they were doing when they heard he had died.

Back in her cube, Janet kicked herself. If only she'd listened to the details of Cassie's invitation to the dance lesson! What was she going to do now?

If Walt weren't going to step up, she'd have to take matters into her own hands. In Victorian novels, the lady always saw the gentleman she fancied—at tea, the village dance, or some social gathering. It was easy for her to drop a handkerchief or bat her eyes discreetly. But this was real life, and she never saw Walt.

Maybe she could say, "I have an extra ticket to the symphony. Would you like to go?"

Too obvious. There must be some plausible deniability for Walt. She pondered. Then Larry interrupted her with—what else? a summons to another meeting.

42

BOTH SIDES NOW

Dan and Matt were going in different directions at work. Dan was the unquestioned technical leader of email, but that seemed like a depreciating asset. The management was increasingly divided between Ethernet hardware and LAN software, their traditional business, and internetworking hardware, now that Cisco had proven that it was a market. Email was far down on their priority list, if it appeared at all.

The original leaders of 3Com, Krause and Metcalfe, were firmly in the Ethernet camp, while the survivors of the Bridge acquisition, especially Eric Benhamou, leaned toward internetworking. The Ethernet adapter business was growing like mad, illustrating the business maxim, "Nothing is as hard to handle as failure, except success." When you have success, more and more people are hired who are committed to whatever strategy brought it about, and they refuse to believe that it could ever stop working.

It seemed to Dan that no matter what the decision was, the argument always came down to, "Do we want to be in *that* business?" A joke appeared on a piece of paper in a stairwell with the question, "How many 3Com executives does it take to change a light bulb?" The answer was, "Fifty-three. One to do it and fifty-two to argue if we really want to be in the business of changing light bulbs."

To the extent that they cared about email at all, the international standard, X.400, was something they could get behind, albeit in a lukewarm way. While all the vendors paid lip service to the Open Systems Interconnect model and professed to believe that someday we'd all be using it, you rarely saw anyone actually running OSI on their network. The Internet people were increasingly taking high-level application protocols, like X.400 for email and X.500 for directories, and figuring out ways to run them on top of TCP/IP, the Internet protocol, since fewer and fewer people cared about the lower level OSI protocols.

Even there, they ran into trouble since the standards were full of extraneous garbage that some country had insisted on, and the group leaders were bureaucrats who could never say no to anyone. In the Internet Engineering Task Force, by contrast, there was a rule of "rough consensus and running code," which created a certain economy in the results. If you were a political type who wanted something fancy, you had to explain how it would work and write the code, have someone else write it as well, and prove that yours interoperated with theirs. The IETF had senior technical people who had earned near-universal respect, and if they thought your idea was dumb, that was usually the end of it.

Still, it would be politically incorrect for a corporate leader to come out and say, "You know, this OSI thing ain't never going to happen," and so they didn't.

Dan proceeded to design a new email system that was closely modeled on X.400 but more compact and efficient so that a gateway to X.400 was a simple thing to do. This seemed like a big career achievement that it was worth staying at 3Com for.

Matt, however, threw himself into 3Com politics. He cultivated the HR people, especially Miss Smarmy, and this was a shrewd move because HR actually had power at 3Com. HR handled hiring, firing, and benefits in most tech companies, and no one even thought to consult them on business decisions. But at 3Com, they somehow convinced management that their people skills gave them a unique insight into the company culture. And it was not uncommon to see them attending large product strategy meetings as equal partners with Engineering and Marketing.

Matt thought he'd convinced Miriam that if he were a sufficiently big cheese at 3Com, then he'd be in a good position to become a VP at some startup, and then they'd *really* be rich. In fact, he only *thought* that was his idea. In reality, she'd been pushing it on him.

Matt still followed Internet developments closely. He seemed to rely on Dan to put them in perspective for him. One morning in March, he said to Dan, "So, did you see the latest RFC on Internet Management?"

Dan hadn't, and he was annoyed with himself for not keeping up with it as much as Matt did. He shook his head.

"There's a high-level decision to develop something called Simple Network Management Protocol in a hurry, for the short-term. SNMP for short."

"Simply Not My Problem?" asked Dan, making Matt laugh out loud. "So, what's simple about it?"

"Well, it's datagram-oriented, for one thing."

They had often talked about this, and it was something Dan enjoyed tutoring Cassie about. A datagram is just a single packet with no attempt to open a connection. It either gets through, or it doesn't, the Internet being unreliable. If you send a packet and don't receive a response, then you send it again. Eventually, you either receive a response, or you give up. This was something the old telephone company engineers could never quite accept. They thought the network should guarantee everything for you since that was the entire point of having a network. In the old days, people used very stupid telephones that couldn't do anything on their own, but now, they had powerful computers. "*Why not use some of that intelligence?*" the new generation of engineers believed.

Of course, quite often a software application did need a connection to put all the packets in order and ensure none were dropped. Making that work properly on a huge network with all sorts of diverse equipment, when any of the packets might fail to arrive or arrive out of order, was one of the great achievements of the Internet.

As an application designer, you could do without a connection and handle it all with datagrams *if* you were prepared to deal with all the issues a connection normally handles. It was like driving a stick-shift car with manual steering and brakes instead of a Buick with automatic transmission and power everything—not for everyone. But that was what they were doing with SNMP. Dan liked that kind of stuff.

Dan said, "Wasn't that how the Simple Gateway Monitoring Protocol, or whatever it was called, worked, too?"

"Yeah, this replaces that."

"Okay. And you said it was short-term? What's the long-term solution?"

Matt smirked, "You know the drill… it's international standards to the rescue! There's also something called CMIS, for Common Management Information Service, which is much more full-featured."

"And naturally, this CMIS thing isn't ready yet, but Any Day Now…"

"Naturally. It's object-oriented, too."

Dan pretended to hold up a box in a TV commercial, "New! With object-orientation!"

"And of course, the management will buy into this CMIS crap and force us to pay attention to it." He was hoping to goad Dan into sending some rash email about this.

Dan sighed, "Meantime, the Internet will pay lip service to it but go with SNMP and just quietly forget about the..." he made air quotes, "... standards." He continued, "I was talking to some of the old Bridge people, and they're totally into this stuff."

"Oh, yeah?"

"They're trying to start up a new product to manage a bunch of devices that all use SNMP."

This interested Dan. It sounded like something with a modern user interface. Most networking gear had an interface that could only charitably be called "functional."

"Interesting. Anyway, what are you working on now?"

Matt replied, "Finishing up this API for the Name Service. Marketing's been asking for it for a while now."

"Send it to me, and I'll try it." Matt said he would.

Later that day, Dan saw Matt's email announcing the API. It was answered by congratulations from lots of executives. Matt's product manager listed the vendors who were now going to develop exciting new applications for 3Com's network. It was a very good day for Matt.

[suggested section break]

That night, he told Miriam about it. Mookie could tell from his tone that this was good news, and maybe he'd get a treat out of it, wagging his tail enthusiastically.

"Hey, that's great!" she said. "Does this mean you will be promoted?"

Matt laughed, "Easy there, cowgirl. These things take time." He explained what the API did and why it was a big deal, but she interrupted him.

"Well, I'm really proud of you, anyway," she said and hugged him. "So, what's next?" He had no idea at the moment.

This was becoming a familiar story. Miriam took a keen interest in his career path and questioned him regularly about his superiors, what they wanted and which ones liked him, and who his rivals were. He tried to tell her that high-tech wasn't like *How to Succeed in Business Without Really Trying*, but she didn't buy it. Once, he made the mistake of taking her to a 3Com party where she could meet everyone, and for weeks, she quizzed him about all the people and what they did. He had to admit her insights about people were better than his, which was not surprising for a clinical psychologist.

Matt thought the work was mostly done. He'd announced the API, people were pleased, and next was the boring part of making it all work properly. This was the normal life of an engineer. But Miriam had other ideas.

"What did those executives I met last month have to say about it?"

He told her about some of the congratulatory messages he received. She noticed the ones who hadn't responded and asked him about them. He had to promise to talk to each one this week and take their temperature—were they pleased? Indifferent? What did they really want? She wanted a report.

Matt was inclined to think, "Well, fuck 'em," and just go on with his work. But she hammered on him that his image was the important thing, and after all, they wanted to become rich in Silicon Valley, didn't they? It seemed like everyone they knew was buying a better house in Palo Alto or moving to Portola Valley or Los Altos Hills, and did they want to stay here in this fucking Eichler their entire lives?

He thought maybe she had a point. These imbeciles in management had no attention span. They didn't care if your software worked as long as it didn't fail too publicly. And if it did, you just feigned surprise and got busy fixing it.

The official development methodology at 3Com, as at most tech companies, called for the Quality Assurance (QA) group to examine the specifications for a product, write a Test Plan to verify that it met all of them, and formally agree that it worked before it could be shipped. The QA people had a motto, "The sourness of bad quality lingers long after the sweetness of meeting the schedule is forgotten."

However, this was ideal, and the reality was often different. This formal QA process was a lot of work, and if Matt or his product manager, for example, had approached the QA group to have his API formally tested, he might have been told, "We don't have the resources for that." Or perhaps, they could have been put on the QA schedule six months later. The QA group didn't consider APIs to be part of their job.

Matt had to do his own QA, meaning he was on his honor to produce something that worked. The users would discover if it did or didn't. In the meantime, he was free to bask in the glory, go to all the management meetings, and try to keep the good news coming. This was not the world he'd been prepared for in college, but apparently, it was the real world.

JANET SAW Matt's announcement of his API and passed it on to Mohan. He'd wanted to do some programming for a while now, and this seemed like a good opportunity to automate some of his boring work. He was always doing the same tasks for everyone who was hired or promoted or quit. Now, maybe he could centralize it all in the Name Service. Mohan was excited.

Mohan was a young graduate of the India Institute of Technology in Delhi. He went to graduate school at the University of Arizona and earned his M.S. and was on a temporary visa to work here. He lived in an apartment in Sunnyvale with three other Indian men. Dan had talked to him a few times and found out that he was expecting to go back to India soon to get married to a girl his parents arranged for him. Dan always thought it would be interesting to hear more from Indians about what life had been like for them in India, but they never seemed to want to talk about it much.

Mohan had done a few utility programs during his time at 3Com, so at least he knew the basics of running the compiler, interpreting the error messages, and so forth. Janet warned him not to bother Matt too much, although a few tutorial sessions were fine. He printed out the documentation and returned to his cube to study it.

Janet was surprised to see the other Indians at 3Com appearing in his cube regularly—Anand from the Ethernet driver group, Ravi from hardware testing, and Vish from the QA group. Mohan relied on them to help him understand the documentation, and no matter how often she urged him to just talk to Matt, he would always ask them first. It almost seemed like it wasn't *his* project—it was *their* project.

After a couple of weeks of this, she tried to set up a meeting with Matt in hopes that he could answer the questions they hadn't been able to resolve. Since Anand, Ravi, and Vish were not officially on the project, she couldn't invite them because their managers might not like it. Mohan would have to brief them afterward on what was said. Dan asked to attend as well.

Matt was notably unenthusiastic about this, but he couldn't refuse, so eventually, the meeting happened. Mohan came prepared with a long list of questions, and Matt dutifully answered them all. Dan had been thinking in broader terms about joint Name Service-Mail applications, but he realized that he and Matt could probably figure that out later, and this was Mohan's meeting.

Mohan had wanted to write the entire big application, which was his ultimate goal. But Dan convinced him that he should start with what he called the "hello world" of Name Service programs. "Hello world" was the slang term for the simplest possible program you could write in any language—it didn't do anything but print out "hello, world." The point was that you had to go through all the basics of writing a program, running the compiler, and then executing it to do that, which sounds simple but often is not. The smart programmer always starts with a "hello world." It's always much easier to extend a program that's already working than to start with a big, complicated program. Dan, Janet, and Matt all agreed about this, although no one could give a good explanation for why that was.

This was a hard sell for Mohan since it seemed so trivial, but Matt and Janet both backed Dan up. It got worse from Mohan's point of view. They couldn't risk having him mess up the real corporate Name Service until his program worked, so he had to use a test system to develop on, and there wasn't one at the moment that he could use. Matt had his own, but he wasn't willing to share it. Mohan hadn't considered that either. Janet asked Matt if he could help Mohan set up a test system, and he grumbled but agreed. Janet donated a machine from her lab to use as the test Name Service.

Afterward, Anand, Ravi, and Vish came by to find out what Matt had said. They had more lengthy discussions comparing Mohan's notes with what the documentation said, and finally, Mohan felt he had enough to start writing code. Janet was relieved.

Mohan's "hello, world" equivalent was a program that inserted a user named Hello World in his Name Service and then retrieved it with a query. As Dan had predicted, this took several days and turned out to be much, much harder than Mohan had ever expected since he hit a whole host of stupid problems he'd never thought of. He felt embarrassed, but Dan assured him this was totally normal on your first try, and now he was a member of the club, and he should be proud! Persistence was an essential trait for a good programmer, and he had just displayed it.

Now, at Dan's suggestion, Mohan changed the program to retrieve a non-existent user called "Hellp, Wprld." After all, the API must behave properly with bad data as well as good data since that will happen in real life. He expected to receive an error code, but the API returned strange results instead. Mohan's first response was to double- and triple-check his code, assuming he must have done something wrong. Then, he had Anand, Ravi, and Vish do the same. Since none of them could find anything wrong, Mohan went to talk to Matt, but he was out. He sent an email instead.

Matt's reply was a little frosty. He clearly assumed that Mohan must have done something wrong and asked him to check on his code a little more. He didn't offer to come over to the lab and try to debug it. Mohan was perplexed about what to do now. He'd already checked his code multiple times, and so had his friends.

Finally, Dan asked him how it was going, and although Mohan was reluctant to get anyone in trouble, Dan ferreted out the situation and looked at the code himself. He didn't feel like getting Matt in trouble either, so he suggested the two of them go over and talk to him together.

Matt asked for more details, but clearly, he took it more seriously with Dan involved. In the end, Matt took Mohan's code and ran it on his own test server, discovered that there was, indeed, a bug, and fixed it.

Mohan had no more trouble with Matt investigating problems. Janet saw the two of them huddled over the test server many times over the next few weeks, running the debugger. Mohan was in heaven. She started figuring out how she could promote him and maybe keep him in her group since he would now be in high demand with the software QA group.

43

A SIMPLE PLAN

I t was February 11, 1988, and Janet was leafing through the *Mercury* when she saw this:

OFFICIALS FORECAST 'NORMAL' SALMON SEASON
EXPECT FISHING as usual when ocean salmon season opens Saturday, a Department of Fish and Game marine biologist says.

"Salmon fishing? Isn't that something Walt does?" Maybe she could use this. She thought about it over and over. She couldn't just invite herself onto his boat, assuming he was even going fishing. Maybe Cassie had some idea.

The next morning, Janet casually mentioned the salmon-fishing season and Walt's boat, and Cassie leaped at the chance to redeem herself. Janet had told her she didn't need people fixing her up, so Cassie had honored that. They wouldn't talk about whether this really was a fixup—they'd just do it.

Cassie found Matt and Dan talking about the difference

between jazz and classical music and interrupted them, "Hey, it's on again!"

Dan asked, "What are we talking about here?"

"The plan to get Janet and Walt together, of course!"

Matt said, "Oh my God, not that again! I thought Janet told you to back off."

"That was then. Now it's salmon season."

They both looked puzzled, and she told them about Janet's previous talk with Walt and Pete about fishing and how he had a boat.

Dan said, "But she can't just invite herself onto his boat, of course."

"Well, duh."

"So, Walt has to do the inviting?" Cassie nodded impatiently.

They all pondered the problem. Finally, Dan said, "Didn't Walt ask you to Pete's wedding last December?" She nodded.

He said triumphantly, "So, you pull a switcheroo! You get him to invite *you* to go fishing, and then at the last minute, you cancel and send Janet instead!"

Cassie pretended to slap him, "I'm a decoy? I'm sure he'd see through that."

He snapped his fingers in disappointment. They all had their own meetings to go to, so they left without figuring it out.

Cassie barely paid attention during her meeting. Janet was relaying what had been said in the executive meetings she went to, and Leisure Suit Larry was sucking up to her in his usual sickening way. She had an inspiration, "*Pete! I bet his new wife wants to fix up Walt, too!*"

She called Pete that night and left a message on his machine. Fortunately, his wife, Barbara, was out so he could call back and talk. Wow, did she ever have plans for Walt! Pete had seen this pattern with his first wife, too—they both wanted his single friends married off immediately. He thought it must be a desire to eliminate the competition for his time or maybe to make sure all his friends were as miserable as he was. He wasn't going to have *any* single friends if she could help it.

He said he'd bring it up with her. Personally, he felt he'd already done his share with the dance lesson. He had to keep working with Walt, after all, so he didn't want to push it.

When Barbara arrived home, he told her about the call and how last fall, he'd convinced Walt to go to a dance lesson. Supposedly, this was so Walt could make a good showing at their reception, but really it was so he could "accidentally" run into Janet. But Janet failed to show up. Barbara berated Pete for not inviting Janet to the wedding. The fact that her mother would have vetoed another guest from his side didn't quite register with her. She decided she would succeed where Pete had failed. She quizzed him on Walt's habits, and pretty soon, she had her plan. Barbara hated being on boats, but this was for a good cause.

The next morning, she waited until Pete left for work, and then found Cassie's number on the pad by the phone and called her back. The conversation was a little awkward at first since they didn't know each other, but they both had the same goal. Pretty quickly, they started scheming. Barbara would arrange a fishing trip for her and Pete on Walt's boat and "encourage" him to invite Cassie and Janet. Cassie volunteered that Walt and Janet had talked about salmon fishing once, and Barbara said triumphantly, "Well, there you go then!" Pete and Walt went fishing together, so this would be an easy sell for Pete.

Barbara thought she had the plan. She'd have Pete propose to Walt that he invite Janet and Cassie to their next salmon-fishing trip. Walt knew them both, and this way, it wasn't obviously a fixup. Pete tried to find a flaw in her reasoning, but he couldn't.

~

JANET WAS a little amused that she and Cassie were apparently a package—The Tech Girls. But the trip sounded like fun. Walt said he had enough fishing gear and life jackets for them, so she didn't need to buy any of that. But if she wanted to pick up a pair of rubber boots and overalls to wear on the boat, that might be good. She went to the outdoor shop and bought the stuff for her and Cassie. She also got a fishing license for herself, but Cassie had to purchase her own.

They were going to launch his boat from the Pillar Point Boat Launch near Half Moon Bay at 6:00 am on Sunday, March 20. She arranged to pick Cassie up at 5:00, which meant she'd wake up at 4:00. When had she ever been up that early? Back in LA when she was married, their friend Steve had taken them out on the ocean in his boat, but he kept it docked in the marina. Walt apparently kept his boat at home and launched it on a public boat ramp.

They drove over 92, which was deserted at that hour of the morning, parked near the boat launch, and put on their gear. Walt, Pete, and Barbara drove up in Walt's truck with the boat on a trailer behind it. There was a surprising number of people out, and the boat ramp already had a line of cars waiting to launch. The sky was overcast, and it was chilly. A gigantic dog jumped out of the truck along with them and was introduced as Bernie "because he's a Bernese Mountain Dog," explained Walt. Bernie was calm and waited for Janet and Cassie to come over and be introduced, which he clearly enjoyed.

They helped Pete load the gear into the boat, and then Walt instructed them to wait on the dock until it was launched. He also told them to put their fishing licenses on lanyards around their necks so that the wardens could check them via binoculars.

When Walt's turn at the ramp came, Pete ran through his checklist like any good first mate, looking like he'd done it many, many times before. He hopped in the boat, and Walt backed it down into the water. Walt got out and unhooked the bow strap and hopped back into the truck. Pete already had the engine running in reverse, so he gave Walt the signal. Walt backed him down a little farther until the boat was floating, and then Walt drove away and parked. When he returned, Pete tossed him the lines, and he pulled the boat over to the dock and tied it up. Barbara, Cassie, Janet, and Bernie climbed in, and they were off.

Walt took the wheel and headed over to where the big party boats were loading up. It was cold when the boat was moving! Barbara brought a thermos of hot coffee, and she poured cups for everyone. Pete explained that since the big boats had to know where the fish were—because unhappy customers were very bad for business—they would follow one from a safe distance. This early in the season, the salmon were pretty far out, ten to fifteen miles, so they'd probably have a long cruise before they put their lines in. They all hunkered down, facing out of the wind. Janet and Cassie finally lay down on the floor behind the windshield near Walt so that they'd be out of the wind. Bernie seemed to realize they were cold and draped his one-hundred-thirty-pound body across their laps, effectively immobilizing them as well as warming them up.

It was only a couple miles before Pete sighted a large group of pelicans diving into the water and coming up with fish. They were in luck! The party boat had ignored the birds and headed out to deeper water, but they decided they'd try their luck here first. Walt cut the engines and checked his sonar.

"About fifty feet down," he said. "We'll troll around here for a bit." He and Pete set up the rods for Barbara, Janet, and Cassie and stuck them in rod holders on the sides of the boat. He explained that they were to watch the rod tips for sudden movement, and if they had a fish, carefully lift the rod out of the holder, keeping the tip up, and do *not*, under any circumstances, jerk the rod to set the hook. This was a surprise for Janet since setting the hook was the usual procedure when she'd fished back in Michigan. Walt explained that these were barbless hooks they were trolling with, so the hook was already in the fish's mouth. If you yanked too hard, you might injure a fish that was too small to keep or yank it out of its mouth.

They waited. Twenty minutes went by with no strikes. Walt said, "Well, shall we try somewhere else?"

Pete said, "Might as well," and he reeled in all the lines. Walt headed farther out to sea until his fish finder seemed to show something at eighty feet. Again, Pete threw in the lines and fastened the rods in the rod holders. Another fifteen minutes went by, and then Janet's rod started dancing wildly.

"Whoa, you have a fish there, Janet!" said Walt. "Grab the rod."

She braced it against her waist and held it with both hands. This was a much bigger fish than she was used to back in Michigan. She tried pulling up the rod and then reeling in like she'd seen on the outdoor shows on TV, but it was *hard*! Pete told her to just keep even pressure on the line instead of doing that. She made a mental note to ask him about that later.

Pete took the other rods on her side and handed them over to Walt to get them out of the way. Walt went to the cockpit and cut the motor. Cassie figured Bernie must be excited, but he'd seen it all before and just watched alertly.

Finally, the fish was on the surface thrashing wildly.

"Whoo-ee, that looks like a keeper!" said Pete. "Bring him in closer, and I'll net him." He put the net in the water.

"At least this part is the same as lake fishing!" Janet pulled the fish over the net instead of making Pete stab at it, and he scooped it into the boat. He laid the net with the fish in it on the deck, where it continued flopping. Bernie had been calm up to now, but he couldn't resist any longer and barked excitedly. Finally, Pete freed the fish from the net and bashed its

head with a wooden club to kill it. He handed it to Janet for a photo. She beamed as she held it with both hands. "Dad's going to love this!" she said to Walt. "You remember my dad, don't you?"

"Indeed I do. Len, was it? Did he teach you how to land a fish?" he asked. She nodded.

Everyone congratulated Janet. Pete put it on his scale and announced that this beauty was eleven pounds. Pete tossed it in the fish well, and they all took their rods and put the lures back in the water. Walt resumed trolling slowly.

This was a productive spot. Next, Walt caught a fish, then Cassie, then Barbara. According to the regulations, anglers were each allowed to keep two salmon, and within an hour and a half, they'd all caught their limits. It was still only mid-morning, but the sun was out, and they weren't shivering anymore.

As the boat owner, it fell to Walt to suggest they head in because it had been such a good day, and the warden might ask why they were still fishing when they already had their limits. Barbara and Pete exchanged glances, and Pete offered to take the wheel and steer them in since Walt had already worked so hard. Walt resisted, but Pete made him slide out of the pilot seat. Walt walked to the stern where Janet was. Barbara caught Cassie's eye and tilted her head toward the bow, and she and Cassie walked up there, leaving Janet and Walt together at the stern. Bernie lay down and watched them.

"A pretty good day, huh?" he said.

"Yes, and thanks so much for bringing us!" He nodded modestly. "Was this your first trip this season?"

"Yeah, first time. We usually try to go at least three times every year."

Janet wasn't sure where to go with that. Finally, "Well, it took me back to fishing with my dad. I wish he could have come along today!"

Walt thought about that for a while, "Sounds like you're pretty close to your dad." She smiled. "I didn't see much of mine after my folks divorced. My mom raised me."

"That's too bad. Is he still alive, do you know?"

"Yeah, I think he's living in Seattle now. Haven't talked to him in years."

They were both silent as they watched the pelicans still diving for fish in the spot where they'd struck out earlier.

At the bow, Cassie and Barbara looked forward for a few minutes but then turned back to the stern to keep the spray off their faces. They couldn't hear Walt and Janet at all, although they were dying to know how it was going. Barbara kept up a steady stream of small talk, asking Cassie if she'd ever been out fishing in the ocean, which she hadn't. Cassie knew she and Pete were newlyweds, so she wasn't sure what she could ask her. "*How's married life so far? Have you started hating each other yet?*" probably weren't good openers. Bernie trotted up to join them.

"This is one big dog, all right! We couldn't even move when he was on our laps!" said Cassie. They both laughed.

"Kept you warm, though, I'll bet!" said Barbara, nuzzling Bernie's ears. She exchanged another meaningful look with Pete at the wheel.

At the stern, Walt and Janet had been silent. The boat was nearing the boat docks. They both looked uncertain about what to say next. Finally, Janet said, "So, I heard that dance lesson really worked!"

Walt was puzzled, "Wait, how'd you hear about that?" Then suddenly, he put it all together—Pete's comments when they were at Janet's house, the dance lesson, the fishing trip, the two of them so conveniently left alone back here while Pete piloted the boat.

"Pete, I'll kill you!" he yelled and started toward the cockpit.

Pete glanced at Janet and then cut the engine, gunned it,

and steered sharply to the left. Walt was thrown sideways. Janet had braced herself when Pete looked at her, and she caught Walt in her arms. He was embarrassed and started separating himself, and she said, "Shall we dance, Mr. Campbell?" and took his left hand in her right.

Pete had brought a cassette of *The Way You Look Tonight,* jammed it into the tape player, and cut the engine to trolling speed. Walt's right hand was already on her back where it should be, and Janet put her left hand on his shoulder. They started moving unsteadily in a foxtrot.

44

WAIT! WHAT EMAIL?

I t was August 1989. Janet never said anything about Walt to Dan, but Cassie kept him informed. Apparently, the romance was proceeding nicely. He, Matt, and Cassie were all so proud!

Janet had moved up a level in management as the company continued to grow. She had promoted Cassie to be Manager of Desktop Services, meaning she was now managing other people who did what she used to do. There was too much work for one person to do anymore, for one thing, and for another, Janet didn't want to lose her to some other group or company.

Leisure Suit Larry had not been promoted, and wow, was he pissed! He was widely expected to quit or transfer as a result, and Janet wasn't bothered at all by that prospect. In the meantime, he spent a lot of time gossiping about Janet's new boyfriend, whom he termed The Blue-Collar Hunk. His favorite gossip partner was Paul, who just happened to be the guy Janet had overheard talking about how there was a lot of boinking at some party. Larry was often seen hanging out with Paul, both sniggering at some joke. They seemed to enjoy playing practical jokes on people and each other, which no one else thought was funny. Everyone learned to lock their screens because Larry or Paul would sit down at people's PCs and send "funny" messages supposedly from them.

Almost no one in Janet's group ever talked to Larry anymore. Paul occasionally asked Cassie questions about how the mail system worked, which she tried to be polite about, but she didn't like him and wondered why he was asking. He said he had a friend at a university who he wanted to communicate with via their Internet gateway, which required some unusual syntax for addressing recipients.

Mohan hadn't been made a manager officially, but his title was Tech Lead for utility programs, which meant that whenever the group needed actual programming done, Mohan was the man to call. He was hoping he'd eventually be able to hire people to work for him, and Janet encouraged him in this hope.

∾

ONE TUESDAY MORNING, Larry quit 3Com, and Dan thought there was something strange about it. He left suddenly without the customary two-week notice, and in fact, without any notice at all. Yet, he had not been fired, and Dan had verified that with multiple people, including Janet. She didn't seem to want to tell him anything more than that.

Even stranger, he'd sent an apology email to the entire company, and Dan couldn't figure out what he was apologizing for! It had something to do with an email that he had mistakenly sent to the entire company, yet Dan had never received it.

He went to Cassie's cube, hoping to learn something. Mohan and Cassie were in a huddled conversation, and when Mohan saw him, he said hi and quickly left.

Dan figured a direct question about Larry was probably not going to result in a direct answer from her. She learned quickly that managers do not give direct answers about anything except occasionally to their own managers. Still, he'd taught her almost everything she knew about networking and email, and she'd taught him something about dancing, so that had to count for a little.

"So, what was Larry apologizing for? I never received any flame-o-gram from him!"

"No? You didn't get that?" she asked.

"Deflect. Always make it about the other person, not you. She's learning this managerial racket."

"No, I sure didn't. Get what?"

"His email about Janet and Walt. You didn't see that?"

"No, Cassie. I said I didn't," he said with exaggerated patience. "What did it say?"

She seemed to become nervous and looked at her watch. As she rose and left her cube, she said, "I forget exactly, but it was something mean about Janet and Walt."

"Something mean. That sounds like Larry, all right."

He'd never liked Larry ever since he said in the committee to name the conference rooms that Mandalay was too hard for people to say. Nothing Larry had ever done since had altered Dan's first impression.

But what did he say in this nasty email, exactly? And to whom was it sent? And why did he think he needed to apologize to the whole company? And quit?

He went by Matt's cube. "Hey, did you see Larry's apology message?"

Matt hadn't, but he brought up his email, opened the message from Larry, and read. "What's he talking about? Was there some message I didn't see? I don't understand."

Dan said, "That's what I'm trying to figure out."

"Did you ask Janet?"

"Yeah, she just said he was not fired but wouldn't tell me anything else."

Matt considered this and reread the message, quoting

aloud in his best smarmy voice, "'Obviously, I never meant this to go to the entire company, but it was still wrong of me to write it at all. I want to especially apologize to Janet for whom I have the deepest respect.'"

Dan interrupted him, "Stop before I retch right now."

Matt laughed, "What, you don't like corporate-speak?" Dan pretended to put his index finger down his throat. "So if I didn't receive the flame-o-gram and you didn't, why did he think *everyone* did? I mean, I did see him meeting with Miss Smarmy this morning, but that didn't seem too unusual. Birds of a feather, you know..."

"Why, indeed?" Dan said, heading back to his cube. He checked the Name Service to see which mail server Larry had his account on, but his employee record was already gone. *"Wow, that was quick!"*

Then, he realized that Larry had to be on the same mail server as the rest of Janet's group. He wouldn't have been assigned to some random mail server. He opened a connection to that server, hoping to look in Larry's mail folder and find some clue. That directory was deleted, too.

Dan had been out of touch with the day-to-day network administration ever since Janet's group had taken it over. He didn't actually know anymore how quickly your data was removed when you left. Mohan would probably know that. Dan went to his cube.

Mohan was a bad actor. He tried not to appear nervous, which any acting coach would tell you is a guaranteed way to appear nervous. "Hi, Dan. How are you?" This was not the way Mohan usually talked. It was too elaborately polite.

Dan was taking movie-making classes at De Anza College and reading books on scriptwriting and acting, and he'd read that the way to act drunk is not to stumble around—it's to walk extra carefully like you're trying not to stumble. What was Mohan nervous about?

"I was just wondering if you knew how quickly the

network resources get recovered for an employee who quits?" Dan asked.

"Right away! We don't want to leave any information a disgruntled person could use."

Dan was pretty sure this wasn't true, based on occasionally seeing mail folders for long-departed employees on the servers.

"Okay, thanks," said Dan. *"Should I ask Mohan why Larry quit? I don't want to raise his alert level."*

"Are you the person who does this, or is it someone else?"

"I still do it quite often. I'm working on a single program that cleans out all the resources when someone quits, but it's not quite ready yet."

He looked expectantly at Dan like he was wondering what would come next.

"Got it, got it. Thanks a lot, Mohan!" Dan said as he left. He'd have to figure this out on his own.

His old boss, Terry, hadn't had anything to do with email for years, but he always loved solving a difficult problem. He went to Terry's cube, "Hey, did you see Larry's apology message?"

Terry hadn't, but he had the same reaction as Matt—he brought up the message, read it, and asked, "What's he apologizing for here? What did I miss?"

He recapped the whole story for Terry, who rubbed his hands together gleefully. It was like a murder mystery for him. "Wow, this *is* a good one! Did you look in his mail folder?"

Dan explained that the mail folder was deleted. Terry said, "Okay, two things. First, we need to find out who actually received this offending message. And second, we have to find it."

This quest brought back so many fun memories of the two of them tracking down some impossible mail server bug. Terry could be a little pig-headed at times about his own theories, but usually, Dan could make him listen to reason.

"Who got it? I guess I can ask around, but so far, I haven't found *anyone* who did!"

Terry thought about that, "Well, we know at least one person *had* it... Larry!"

"Right, but that evidence is deleted."

"Maybe *that's* the place to look. Who deleted it?"

Dan recalled talking to Cassie and Mohan. "Someone in Janet's group, I'm pretty sure."

Terry chucked, "Someone who didn't like Larry?"

"That was all of them." They both laughed.

Terry was always happy to give Dan work to do, and he said, "Well, let's see... Larry had to be sending it to someone. They can't have deleted all his old messages in other people's inboxes. Can you find out who he talked to the most?"

Dan thought for a second, "Not really. Once you fetch a message, it's gone from the server, and it lives on your PC, as you well know. So, their mail folders would only have Larry's messages that they haven't retrieved yet. He seems to hang out with Paul a lot."

"That's right. The server doesn't have any permanent record of your old mail, does it?" Dan shook his head. "So, what could it be? What could it be?"

"I suspect an inside job!" Dan said.

"Meaning what? Inside by whom?"

"By Cassie or Mohan. Or Janet."

"Why do you suspect them?"

"Something about the way they acted," said Dan. "Like they knew more than they were telling me."

"Okay," said Terry. "You've talked to them, but I haven't. Now, what do we do?"

"Not sure," said Dan. "We can't exactly seize their PCs."

"Not officially, at least!" laughed Terry.

"I don't feel like sneaking onto someone's PC at night, sorry. I prefer not to be fired."

"This *is* a tough one," said Terry. "Let's think... how would you pull off a trick like this?"

Dan muttered, "With all my intimate knowledge of the mail system?" Terry nodded. Dan thought out loud, "I guess I would alter his copy of the message so that he thought it went company-wide."

"Even though it didn't?" Dan nodded. "How would you do that?"

"I guess... I'd have to get onto the server before it was delivered and alter it there."

Terry said, "Or diddle it on Larry's PC. Remind me... aren't the messages encrypted on the server?" making the air quotes around encrypted.

Dan laughed again, "If you want to call that encryption."

Terry said, "If I remember correctly, it was just exclusive-or-ing it. Does anyone know that besides us?"

Dan thought again, "Not that I know of. I think once I showed some things to Cassie, but I don't think I told her where the encryption programs are or what they did."

"Maybe she just got on his PC and altered the message with a text editor," offered Terry.

Dan stood up, "Yeah, maybe. Need to figure this out."

He laid the problem aside for the rest of the day to let fresh ideas bubble up from the unconscious. Sometimes, that was the only way to solve a problem.

45

OH, THAT EMAIL

Dan was not a huge fan of classic detective fiction, but he did remember one adage—the criminal always returns to the scene of the crime.

If you, with "you" being the person who pulled this off, did something like this, you might not be smart enough to just shut your mouth and never tell anyone. It would drive you crazy not to know all the details of how your scam worked out. And especially, you'd be worried that it *didn't* quite work!

So, what would that mean if someone tricked Larry into thinking he'd sent a nasty email to the entire company when he hadn't? Maybe the perpetrator, "the perp" as Dan and Terry liked to call him, would flip out and betray himself if he thought his scheme had misfired with Larry's email really going out to a lot of people!

Dan set about laying the trap. He didn't have the email in question *yet*, but maybe, that wasn't necessary. He explained the scheme to Terry, who came up with a better idea. Terry sent an email that was *ostensibly* to everyone in the company but in reality, it only went to a few.

Recently you saw a "goodbye" message from Larry
Whitlock apologizing for an inappropriate email, and
yet you probably never got that email. We're very sorry
for your trouble, and we're trying to figure out what
exactly happened. If you'd like to help us out: can you
email me or Dan Markunas your copy of the original
email, IF you got it? This will help us a lot.

It ended with some standard corporate boilerplate, but the
important thing was that it appeared to go to most of the
company. In reality, Terry jiggered the mail server so that only
a few people received it. If the perp asked around, he or she
would start worrying that they didn't understand the mail
system because Terry's message seemed to go to everyone but
didn't. They might panic and give it away!

Everyone in Janet's group was included because they were
all considered suspects. Larry had hung out with Paul a lot,
and they were always playing stupid pranks on people. So,
Paul and his entire group were included. The other recipients
were there just as a cover so that the real suspects wouldn't
figure out what was going on.

Then, Dan and Terry waited for the answers. Almost
everyone replied that they hadn't received it, which was what
they'd expected. Cassie and Mohan came by and talked to
Dan and told him they hadn't gotten it, but they thought
maybe Janet had. Cassie also told him that Paul had been
asking her some suspicious questions about email lately.

Paul didn't respond at all, and neither did Janet. Kristen in
HR called Terry, but not Dan, and left a voice message asking
him to come and talk to her. Dan was amused because he had
always been completely unable to conceal his feelings, so she
probably could tell he hated her.

Dan suspected that Paul and Janet were the only ones who

actually received Larry's message since they didn't respond. They had a motivation to deny it. Paul because it was nasty, and Janet because well... because she was a manager who wasn't about to tell anyone anything about personnel matters. But he still wanted to hear what Kristen told Terry.

Terry had been sworn to secrecy and initially refused to tell him anything. Dan figured he'd crack eventually if he worked on him.

He pieced some of the story together. Kristen received Larry's nasty message and somehow was convinced it had gone to the entire company. So, she had called Larry and left one of those "would you please come talk to me when you get a chance?" voicemails, and he had panicked and quit on the spot. She swore that he already had an offer from another company and was quitting anyway, but neither Dan nor Terry believed that.

Dan asked Terry, "So, did you see the actual Larry message?"

"Well, sort of. She showed me a printed version of it, but she wouldn't let me keep it or even study it for long."

"And?"

"From what I saw, it was just some dirty talk about Janet and her boyfriend, whatever his name is."

"Was it Walt?"

"Yeah, that sounds right. Anyway, I couldn't figure out how she got it or why she thought it went to the whole company."

"Oh, man, Terry. You fucked up! Why didn't you just grab it and run out of the room?" They both laughed.

"Anyway, who were the recipients? Did you at least see that much?"

Terry said, "I did see that much. It was to Paul."

"No one else?" Terry shook his head.

"And, it wasn't a forward of Larry's message?" Terry shook his head again.

Dan couldn't think of anything to say. Finally, "Okay, we're not getting the entire story here."

Terry laughed, "You think?"

"So obviously, Paul received the message." Terry nodded again. "Should we go and talk to *him*?"

"I don't know the guy at all. Do you?"

Dan made a face, "I might have talked to him once or twice. Not my favorite person."

He thought a while longer, "Cassie told me he'd been asking her questions about how email worked."

Terry's face brightened, "Really? What kind of questions?" Dan didn't know. Terry said, "Well, I think we have our primary suspect. Can you find out from Cassie what, specifically, he'd been asking her about?"

Dan said he would.

Cassie was talking to one of her new underlings when Dan walked over, so he waited until the person left.

She said, "What's up?"

"You said Paul had been snooping around the mail system, right?" She nodded. "What areas, exactly?"

She closed her eyes and thought, "Trying to remember… he seemed very concerned with group expansion and how the email header was parsed."

"Like what? Like how it talks to the Name Service to expand the group?"

She said, "No, no. Like how you split up the recipients in the first place."

Dan was dumbfounded, "What's there to know? You look for commas and keywords, end of story!"

She also looked puzzled, remembering it, "That's what I told him. He didn't seem satisfied, though."

"Jeez. What was he trying to do, do you think?"

"Beats the shit out of me. Some prank to end all pranks?"

"Well, he did that, all right. Getting a guy fired who supposedly was his friend."

Now Cassie was intrigued, "Larry was fired?"

"Who knows? I'm not going to believe anything Kristen says, that's for sure."

Cassie was becoming more cynical all the time, but this was still a shock for her. "So, you think Kristen *fired* him? And Janet's not telling us?"

Dan just shrugged, "The question is... *how* did he do it?"

Cassie was silent. Dan left and went to tell Terry what he found out.

"We have our working hypothesis that Paul was the perp. I don't know about you, but I'm more interested in *how* he did it. He can be fired or not. I don't care."

Terry nodded, "Yeah. There might be some bug in the mail system we need to fix."

Dan said, "So, how do we get hold of that email? We know Kristen has it."

Terry mused, "We could have some executive ask her for it. Someone she can't refuse."

Dan thought about that, "Captain Bob? Or we could swipe it out of her office!"

Terry laughed, "Do you feel like being fired? I don't, particularly."

"Yeah. Another alternative is to maybe trick Paul into doing it again!"

"Or watch his email and see if he brags about it to other people?" said Terry.

"Let's try and avoid anything overtly illegal, like snooping on the mail. At least for now," said Dan. "Maybe we can have some friend of *ours* to just ask him!"

"I like the way you're thinking," said Terry. "Who else does he hang around with?"

Dan's face brightened, "Now *that, we* can figure out!"

"Without watching his email?" Terry asked. Dan nodded and walked over to Matt's office.

46

THE END

I t was Saturday, March 11, 1989, and Walt and Janet were getting married, with Pete as best man. Dan, Matt, and Cassie sat together in the third pew on the bride's side. Miriam had sent her regrets, which everyone knew was because she hated Walt. Dan and Matt had never seen each other in a suit and tie before, and Dan figured they probably never would again unless someone died.

While they were waiting for the show to begin, Cassie leaned over Matt and asked Dan, "So, Dan, did you know Janet's first husband when you were both at Xerox?"

"I think I met him once."

Matt interjected, "Wasn't he an engineer? She's sure avoided that mistake this time around!"

Cassie said, "Nothing against *you* guys, but Walt is a hunk!"

Walt and Pete came in and waited at the altar. The processional began, and Len and Janet came down the aisle. Len looked like he was holding back tears, while Janet felt sure she looked more radiant than the first time with Ken.

At the reception, Cassie, Dan, and Matt sat at the same

table, along with some of Janet's relatives from Michigan. Dan thought it was odd that they were the only 3Com people there —didn't Janet have an entire army of people in her empire now? He figured she must be better at keeping work separate from real life than he could.

The first dance song was "Girls Just Want to Have Fun." Dan thought it should have been "Shop Around," but Janet never listened to him. Anyhow, they all danced for the first three songs.

It was a long afternoon, and Dan and Matt couldn't avoid talking shop forever. 3Com stock had just hit twenty-six yesterday after being stuck near twenty forever. But they knew the management ranks were deeply divided about what to do next, and it was dispiriting.

The bride and groom made their circuit around the room, visiting each table. Dan knew all about Matt's history with Walt in the remodeling job, but they both hid it well and exchanged very brief pleasantries.

Janet and Dan hugged, "Congratulations, Janet. You look so beautiful!"

"Thanks so much for coming, you guys!" she said.

Cassie asked her, "So, where are you going on your honeymoon?"

Janet said, "We're going to Hawaii! Walt's never been."

Just then, Janet's father Len dropped by. She introduced him to Matt and Cassie, thinking that Len and Dan must already know each other. They didn't, but Len introduced himself. They all drank to the bride and groom.

"*Len is the happiest person in the room!*" thought Dan. "*If smiles were lightbulbs, we'd all need shades.*"

"So, Len, you live back in Detroit?" asked Matt. "How is it there?"

"Oh, you know. Struggling along. I still have a job, so I guess I can't complain."

They talked about Detroit and Chrysler for a while, and then Walt interrupted and grabbed him for yet more introductions to his family and friends. Janet hung around.

Matt asked her, "So, Janet, are you planning to hang around 3Com for a while yet?"

The walls went up instantly. After knowing her for so long, Dan could decode that look, *"You're not getting anything from me today, pal!"*

"Oh, I don't know. It's fun for now." She looked to see where Walt and Len had gone off to and walked toward them.

Pete came and sat down at their table. They all drank some more champagne.

Matt leaned back, "Good times, good friends... getting people fired!" They all laughed.

Cassie said, "So, I tried that semicolon trick again, just to see if it crept back in!"

Dan laughed, "And?"

"Still fixed. Good work, Dan!"

"Good work for Matt, for sleuthing it out!"

Matt smiled modestly, "Aw shucks! It was nothing. Just needed some acting skills to convince him I was panicking that the Name Service was broken!"

Dan almost spit out his champagne.

Cassie said, "I still marvel. And your wife, the shrink, helped with the acting?"

"She, um... gave me a pointer or two." They all smiled.

Cassie turned to Dan, "And, you're still sticking to your story about how the semicolon thing crept into the mail code?"

"That's my story, and I'm sticking to it. It was there when I started."

Matt looked at him, "So, *someone* thought you should be able to use a semicolon as well as a comma to separate names?"

"I have my suspicions as to who that was, but since that person still works here…"

Pete had been listening. None of this made much sense to him, but his red face, loosened tie, and contented look made them all think he was feeling just fine.

Matt laughed again. "Oh, man, oh, man. Miriam still can't believe it. You type paul:hq;3com instead of paul:hq:3com, and it goes to all of 3Com."

Cassie said, "Or would have."

Dan replied, "Right, right. Larry didn't actually do that, of course."

Matt had never *stopped* laughing, "That's the best part of the prank. We always hear about people mistakenly screwing up, but this clown didn't even do that."

Dan made the gesture of holding up a pistol to his temple. Larry had quit for something he didn't do.

Pete perked up, "You techies. Do you ever do any actual work? Does one of you want to explain this to me?"

Cassie volunteered and walked him through how Paul had snuck onto Larry's PC and sent the message again, with that one-character change—first to Kristen and then to Janet.

"Okay, so? I still don't get it."

"Well, Kristen is kinda dense, so Paul had to go and explain it to her."

"Explain what?"

"That the 3Com had caused it to go to the entire company!"

Pete had a wide-eyed, innocent look, "Couldn't she tell that it didn't?"

They all laughed so loudly that the people at the next table looked over.

"So, this Kristen person isn't too bright, huh?"

No one answered, so Pete just shook his head.

"And you people earn the big bucks."

Dan said, "But you guys are happier. And now, Janet will be, too."

THE END

AFTERWORD

This is a brief summary of what happened in the previous book, *Inventing the Future*, for people who haven't read it and want to catch up. I tried to use some exposition in the text so reading this wouldn't be necessary, but one never knows.

If you *do* want to read it now (and why wouldn't you?), then you may wish to skip this section, which is why I put it at the end rather than the beginning.

Book I: Inventing the Future

Dramatis Personae:

Dan Markunas: a young engineer who's had one previous job out of college. Joins Xerox El Segundo in early 1977, when the Star wasn't even called that yet. Dan is single. Dan is me.

Janet Saunders: a young engineer, also with one job out of college, at TRW, which is right down the street from Xerox El Segundo. Janet is married to Ken, whom she met at MIT.

Grant Avery: a slightly older Xerox veteran, who's transferred to Palo Alto from Dallas. He's brought in to bring some seasoned management to the Office Information Systems project.

Other important characters who appear, but we don't get to see inside their heads. Some of them appear in later books; some not:

Ken: husband of Janet

Len: Janet's father, a financial analyst at Chrysler. Len lives in the Detroit area, where Janet grew up.

Mark Banks: project manager of Star in El Segundo

Tom Burnside: Dan's boss, a mild-mannered guy.

Brian Lerner: another engineer in El Segundo

Porter Berwick: "the Jerry Garcia of programming" in Palo Alto. Porter knows everyone and everything.

Henry Davis: Palo Alto user interface expert. The inventor of icons.

Tim Field: Palo Alto hardware designer of the Ethernet transceiver.

Main events:

Xerox is embarking on The Office of the Future, diversifying from their copier business. The effort is to be *based* on Xerox PARC's groundbreaking research, but it is not, contrary to popular ignorance, actually being *done* by PARC. Rather, it's a separate division SDD, assigned to make a product. Dan and Janet are hired into the El Segundo group, and Grant is hired to be a manager for the operating system, in Palo Alto.

The OIS (Office Information Systems) effort is slow to get off the ground. There is much corporate intrigue, and the computer eventually called "Star" is called the "Display Word Processor" at first. Grant is in way over his head managing the operating system; the Ph.D. engineers mostly ignore him, and his calls to stick to the schedule and follow the Xerox development process fall on deaf ears. In a few months he transfers to the "Planning" department, and tries to act as an interface to the main Xerox bureaucracy. Grant has a crush on Janet, but she's married.

Janet works at TRW and her husband Ken works at Hughes Aircraft. They have an active social life with Ken's friends at Hughes, and most of them are bemused, at best, by Janet's work at Xerox. Ken makes fun of it constantly, which leads to a growing tension between them.

Dan becomes the manager of Records Processing. Janet has an interview at Hughes, gets an offer, and turns it down to become the Release Manager on Star. This leads to an explosive fight with Ken. Grant resolves to transfer down to El Segundo to work on the Tor electronic printer project, since he thinks Xerox has a better chance of marketing and selling laser printers (he was right, by the way).

Eventually, Janet gets a divorce from Ken, and Grant moves down to El Segundo to work on Tor. He thinks that, now that she's divorced, he has his chance! However, she just doesn't see him that way. They go out once, but eventually he gets the idea that it's not going to happen.

Even though he's in El Segundo, his colleagues still see him as their interface to Palo Alto. Since they're using Pilot, the OS he used to be in charge of, he still has to go there and stay involved. Eventually, his search for a new chip leads him to Fuji Xerox, the Japanese subsidiary, and they offer him a temporary assignment as liaison.

Star is introduced at the National Computer Conference in Chicago, to major headlines. Janet and Dan are there, and Janet notices Steve Jobs and his Apple retinue attending every hourly demo. She gives one of them her business card, they invite her up for an interview and offer her a job on the Lisa, and she accepts it. There are (mostly) no hard feelings on the part of the El Segundo people; they realize, as she does, that Xerox has no chance of success in the computer business.

Grant accepts the job in Japan. Dan feels, initially, that Janet's leaving for Apple is a betrayal of all they'd worked for, but in the end they part friends.

NOTES

4. Marking Time in El Segundo

1. Yes, I really did this.

5. Just Before the Dawn

1. This part is true: CSNET was real, and the University of Minnesota was not one of the initial participants. They joined later. Everything after this about the University is fictional and is a composite of what was going on in the world then.

6. Life in the Circus

1. Lisa did use Hungarian in the memory manager for a while, but nowhere else.

8. The Revolution WILL Be Televised

1. Believe it or not, the French did have the Minitel, long before Internet came along. I saw one in 1989.

10. Matt and Miriam Go for a Drive

1. This part about ARCNet is fictional. Minnesota did not have ARCNet, as far as I know.

11. The Garage Industry

1. This part is true. Some of my neighbors even remember it.

12. Back to the Frozen Tundra

1. Ted Nelson really was at Datapoint for a while.

15. A Name and a CEO, Finally

1. All true. We did play EA, and Trip did hit a home run. I don't remember the final score.

22. Do You Know the Way to Mandalay?

1. Reflex was a bestseller for Borland for several years, after they cut the price to $100 and sold it through mail order.

30. The March of Science

1. I spent a LOT of time on OS/2, back in the day.

ACKNOWLEDGMENTS

The author gratefully acknowledges, first, the wonderful Foreword by Dan Gillmor, cover by Jonathan Sainsbury, and most of all my editor Samantha Mason.

For letting me use his real name: Bob Metcalfe, aka "Cap't Bob."

Others whose help is gratefully acknowledged:

David Crocker
Una Daly
Robert Gaskin
Derry Kabcenell
David Liddle
Frank Ludolph
Christopher Minson
Gordon Peterson
Jay Rossiter
Robert Stephens

ABOUT THE AUTHOR

Albert Cory is the pen name for Bob Purvy, a retired software engineer who worked on the Xerox Star. In his career, he also worked at Burroughs, 3Com, Oracle, Packeteer, and Google. Bob lives in San Jose with his dog Ernie, who was named after Ernie Banks, the greatest Cub who ever lived.

ALSO BY ALBERT CORY

Inventing the Future (2021)